A Touch of Innocence

Katherine Dunham with her brother, Albert Dunham Jr. (*from the collection of Katherine Dunham*). Used by permission of Katherine Dunham.

A Touch of Innocence

Memoirs of Childhood

by Katherine Dunham

The University of Chicago Press

Chicago and London

Published by arrangement with Harcourt, Brace & Company

The University of Chicago Press, Chicago 60637
The University of Chicago Press, Ltd., London

University of Chicago Press Edition 1994
Printed in the United States of America
01 00 99 98 97 96 95 94 6 5 4 3 2 1

ISBN 0-226-17112-4 (pbk.)

Library of Congress Cataloging-in-Publication Data

Dunham, Katherine.
A touch of innocence : memoirs of childhood / by Katherine Dunham.
p. cm.
Originally published: New York : Harcourt Brace, 1959.
1. Dunham, Katherine—Childhood and youth. 2. Dancers—United States—Biography.
GV1785.D82A37 1994
792.8′028′092—dc20
[B] 93-46125
CIP

Cover photo: Katherine in the goat-cart of a traveling photographer (from the collection of Katherine Dunham, used by permission).

⊗ The paper used in this publication meets the minimum requirements of the American National Standard for Information Sciences—Permanence of Paper for Printed Library Materials, ANSI Z39.48-1984.

TO B.B.

A Note to the Reader

This book is not an autobiography. It is the story of a world that has vanished, as it was for one child who grew up in it—the Middle West through the boom years after the First World War, and in the early years of the Depression. And it is the story of a family that I knew very well, and especially of a girl and a young woman whom I rediscovered while writing about the members of this family. Perhaps from their confused lives may come something that will serve as guidance to someone else, or something that will at least hold attention for a while as a story.

K. D.
June, 1959

Contents

A Touch of Innocence

One
The Rabbit Hunt

*

She stood first on one foot then the other, leaning on the BB gun and gazing across the dreary field of winter corn which seemed, overcome by the leaden sky, to be trying to curl back into the snow that lay ankle deep as far as the eye could reach. Its sweep was interrupted by the black jagged ribbon of a stream winding along one edge of the field and by a tired storm fence leaning at a crazy angle as it trailed along the other edge and finally lost itself in a drift.

Somewhere beyond distant sparse trees there must be a farmhouse, and the child thought for a while how it would feel to be inside it. She drew deeply on the mucus escaping from her chapped nose and swallowed hard, trying to shut out the bitterness of the cold and the intensity of her loneliness by conjuring up that unseen interior.

On a Sunday in the country the "big" meal would be at noon and so would be just about over. It would be better if the dishes were washed, too, and the family (mother, father, brother, and sister, like her own) all seated in the spacious linoleum-floored kitchen. No, it would be better in the living room, opened once a week, with a fire in the huge pot-bellied base-burner covered all over with isinglass windows like merry eyes. . . .

Her thoughts took flight beyond what she knew from country Sunday visits now and then, into a world of fancy, often evoked when times were hard to bear. The First Mother (spoken of only on rare occasions and secretly, with the child's brother, who, being older, held memories not patched and faded) would be seated at the harp. She would of course be pale, sad-eyed, a little aloof; because to the child all fine ladies should be just a little aloof and never never let out sounds or show things that would attract the neighbors' or anyone's attention, unless in such a way as to make them think that everything was pleasant and charming in the happiest and most well-to-do of families. The father would be as he had used to be—younger-acting and playful and companionable—before bitterness and a foreboding of defeat set in, perhaps before he began to question himself, to realize that for the second time he was married to a woman who could have been in years his mother. On this Sunday, in this house, safe and warm and filled with the orange glow of the base-burner and the rosy glow of love, he would be reading something amusing in the *Sunday Tribune* and chuckling to himself about it, stopping now and then to read an item aloud.

What more could she construct in her fantasy for the brother and sister than that they be allowed to pause, unmolested and out in the open instead of hidden in a closet with a flashlight or candle, lying on the tan carpeting in front of the burner, close to where the ashes dropped glowing through the grate and into a small pit below, reading the pulp of the day: dreaded Dr. Fu Manchu, the thought of whom made one go around the block rather than cross in front of the Chinese laundry; *Science and Invention*, obviously published to delude the gullible into imagining conquests beyond what already seemed unreal, even ungodly, such as wireless and airplanes for everyday use; books of comic strips; and some others that her brother reserved for himself alone. . . .

Two streams had emanated from her nostrils during these reveries, and by now her eyes had overflowed with tears of cold and of an insupportable longing. She wished that the hunters would come back. The bitter cold and the desolation of the cornfield had congealed blood, bone, and cartilage into a condition that she felt sure was like death or might even be a state of near death. She lifted one foot, was surprised that it moved, and took a few steps toward the delivery wagon, black (though in fact it was dark green) against the slate sky, its dull gold hand-painted letters saying WEST SIDE CLEANERS AND DYERS, and underneath, 237 NORTH BLUFF STREET, and in one corner TEL. 4513, and in the other corner, A. DUNHAM. She walked wide-legged to keep from chafing her already raw thighs, where the hated gray-flannel long underwear hung sodden with urine, released twice as she had stood there in the cold, so she wouldn't have to go behind a tree and expose bare flesh to the bitter still air and squat like a *girl*—so letting them know, if they came upon her, that she was weaker and different and therefore should have been left at home.

She eyed the stream, drawn by a perversity stronger than herself, knowing that if she moved near enough to hear its murmured complaint the suggestion would overrule her reflexes; and this time, from the already sodden gray flannel, the wetness would move down calves and into wool socks and galoshes. Her brother would shake his head the moment he saw her and smile wryly with a twinkle in his eye for her only, and she would hang her head in shame, already suffering in anticipation the episode from which there would be no escape that night: the long-delayed bedtime, after the dinner of fried rabbit or rabbit stew if the hunters were successful, or of leg of lamb if they returned empty-handed.

The kerosene stove, the kerosene lamp on the piano in the living room, would help at least a little to diminish cold and shadow; and when undressing time came—resolve though she might to face the glacial cubicle that was her room now that she was too old to sleep with her brother—

she would end by crawling miserably behind the stove and reluctantly start peeling off middle garments, to arrive all too soon at the tell-tale, still damp underwear. And though she herself would hold her breath or breathe lightly and only on the top surface, invariably her brother would look up from his book—a serious one, thought-provoking for the brilliant philosopher to come—and glance slyly at her, then concernedly at their father to see if he was really asleep behind the newspaper or if he would look over it and say, "Young lady, it's about time you learned not to wet your underclothes," and then say, "Get the strap," if it had been a black-mood day or just grunt disgustedly if it had been an average day. Her mother would stop her reading or mending to say, "Oh, Katherine, that is disgraceful, a girl of your age who doesn't even know when to go to the toilet certainly shouldn't be allowed out." But worst of all was the quizzical look her brother would give her, because it seemed to destroy once and for all her half-formulated idea of herself as the girl of his choice, the ideal sister.

Standing between the delivery wagon and the stream, she became more dismal at the thought that, seeing the wretchedness of her condition, her brother would ask her why she hadn't gone to bundle down among the carpet ends in the back of the wagon. She knew but she would not be able to tell him. She would never be able to put into words the primordial need to be near where he was, so that even when she couldn't follow because she was a handicap to their tracking—slipping and falling and hurting her ankles in treacherous hoar-covered wagon ruts frozen glacier-hard and sharp as knife points—and had to turn back and follow the tracks to the wagon, still she felt less alone if she stayed out in the open, where there was a chance to hear the occasional "ping" from the twenty-two or louder reverberations from her father's shotgun, or maybe even see her father's pulled-down gray felt hat or her brother's blue knitted earmuff hood.

Again marveling that she could move at all, she walked over toward a giant elm tree, to which a few brown leaves still clung. Halfway there she heard the twin reports of the twenty-two and the shotgun. She wondered if there would be two rabbits or if one would bear the clean hole of the twenty-two and at the same time the perforations of the buckshot, which sometimes buried deep and was recovered only when bitten down on, hidden under meat and gravy. Her teeth grated at the unpleasant recollection, and this physical sensation seemed to bring to life the numbed nerve ends and aroused an urge to recover from utter mortification before the hunters returned.

She moved to the tree and hit first one foot and then the other against its rough bark. The aching sting that traveled as far up as her knees was reassuring. A leaf or two fell on her gray knitted hood, and when she started to remove these she discovered that, while shoulder and elbow still responded, her four fingers separated from her thumb in fur-lined mittens refused to unbend from the barrel of the BB gun. Frightened now, she began to swallow hard and fast to hold down the gasping sobs that were trying to push out of her throat. To keep from a breakdown into complete "girl" or "baby" helplessness, she stuck her tongue out and took into her lips the edge of the blue steel BB-gun barrel. But the comfort she sought was rudely displaced by the sharp pain of contact between the warm moist tip of her tongue and the icy steel. She jerked her head back; the shock diverted her attention from her other grievances, and the sudden indrawing, away from the instrument of pain, caused a flow of life into her rigid fingers. Gently she let the BB gun slide between her legs into the snow; then she gingerly eased fingers and thumbs from the mittens and made a fist inside the shelter of her palms. Circulation seemed still to be there, and gradually the blood flowed again, and she could feel a slight sting of warmth in her fingers. The raw tip of her tongue burned, and she dared not touch the end of her nose, raw, too, from the constant flow of mucus. She fell again into waiting, comforted a little by the nearness of the tree.

A fine snow began to sift from the ominous blanket of sky, and a wind starting low on the cornfield rattled the numb stalks as it swirled the powder-dry drift, which stayed close to the ground for a while and then climbed up to lose itself in the falling flakes. She saw the hunters approaching in the distance, obliquely stumbling now and then in sleet-covered furrows, each with gun in one hand and furry spoil dangling head down from the other.

Her own interest merely token, she had on other occasions followed the chase through woods and across fields, her heart thumping madly, as startled as the flushed quarry, dragging the BB gun, and once or twice taking fraudulent aim and firing just to seem really a part of things. But though she dared not admit it, the idea of killing was distasteful to her; and the sight of the victim stopped in panic flight by rifle or shotgun—splattering the white snow with red dots, perhaps not giving up immediately or still trying to hop or contort out of pain to safety—brought revolt and repugnance; and some vague element of the abomination became transferred to the doers of the deed. Not to her brother so much: there was no violence in his nature, and no fear was conjured up at the sight of blood that he had let, because he seemed to have killed impersonally, as an expected duty. Her father's smile of satisfaction and the bloody burden he carried, however, gave her a squeamish sensation, which she felt should be associated with him but could not understand.

As they neared her, crunching across the road in front of the delivery wagon, she reached down into the snow for the gun at her feet and started toward them, hoping that what had happened to her during their absence didn't show and that she looked brave and unconcerned and useful, in what way she didn't try to define. She glanced anxiously at her brother and wiped her aching nose with her blue wool coat sleeve so that she would look less un-neat. He was staring into the tree above her head.

"Hey, look!" he said, gesturing with the rabbit. "Look, Kitty!" ("Kitty" was reserved for times when he himself felt playful or when he knew that she felt alone and needed love and warmth.)

Well out from under the almost bare branches, dusted now with the white snow powder, she turned to look up. She blinked water out of her eyes to see better and a second later wished that she hadn't looked at all. One of the forks in the tree seemed swollen: a tumorous, bark-colored growth bulged at the point where limb joined trunk. With her eyes cleared of moisture she could see the slightest movement in the bulge—a settling into position, a shifting into deeper closeness. A revulsion quite different from that caused by the sight of the dead rabbits came over her. Her spine and a band around the center of her stomach seemed to be in the grip of some creeping thing. She was looking at a knot of hibernating snakes, perhaps water moccasins, perhaps only harmless field or water snakes, but nevertheless congenitally loathsome, intrinsically repulsive—to her, the quintessence of everything abhorrent.

"Shoot, Katherine," her father said, pointing upward, too, with his rabbit. "Go ahead. See if you can hit one."

Unconscious of her movement, she stepped back from the tree, at the same time raising her loaded gun. Still mittened, she forced her forefinger into the trigger and pulled, discharging all of her loathing at the noxious bundle under which she had stood unaware a moment before. The bullet must have hit, because some extremity, head or tail, uncoiled itself sluggishly, reached blindly into the cold air, then recoiled again. Her father laughed at her, while she stood and forced down the thin saliva that oozed from the depressions under her tongue and made her want to be sick.

The hood of the delivery wagon was covered with blankets, but in spite of this and other precautions, there was always the tense, shivering wait while the starter was tested, hopefully and persistently to the last, slow, grumbling protest of the unwilling motor and weakened battery. Then always the hand crank was resorted to.

Her brother would climb out first and sometimes, though he strained to the point of sweating, he was frustrated by the groaning motor. Then he and her father would switch positions; her brother would sit next to her and manipulate the mysterious lifeline, while her father puffed and panted and said "Damn!"—until, with a vicious kick that sometimes ejected the crank into the snow—in its flight striking vindictively at the hand that gripped it—the motor would turn over, and her father would catapult around the side into the driver's post. He would take just enough time to throw the crank under the seat as her brother stood up to transfer the controls and then slid past her to sit on the outside, so that she would be somewhat protected from the cold.

And then would begin the long journey home, with familiar landmarks seeming deliberately retarded by her urgency. A storm-windowed farmhouse sending out one curl of smoke, as differentiated from another sending out two; a steepled church at a crossroads, with its biparietal outhouse; the truck garden of Nick, the Greek, shut down for winter now; the long stretch of Plainfield road, its closer-together, occasionally lighted cottages indicating the nearness to town; finally the careful descent down the slope of Buell Avenue with much use of brakes and shifting of gears; then the top of Western Avenue and the even more hazardous descent down a steeper slope, where one had to be expert on roller skates and cautious on a bicycle and where sometimes in the night the accustomed stillness had been ruptured by futilely grinding brakes and screeching tires, prelude to a collision and the split second of stopped-time stillness that followed.

From the top of the hill she could see, immediately after the crossing of Bluff Street, the beginning of Cass Street and the Cass Street Bridge. Over this bridge on one memorable occasion, on a starry winter night not so cold as this one promised to be, she had risked punishment by strap to do the unmentionable, the thrilling-to-the-utmost, the longed-for-in-secret by every child in the town. Going out with their sled, she and her brother had promised to stay on Bluff Street; but on this occasion, overcome by some sense of daring, some perversity, some madness brought on by a full moon, they had decided—taking turns at policing the four corners for danger—to start at the top of Western Avenue and bellyflop down the vertiginous descent at meteor speed, across the Bluff Street intersection.

There had been the trudge up, the last-minute look down, the signal for the take-off, the impact on belly of sled. Speed gathered on speed, and, helpless under momentum, she had screwed her face into a knot against the needle sting of upflung snow, and, not having known before that snow smelled, had smelled its whiteness along with the smell of steel and sulphur from the sparks flying up from the runners. The approach to the bottom of the hill marked the greatest danger, and passing over it the greatest triumph. Pressed flat, shooting past the very spot where the hideous accidents occurred, she could imagine the wheels crushing her body, bursting skin, cracking bones, smashing her skull so that her brains spattered out and froze to the ground.

The intersection was passed so quickly that fright and rapture mingled in a suffusing triumph, and before she knew what sensations had passed through her she was skimming lightly and safely over the stretch of bridge and coasting slower and slower to a gentle halt against the wooden elevation that divided pedestrian from vehicle. Trembling, eyes streaming, cheeks stinging, walking as though for the first time and as though descending from a great flight into space, she had dragged the sled back across the bridge to her waiting brother and taken her guardian's post.

This was in many ways more tormenting than the jeopardies of her own descent. Suppose some car was approaching without lights. Suppose she misjudged, and a vehicle presumably crawling on the ice-covered pavement was in fact moving at top speed, to mete out the extreme of punishment and make her her brother's murderer. Suppose he would be the one lying there mangled, brains frozen to pavement, sled smashed into splinters, runners twisted beyond recognition, gray overcoat soaked with blood and intestines? She stood with her hand raised in an agony of incertitude until, impatient, he called out from the top; and the voice drifting down from the waiting figure poised under the flickering street lamp at the top of the hill activated the waiting figure motionless under the flickering street lamp at the bottom of the hill. With a last anguished look in all directions, she dropped her arm. Then she stood in wait for him to catapult past the corner of Bluff Street, past the danger spot, and felt—as she stood planted square in the middle of the street, vulnerable herself to vengeful parents or oncoming vehicles—that with her own small body she would hold off any danger to him. Blind seeker after an unattainable planet, Iphigenia already begun.

She held her breath now as they descended the hill in the delivery wagon, but tried not to show that she recognized, inexperienced as she was, her father's lack of driving skill, never to be overcome.

Two
The Closed Room

*

People were always amused when Katherine Dunham told them that she remembered the circumstances of her birth. At five and a half she told her new mother all about the other mother who had died, and about riding home from the hospital in her mother's arms, and how the horse had shied at the shadow of a butterfly as the pale lady with black hair piled in a pompadour stepped from the surrey.

It was a warm day just nine days after the twenty-second of June. As the horse shied, her father took her in his arms, then gave her back to her mother, who walked up the driveway trailing her white linen dress and looking down at her seventh child—her second by the child's father, the young tailor.

Katherine Dunham tried once or twice to go back even farther than that and tell about the nine babies in a row at the hospital, all in baskets and all screaming for attention at the top of their newly discovered lungs, and how she howled louder than all the others when her father picked her up and put her into her mother's arms. But at that point the attention of listeners, willing to indulge her fantasies thus far, began to wander, discouraging her from further retrospect.

What she knew nothing of was Albert Dunham's trip to

the village of Glen Ellyn shortly after his wife, twenty years his senior, had been delivered of their first child, Albert Millard Dunham, Jr.

Albert Millard Dunham, the father, was fully aware that his marriage was unusual, and not just because of the discrepancy in age between him and his wife. There was her fair skin, her French-Canadian background; in addition, she was a divorcée, with five children and four grandchildren. All these factors provided material for social discrimination and malicious comment and gave rise to a variety of disagreeable situations which could be avoided, as he saw things, by a removal from the City's congested South Side, already stirring uneasily at hints of invasion by raucous Southern cousins. Her charm, beauty, intellect, and musical accomplishment had placed Albert Dunham on his knees before Fanny June Taylor; her property holdings on Prairie and Indiana avenues and her assistant principalship at one of the big City schools made it easier, once the marriage had become a fact, to leave the City and make a home in the suburbs.

Just beyond the train stop of Maywood was the village of Glen Ellyn, untouched at that time by the economic pressures or racial discriminations or restrictive codes of the City. It was composed essentially of the middle class—upper white-collar workers, lesser business executives, commuters to the City at seven o'clock and back again at seven, with, in addition, a few retired gentleman farmers and building contractors and modestly well-to-do bankers and businessmen, who represented the noncommuting elite. There had been no occasion for concern over invasion by persons of unorthodox colors, creeds, or religions. The rare chauffeurs and numerous maidservants and cooks and gardeners were almost all Negroes; like the office workers, they commuted, but in the reverse direction. Years before Albert Dunham's arrival on the scene, a distant relative of his, Marie Clark, had worked her way through kitchen after kitchen of the village, while her husband, Earley Clark, clipped and mowed his way through as many gardens and lawns; until, like blemishes grown so familiar that they are at last unnoticed, they had settled in the lowlands of the village, bought property, become voters and taxpayers. By then it was too late for decent action, so they were indulgently overlooked or referred to with the affectionate condescension reserved for retired family retainers or illiterate relations.

It was through the intervention of Marie and Earley Clark that Albert Dunham, chafing more than ever at the inconvenience of the City because of his newborn son, came upon a choice property in an outlying area still in the stage of subdivision. When he first looked at it, a dirt road had just been cut through a wheatfield and cement sidewalks were still fresh in their wooden frames. A few brick bungalows were under construction, a few were finished, and new grass was sprouting in front yards behind sparse green hedges. After much bargaining, many trips, and with the last-minute intervention of his wife, the young man finally took title to a plot of wheatfield; in a short time the foundations were laid and the framework was started for a two-story wooden house.

A neighborhood committee was waiting for one false move on the part of the interloper. The people of Glen Ellyn had discovered, soon after the purchase, that the dark young man was married to, not just acting for or employed by, the tall, fair-skinned woman who often accompanied him to offices of realtors, contractors, and builders, and this caused no end of chagrin and unconcealed resentment. The neighboring landowners felt duped and misled but lacked a definite incident to seize upon; they sulked, held meetings, and foresaw the irreparable decline of property values. It happened that most of the scattered dwellings completed or under construction were of brick; a hastily set up zoning commission, drawing boundaries as irregular as the markings of a rabbit warren, concluded that Albert Dunham's lot fell into a division reserved for brick houses. The owner of the wheatfield, a farmer in the process of retiring on the profits of these subdivisions, saw in this strategy a double-edged knife with one side of the blade turned toward himself. He opposed the coalition and won. But he could not change the spirit of men, and the next night an ineffective, home-manufactured explosive shattered the downstairs windows, which had just been installed. Albert Dunham's reaction was swift and to the point. Told what had happened by Earley Clark, he descended from the six o'clock interurban armed with a double-barreled shotgun, determination in his stride, murder in his eyes. The neighbors had counted on no such reaction and withdrew behind their piles of red brick and cement bags to confer, or peeped between starched bungalow curtains, watching the angry young man inspect the damage, look about defiantly, and then install himself in the tool shed on the front of the lot. Here he settled down for a vigil that extended through that night and every night, until the last coat of paint had been applied to the house and the carriage barn behind it.

The house was roomy, planned to accommodate, in addition to the immediate family of Fanny June Dunham, several members of her extended clan, who, until her death, took advantage of her generosity. The rotation of these guests was so regular as to make them seem fixtures. The eldest daughter Louise and her children hardly said goodbye before they were again on the doorstep, with suitcases and parcels and tales of abuse by a drunken husband and father. The youngest daughter by the previous marriage visited at regular intervals, and her visits were protracted, beginning as they did at the earliest stage of her successive pregnancies and lasting through parturition. The middle daughter—also named Fanny June—had married before her mother's second marriage, and it was George Weir, her husband, who had been responsible for the meeting that resulted in Albert Dunham's marriage to the much-courted divorcée.

George Weir was of the color classification known as "octoroon" and freely circulated between the two opposing color groups of the City. He also was a tailor's apprentice, and when the ambitious Albert Dunham decided to leave the firm of German tailors where both young men were employed, George Weir joined him in the daring adventure of an independent business in the Fair Building, a structure in the very center of the City which in those days was considered a skyscraper. Here they attracted much of the clientele from their former employers, and only they knew of the scanty meals they shared sitting cross-legged on the cutting table or of the coffeepot that simmered in the washroom from early morning unil late at night, giving them stimulus when food had been too scanty.

George Weir introduced his friend to his bride, and Albert Dunham met and fell in love with the bride's mother. By the time he felt that he could ask her to marry him, George Weir was the father of a girl, Helen. By the time the Weir family paid its visits to the house in Glen Ellyn, a boy, Everett, was out of diapers. George Weir was happy with the life of the City and with his children, so fair of skin that they like him would have free access to all of the accompanying benefits. He had no aspirations beyond the immediate enterprise, which daily was proving more lucrative.

His partner, on the other hand, was set on suburban or even country life and could wish for nothing more desirable than the transformed wheatfield and the two-story frame house with the carriage barn behind—even though he had not bargained for the heterogenous household that he had inherited with his handsome wife. But he was aware that, despite her devotion to her new life and the responsibility she felt toward first the son and then the daughter, Fanny June was inevitably torn in her affections by the demands of her grown children. She was, in fact, unable to refuse the hospitality or even the financial help needed from time to time by one or more of them. But the least worrisome of her many responsibilities was the family of George Weir.

Katherine Dunham liked her unnaturally placed niece and nephew well enough, but even before she could talk intelligibly she took a strong dislike to the children of her half sister Louise and to their father also. One of her reasons for disliking the girl child in particular was that she always ended up wearing her clothes. And she mistrusted her half sister Louise's husband because she had once seen him in the ugly condition of drunkenness that resulted in violence. He was careful to call at the house only in the afternoon, when he was certain that the parents had left for the day, and he always went back to the City before they returned.

Henry, the youngest of Fanny June's children by her former marriage, was one of the permanent residents of the gray house. When left alone, he seemed quite tractable. When aroused, he fell into a fury, striking out at anything near and uttering cries only partly human. Katherine Dunham was fond of him because sometimes when she lay all alone and bored in her crib, he would creep into the room and lean over and look deep down into her eyes as though searching for understanding. They would communicate in their secret language, and what he said pleased the child, who always laughed. Sometimes he would sit for a long while catching stray flies that wandered into the room in summertime and show them to her before throwing them out of the window. Their frantic efforts to escape distressed him, and she felt that he caught them and threw them out not only to please her, but to save them from the flyswatter. When Louise and her husband and children and callers teased Henry just to see him tormented into a speechless rage, she would feel very sad and want to stroke him or murmur something in their own language. But he was too far gone by then to be reached and would be led, frothing at the mouth and with eyes rolling far back in his head, to Grandmother Buckner's room, because she was the only one who could calm him, being a little different in behavior from the others herself. Once the child heard her mother, as she sat stroking the unhappy boy's head, offer an explanation about Henry's erratic behavior and frequent communications with inhabitants of a world that only he could see. He had fallen from a highchair as a baby and fractured his skull and he had never been in possession of all his senses since then. Henry was fortunate enough to die early.

Grandmother Buckner tried again and again to tell the polygenetic members of the Glen Ellyn household what she knew from her Indian forebears and what she had learned from the family of dolls that lined the shelves of her bedroom. The only listeners were her daughter Fanny June and two small children apparently attached in some way to her daughter, but just how and in what relationship the old lady couldn't quite figure out.

Her daughter had always been a good child, as far back as when she was a little girl, dark-eyed and long-haired, in Winnipeg. Visits to Fanny June's old Indian grandmother, Grandmother Buckner's mother, had not frightened her, as many second-generation children of such unions had been frightened. Mother and child would drive deep into the country, sometimes in winter when the snow was piled higher than the rooftop of the log cabin where the old Indian woman lived alone. Then they would have to go by sleigh, and the little girl would never complain of the cold or cry at the sounds of animals when the horses turned into the woods near the log cabin. They would stay overnight, and the old Indian woman would prepare infusions of herbs and dried berries to make the little girl strong, because she was always frail and pale and too tall for her age. They would drive back the next day, and Grandmother Buckner would feel pleased with herself because she had taken the child, against the wishes of her school-teaching, French-Canadian husband, to the people he called "heathen."

When he died, Grandmother Buckner—whose people were English farmers and had little use for the descendants of the French settlers—changed her name from Guillaume to Williams and married the man whose name she carried thenceforth. The daughter, Fanny June, proved to be exceptionally apt in school, and soon after the family moved to Windsor, the mother decided to send the girl, then fifteen years of age, across Lake Michigan into Detroit for further schooling. Immediately after graduation from a school for elementary schoolteachers, the daughter fell in love with and married a man named Taylor, about whom little was known by the family except that he had sired five children and that his own father had been a Russian Jew. He was swarthy of skin, so everyone supposed that he had on his mother's side some mixture of Indian or Negro or Asiatic blood or perhaps all three.

Grandmother Buckner stayed in Windsor until her second husband died. As she was packing her belongings to make the trip to the Middle West to live with her daughter, she fell from a stepladder and broke her leg. Incompetent medical care led to its amputation, and it was during this confinement that the old woman, feeling herself alone and not being at all sure of welcome by her daughter's new husband in an already multiplied household, began collecting dolls. She had always wanted a large family, and the dolls were a kind of substitute for all the sons and daughters she had never had; they also became the friends and counselors of her declining years.

Some of the dolls had belonged to her when she was a child. These were dressed in worn and faded gingham, some in fringed suede or buckskin jerkins and skirts. They were very old, and if they had originally been painted, time and the affectionate handling of a lonely child had removed all traces, leaving only the crude torso and features fashioned long ago by some north-woods craftsman. There were dolls that had belonged to her daughter Fanny June and to Fanny June's daughters also. These had china features, with bodies of cloth stuffed with cotton or sawdust. One or two of the most elegant had bodies of fine kid leather, and delicate hands and feet of china, and heads and shoulders and elaborate coiffures of china or porcelain. Some were babies in long, time-yellowed baptismal dresses. Their faces were round and for the most part blank. One or two tried to smile, but because they were paintless, with an eye missing or the end of a nose chipped off, the effect was grotesque. Some of the dolls were more recent, gifts from the indulgent daughter who recognized the withdrawal of the old woman from a world she neither understood nor wanted to be a part of, but from which at the same time she would have liked to have some regard.

Her grandchildren laughed at her when she brought the dolls to the table to share her meals, and, if she left the room for a moment, brought their friends to look at the array. She would run them from the room, stumping after them as fast as she could on her wooden leg, sometimes forgetting that she was waving one of her precious family in the air as a weapon. Henry was often with her, and he, too, would join in the routing of the enemy, which only occasioned more taunts and jeers and laughter, until the old woman, exasperated and worn out by her efforts, would retreat to her room and bar the door with chairs and tables.

Of all this Fanny June remained unaware, seeing only the steady unhappiness and decline of both the misfits, the solemn introspection of her young son, and the concern of her young daughter. Sensing the affection that the children felt for the old woman and their defective half brother, she took them from time to time to her mother's room and explained the doll family and told them not to be afraid of Grandmother Buckner as the other children were. They examined the wooden leg as the old lady held her skirt for them to see, and looked with great interest at the doll in the old-fashioned babies' highchair, and the one always sleeping in the little wooden crib, and at the others on shelves all around the room. The old lady talked to the dolls and listened to their answers. She fed them bits from her own meals, which were brought to her on a tray after she refused to leave her room. Those with cavities for stomachs were neatest; the others were forced all the same to partake of the repasts, which included cooked cereal, soft-boiled eggs, mashed potatoes, and different kinds of fruit. Like overstuffed Roman senators or unco-operative children, they sat with bits of food smeared around their mouths and over the front of their clothing, taffeta as well as gingham. Since Grandmother Buckner had done with washing them when she took to her room to stay, the food remained stuck to their vacant smiles and overflowing from their partly open lips.

The youngest half sister seemed to have installed herself and her children permanently in the Glen Ellyn house, and although her husband continued to live in the City, he paid frequent and fruitful enough visits to ensure the enlargement of his family. A hardship was worked on the two children of Fanny June and Albert Dunham, who had to relinquish their room to the half sister and her children. The brother slept on the parlor couch, and the girl's iron-barred crib was moved into her parents' bedroom. The air was heavy with trouble, both present and to come, and in the midst of it all the child reacted by standing for long stretches of time looking out of the front window at the houses that had sprung up on all sides, trying to identify the few neighbor children that she knew, trying to recall her waking and sleeping fears of the night before.

At night when she was undressed and placed inside the crib and the protective iron fence was hooked into place, she always looked around the room, stealthily so that the others would not know of her secret fears, to see if there were any indications of "Them." A light would be left burning on her mother's bedside cupboard if it were dark, or the shade only partly drawn if it were light outside. Then she would be left alone to listen to the sounds of a still, closed room and to wait for Them. She always went to sleep and didn't even awaken when her mother and father went to bed. Later in the night, however, something would happen that would start her wide-awake, and she would sit up in bed damp with perspiration and cold with fear. There would be no identifiable sound, and she could see no strange form. But she knew that the creatures were there, and that They were in some way interested in her, and that They would do her harm if they could. She knew just what They looked like, and there was nothing especially outstanding about their appearance; it was an evilness which exuded from Them that began a fortification inside her, once she realized that this was something she had to face alone.

On one occasion she had cried out in the night, and her mother had taken her into her own bed. But this hadn't pleased her father, and she was afraid to be ejected altogether from the room, where she felt at least some protection in the black of night, at least some comfort from the regular breathing of her father and the fitful breathing of her mother. If she were moved into the open space of the parlor, her brother would be there, but he was, to her, not much more equipped than she to deal with such malevolence; and, besides, there was no door between the parlor and the hallway where (it had somehow become imbedded in her consciousness) these creatures had their abode. In the daytime she looked upon the halltree in the hallway with mistrust and avoided it altogether when she was alone or at night.

But They were somehow also connected with the upstairs part of the house, where there had been other mysterious happenings, and where later the greatest mystery of all was to take place, the closed door behind which her mother lay to await her death. In the room in the middle of the night They lay in wait for her, and once she knew that there was no outside aid, she lay waiting for Them. They were called "Crandalls"—why, she didn't question; They just were. And They wore gray striped baseball suits and caps, which she must have seen once when her father took her to a baseball game. The faces were formless and evil, with no defining color or features, and more of the dead than of the living. They wanted her badly, but though she might be afraid of them, she was not afraid enough to give in to them. They were familiar to her and were a family, and more than this she could not figure out. Her brother, in whom she confided, could help her only by accompanying her to the halltree and taking off all the coats and umbrellas and showing her that no people lived there. He also took her to any upstairs room that happened to be unoccupied and made her look under the bed and in the closets, and she let him believe that she had dreamed it all. But within herself she knew that They were there waiting and she thought of these things when she stood in front of the plate-glass window of the parlor, looking out at the children playing in the front yard across the street.

As she learned to walk more freely by herself, her world took on new sizes, shapes, and colors. The changing season helped, too, and as spring warmed into summer, she took a great interest in the barn and in the end of the lot where it merged into fields no longer planted in wheat, but green with long grass and dotted white with daisies and yellow with buttercups and blue with gentian and pale wild violets. She noticed her brother more, because his was the task of following her, of finding her when she wandered into hiding places, of trying to keep her out of trouble, of trying to answer her never-ending "why's" about things and people and events. With others she was silent and withdrawn. With him she always sought communication, half the time not waiting for answers, which he gave only after deliberation and full certainty, feeling the responsibility of his position as guide and mentor.

Somewhere, either at the end of the lot on which the house stood or farther out in the middle of the daisy field, was a hoary old apple tree. It stood alone, the next trees being on the property of a neighbor on the other side of the path that loosely marked a future road. The subdivision could still be considered in a pastoral stage, particularly on the side of the road where Albert Dunham's house stood. By accident or intention the fields behind the house and on each side were still vacant, and for this the father was grateful. The carriage horse was put to pasture in these fields and the skittish mare was led around an improvised exercise track on Sunday mornings.

During the lazy summer afternoons the children, who by now had settled into the foursome of Helen and Everett Weir and Albert and Katherine Dunham—on rare occasions joined by children from one of the more friendly families of the area—would gather under the apple tree to play at housekeeping, exchange confidences, make necklaces of the daisies and wood violets they collected in the field and under the apple tree, and climb into the upper branches of the tree itself.

A new world opened for the child with communication on the level of the others. The excitement was not so much in talking, because her niece and nephew were so voluble and clever that they automatically took over the conversation wherever they were, even with elders, who never tired of the witticisms and repartee that they had developed as a kind of defense mechanism in the competitive world they had known in the City, and in the often conflicting inner circle of their own family. Her brother did not say much, but what he said was always wise, and she found herself listening more and more to his counsel and trying more and more to please him and make up for not being a boy.

The excitement of articulation in a comprehensible language came in mastering numerous jingles and songs, some of which were re-edited from the original by her niece and nephew into cleverer or more amusing versions, as, for example, in the case of a song called "Under the Old Apple Tree":

"In the shade of the old apple tree
A hobo sat down on a bee."

She sang this version lustily, with, when she sang it in front of grownups, consequences remarkably close to those of the hobo's experience. But they were proud of her recitation of

"I had a little pony whose name was Dapple Gray
I lent him to a lady, to ride a mile away."

Saddened by the thought of the unhappy pony, ridden under whip and lash and through mud by the ungrateful lady, she would say the verse over and over in a monotonous chant, until she had worked herself into a kind of abstracted melancholy in which she and the pony and the mud and the switch were all one in a dreary, thankless world.

The melancholia of this period was rooted in actual events. One of these was the disappearance of the white mare Nellie from the stable, on a late spring night during one of the electrical storms that hit the Middle Western States without warning—sometimes with accompanying winds that turned into tornadoes, sometimes simply splitting trees and setting fire to barns and causing lightning rods to discharge into the overcharged atmosphere like Fourth-of-July sparklers.

On one such storm-charged, rainless night the mare panicked in her stall and attempted to escape under the stout oak beam that barred the exit; she broke her back in the attempt. The storm and the noises and the shouts woke the child, and she was glad of an excitement stronger than the presence of the leering "Crandalls." She could see the lightning all around and, in its flashes, the grass of the fields bowing low under the sweep of the wind, and the old apple tree yielding up twigs and leaves and blossoms and finally whole branches. She could not see the barn, but she could see that her father was not in his bed; and soon she heard, above the noise of the storm and sound of voices calling and shouting, an explosion like the banging of a large door. As she looked at the empty bed in the flashes of lightning, she began to try piecing together something else that had been worrying her for some time. But as the questions were taking form in her mind, the storm subsided, and she dozed off; and by morning she had forgotten all but a dim uneasiness.

The excitement about the mare took her mind off this worry. She was told to stay in the front part of the house until well into the afternoon, even though the day had become calm and beautiful after the storm, and she would have liked to visit the apple tree and gather the fallen branches of blossoms. When no one thought that she was listening, they talked of the pity of the white mare. Her father had stayed home from his work to survey the damage of the storm and was in an unusually disagreeable mood, not wanting to talk about the horse and finding the children too much underfoot. When she asked why it was a pity about the white mare, and what was a pity, and where was Nellie going now, the adults looked at each other in surprise and said that Nellie had run away in the night. But, standing at the front window, she had seen a wagon, pulled by two horses and with several men and lots of rope and iron bars on it, turn into the driveway. She couldn't follow its progress because the back part of the house was forbidden to her until afternoon, but she waited patiently, and after a while the wagon went out of the driveway again, and Nellie lay on it while two men kept trying to adjust a tarpaulin to cover her from sight.

She passed this off as another of the strange whimsies of adults and wished that she could move on to something else now and not worry about what had been gnawing at the back of her mind during the storm last night. There was something mysterious about it, and the reason came to her as Nellie's limp body, legs thrust awkwardly into the air—she who had been so proud and graceful—jolted around in the wagon as it turned out of the driveway and off down the road away from the house. The mystery was connected with the empty bed during the storm.

She woke less often in the night than during the cold dark winter months, but she was aware of the fact that there was now only her father's steady breathing from the large bed and that the fitful breathing of her mother, which sometimes of late had been interspersed with groans and once or twice with weeping, no longer accompanied his. Once she had experimented with sliding from her crib, which was now uncomfortably small for her and therefore left with the fence down, and tiptoeing to the side of the bed where her mother had always slept to see if she had simply not been hearing correctly. She was frightened to discover that in fact her mother was not there, and she crept back to bed to think about it; but then she fell asleep and in the morning didn't remember.

A few days later she did remember and asked where her mother was and why she never came from the City in time for supper any more and why she was always gone in the morning. Her brother didn't answer, and the others repeated what they had said on other occasions, that her mother was very busy and returned always after the child was asleep and left before she awoke. She tried staying awake when she was put to bed but always fell asleep before either her mother or her father came into the room, and was cross with herself the next day when she thought about it. After the storm this thought was continually with her, especially because on Sundays also her father was in evidence but her mother was not. Once she complained so much and followed everyone about making such a racket, trying to solve her loneliness and fill in her loss, that a conference of the grownups was held and some decision reached in her favor.

That night, just at her bedtime, her mother came into the room as she had done so often, dressed in the clothes that she had worn to the City to teach school in, wearing a straw sailor hat with a black bow, on top of hair piled high into a shining black pompadour. The child could not know the effort that this deception cost Fanny June, nor was she more than vaguely aware of the whiteness of her mother's skin or of the deep shadows of suffering under her sunken black eyes. She could not tell that her mother could scarcely walk, much less carry the nightshirted, ecstatic child to the darkened kitchen, where by lamplight, as on so many occasions before, she went to the screened-in cooling shelf of the pantry and came back with a pitcher of milk and poured a single glass and, with the child on her knee, took a sip and then held the glass to the child's lips. The child paid no attention to the fact that all the others were suddenly out of sight or that the shades were drawn even though it was summer and the nights darkened later. She did not know that this would be the last time that she would see her mother alive.

Fanny June Dunham must have known for a long time that her illness was a malignant one. She must have hated to have her husband know it and to realize that the blow of her death would be a bitter one to him, and the responsibility of the children's upbringing a cruel one. And she didn't see anyone prepared at the moment to take over the task on her departure. Her daughter Fanny had her hands quite full and, moreover, was absorbed in her own interests. A sister of Albert Dunham, Lulu, was fond of the children and they of her, but she lived in the City in what was virtually a tenement, and all sorts of odd people circulated around her just because she was goodhearted and unsuspecting and generous. In the opinion of the mother, that was not a proper environment for children, especially for the oversusceptible daughter. The son seemed to have a mind of his own and was wise enough to choose and discard and select from life around him those things that would serve him best, and to look at people from a great distance and with far more discrimination than his years warranted.

Tears ran down the mother's face and over her lips and into the glass as she sipped the milk to please the child, then held it to the child's mouth. The child reached to her and patted her cheek, feeling safe and eternally secure and so full of contentment that she thought only of the goodness of things; though the exact picture as it was, tears and all, remained with her as her last remembrance of her mother.

Death came slowly and painfully to the woman in the closed room, and as she wasted into death she wanted to be alone. The daughters and their families had moved into the house to wait with her, and a nurse came from the City and sat through the long nights. The young father stayed more at home through the winter and made every effort to know his children better, even at the sacrifice of his business, which needed more of his attention at this time than at any other. The child hung around the fringes of these vicissitudes, picking up what information she could and storing it for later assimilation. She was thwarted in her efforts to gain access to the upstairs room: the mother did not wish to be remembered by her children as she knew herself to be during her dissolution.

On Sunday afternoons the father would take his daughter on one knee and, with an arm around his son, would try to recapture his own Memphis childhood long enough to relay to them stories that his father and *his* father had told among themselves, with the children listening in front of a fire where hoecake browned in the ashes. He hit with great success upon the saga of Br'er Rabbit and how he outwitted Br'er Fox and all the rest of the Tennessee woods animals, until the Tar Baby outwitted *him*. Br'er Rabbit dressed up and leaving church on Sunday and bowing low to Br'er Fox, who waited outside licking his chops and planning how to work out an ambush for Br'er Rabbit, who had selected Br'er Lion as walking companion through the woods that morning and therefore felt very smug and took off his hat and bowed low to Br'er Fox, grinning all the time. Br'er Rabbit courting the same girl as Br'er Fox and always arriving by a short cut, so that by the time Br'er Fox arrived hot and tired, Br'er Rabbit was sitting cross-legged in the porch swing, fanning himself and drinking lemonade and making pretty speeches to the lady. And then sometimes Br'er Rabbit singing another tune, finding himself all alone in the woods, with Br'er Fox burrowing into his doorway or staring greedily at him through a clump of bushes where he had injudiciously taken a nap; and Br'er Rabbit having to do some fast talking and many times just barely escaping Br'er Fox's cooking pot . . .

The child would demand over and over again the description of the Tar Baby that the farmer made and put in his corn patch, knowing Br'er Rabbit's inclination toward courting fair ladies, and how the Tar Baby melted in the hot Tennessee sun and wouldn't answer when Br'er Rabbit addressed her in the courtliest of manners—so that he became angry and hit her and stuck to the soft tar and would have been apprehended by the farmer and severely chastised and maybe even eaten if his enemy hadn't come along and, after taunting him, let himself be talked into releasing him, only to be made fun of later for his gullibility as Br'er Rabbit gaily skipped off to safety.

So the mortal feud unwound itself through episode after episode, and when Br'er Monkey and Br'er Lion entered the scene, the flavor of ancestral Africa delighted the child, and her pleasure was unmarred by any attempt to rationalize the seepage of this distant continent into not-so-far-off Tennessee.

The boy listened but preferred the tales of Great-grandfather Dunham, who, of his own free will and dodging, as it were, between projectiles from the muskets of the Union troops, had hitched two steeds to the Big House family carriage and maneuvered the young and the womenfolk of the family—with silverware, heirlooms, and all—to safety across the line. The father explained that the father of John Dunham, his own father, had been a Malagasy, which meant that he had been one of the few of the slaves recruited on the east coast of Africa, and that they came from an island named Madagascar. In their blood flowed the blood of Malay people as well as a type of African different from the Guinea or West Coast African people, one of whom the father of John Dunham took as a wife.

On winter Sunday evenings the child missed the sound of music as she lay in her bed waiting for sleep. Before, when her mother had been with them, there had been music from the small organ in the parlor and sometimes the delicate tinkling tones from the instrument in the corner under a cover that they were never to touch. It was called a harp, and once she had stood in the doorway of the parlor and watched her mother seated behind it, face against the wooden frame, arms extended to embrace it as it tilted into her lap between her knees. Her mother was moving her fingers over the instrument and changing little pegs and listening to the result as she plucked the strings, and her father sat near by doing the same thing to the guitar that he loved to play on Sunday evenings. After the child was in bed again, they seemed to reach some sort of tonal rapport, and she fell asleep to music that they were practicing together.

With her father alone, there was seldom music. Once she saw him come down from the room upstairs and go straight into the parlor, where the fire had gone out in the grate, and sit with his face buried in his hands, while his shoulders shook and sounds like crying came from between his fingers; but then he stood up and went to the guitar and took it from its case and sat and began to make the plucking sounds while he turned screws at the top, and his face was in the light, and while it looked wretchedly unhappy, it was not wet from tears, so he could not have been crying.

Katherine Dunham loved new clothes, especially because, long before her old ones were outgrown or outworn, they were swiftly appropriated by the rapacious Louise for her own daughters who were the child's approximate age. During the last winter in Glen Ellyn she wore rompers and overalls almost always, inheriting her brother's outgrown ones when no one seemed to have time to replenish her depleted wardrobe. She remembered with nostalgia the times when her mother had dressed her on Sunday afternoons in woolen dresses with flounces or cotton dresses with stiffly starched pleats before a Sunday buggy ride. Her lower lip thrust forward as she saw the same dresses on the two disagreeable half nieces who, with their mother, were again among the multitude feasting on the hospitality of the dying mother. The fact that she might not now fit into the dresses made no difference whatsoever.

Her deprivation was given emphasis by these constant

reminders, and as her own condition became sorrier, her dislike for her relatives increased. Her father no longer troubled to cut her hair on alternate Sundays, and the difference in quality between her own and that of her relatives was brought home to her by the fact that the longer it grew the more unmanageable it became; no one was able to untangle the snarls and knots, so that after a while it resembled more the brier patch in which Br'er Rabbit outwitted Br'er Fox than hair on the head of a three-and-a-half-year-old girl. She would stand in front of a mirror long enough for her to see into, and she would comb at and pull at and scrape over the nappy surface without ever being able to approach the roots, and tear away at the matted ringlets until her scalp was too sore to touch. Applications of Vaseline did not help, and she felt trapped by her unbecoming attire, her unkempt coiffure, and the gathering gloom of the household, underneath which ran currents of cross-purpose reaching beyond the life and death of the woman upstairs.

By now Albert Dunham had learned that the greater part of his wife's worldly goods had been cozened from her by her children, that a house on Prairie Avenue and a flat building on Indiana Avenue in the City had gone for the reparation of some folly of one of the daughters or for the hospitalization and burial of Grandmother Buckner, who had gone with her dolls to the cemetery in Glen Ellyn the spring before, or to committing Henry, who had become dangerously unruly under vicious baiting, to an institution. Her insurance had been borrowed against in full for this last illness, and, foreseeing disaster, she had denied herself the comforts of hospital care and even tried with her last feeble energy to persuade her daughters to dismiss the nurse who ministered to her at night and increased the dosage of sedatives as ordered by the attending physician. As he stayed at home to take stock of things and to try and prevent his household from falling into total chaos, the distracted father saw for the first time the true pattern of his brief conjugal life, instead of the idyllic moments of his courtship and the first bloom of fatherly conceit and the pride of possession. He had been immersed in love of the wife who had, in accepting his youth, gratified in full measure all his innermost and strongest yearnings. Now grief over her loss was already turning him toward bitterness; the thoughtless dependency of her grown children, at the expense of a good deal of his own effort and of the future security of her two youngest children, instilled in him a resentment that stayed with him for most of his life, so that mere mention of one of "that" side of the family had the same effect as mention of a Hatfield to a McCoy. The household seethed with resentments; with the arrival of the child's Aunt Lulu and the more frequent visits of Marie and Earley Clark, the schism became one of color—the "near whites" against the "all blacks."

Aunt Lulu was welcome to Katherine Dunham, because she brought a present of clothing and because her first deed, even before visiting the upstairs bedroom, was, on seeing the disorder of the child's hair, to set about dividing it into microscopic partitions and, with a gentle, professional touch, brushing, oiling, persuading the crinkles from their tangled state into some sort of order. Then she undid her parcel, and there was—instead of a dress with flounces and ruffles and pleats which stood out starched below the waist—a skirt of dull gray wool, and a gray sweater which buttoned down the front, and a gray knitted hood with knitted roses on each side and two long knitted bands with which to tie it under the chin. Her Aunt Lulu, thinking way ahead, had bought them all far too big for her. The skirt reached her shoe tops, the sweater her knees, and the hood hung over her face almost hiding it, even when the ties were pulled so that they crossed each other. The roses, instead of adjusting over the ears, hung down below her chin like fat woolen whiskers. She was not happy about all of this, but the hairdo made up for much: the fact that it was new and obviously not soon to be outgrown compensated to some degree for the outfit's dowdiness, of which she was conscious even without the side glances from the "other" side of the family or the expressionless stare with which her brother made his inspection.

One cold day late in January the upstairs bedroom released its guest. The girl was not present for the act itself, the children having been ushered into the attic for the occasion. When later she saw her mother, it was in the chill, darkened parlor, where the two factions of the family had arranged themselves on opposing sides of the room, with the glass-covered casket between. A man in a black suit read from a small book. People on both sides of the coffin wept; at some words from the man who was reading, the ones on the other side looked in the direction of her brother and herself and wept harder. Her father sat beside her, and she pulled back the gray hood and tilted her head down and to one side so that she could look up into his face, because his head was bent.

His hands were folded tight together in his lap between his knees, and he was looking down at nothing. His face looked terrible and miserable at the same time, and she wondered if she should cry as the others were doing, even the children, nervous from the long wait for something that they couldn't understand and infected by the unaccustomed behavior of the adults. She looked at the quiet face of her brother and decided not to cry, but to keep her sadness inside until its reason was made clear to her. When the man finished reading, everyone bowed his head and the room was very quiet, with only little sounds from her Aunt Lulu and her half sister Fanny. She saw her brother glancing at her and stopped squirming and looking around until people lifted their heads again. Then they all stood up, and there seemed to be a question of who would move first to walk over to the glass-covered box and look in. Her father lifted her, and she was the first. She looked at someone she scarcely knew, then looked away quickly, as though prompted by a gentle hand that turned her head aside so that this memory would not outshadow all of the others. The flowers were pretty, and her new sweater matched the gray of the velvet-covered coffin.

Three
The Gray Sweater

*

After Fanny June Dunham had been buried and the house in Glen Ellyn closed, to be auctioned off later for the payment of accumulated debts, Albert Dunham gifted his partner George Weir with his share of the tailor shop in the Fair Building and put upon himself the sackcloth and ashes of a traveling salesman of men's suitings. Certain that he had been misused by life beyond restitution, he took his two children from his wife's relatives and placed them in the charge of his sister Lulu Dunham. So they found themselves snatched without warning from a solid if disturbed pattern of family life, with regular hours of feeding and sleeping and waking, and plunged into the bewildering network of the City's black ghetto.

Lulu Dunham was a beautician by trade, with parlors on the fourth floor of the Fair Building. By day she was surrounded by starched white curtains and spotless screens which shielded manicure table and shampoo board and polished glass jars of cosmetics. Underfoot were soft carpets; overhead was discreet lighting; for her affluent clients there were lounging chairs in the outer salon and a reclining chair in the inner one. But she, like her brother, had her economy closet where, behind a screen, a coffeepot sat on a small table over an alcohol burner. There were always, as well, a cardboard carton of cream puffs from the day before and a few plates with cold remnants of food stuck to them.

Albert Dunham, the son, had by this time started school, and during the day the sister was left alone with her Aunt Lulu. She spent happy mornings dusting and polishing the parlors, carrying soiled linen to the basket in the corridor, putting clean linen in all the wrong places. The customers before midday were few, and she had time to unscrew and screw on again the tops of most of the jars, while her aunt patiently followed, righting her mistakes and listening with endless forbearance to the stream of confidence that she alone seemed to evoke from her niece.

The happiest moment came just before twelve o'clock, when Lulu Dunham put a sweater over her white nurse's uniform, took the child by the hand, and threaded, through elevator and passageway and back staircase, the labyrinth leading to the cafeteria of the department store that occupied most of the building. Tantalizing smells filled the corridors as they approached, and the child could hear the sounds of clattering cutlery as it was poured into bins and sorted onto trays, the tinkle of cups hitting saucers, thick glasses clinking against each other, the hum of voices talking rapidly and calling out orders, the shuffle of feet from elevators and stairways and hallways. The smells made her mouth water, because breakfast might very well have been a day-old sweet roll and a swallow of her Aunt Lulu's lukewarm coffee; the sounds excited her, because this was a world of business and activity and a kind of order which she enjoyed feeling part of, small and unobtrusive and anonymous though she was.

Her aunt carried the dirty dishes from the day before neatly wrapped in a towel which had "Lulu Dunham" stitched across one corner in red. She handed the dishes to the attendant and took her place at the head of a line just forming in front of steam tables, with pans and glass shelves full of every kind of delectable foodstuff, most of them foreign to the child.

The clerks behind the steam tables would always have a friendly smile for the small dark lady in the white uniform, and before long they were leaning out to say a word to the child who clung wide-eyed to the skirt of her aunt's sweater and never acknowledged the greetings, either by smile or word. The clerks served Aunt Lulu generously, not just because she was well liked and a fixture in the building, but in recognition of her delicacy in avoiding a situation that could have caused embarrassment had she not brought her dishes every day and taken her food upstairs to eat.

After lunch there were always customers in the waiting room of the beauty parlor. The child would sit scribbling at the table in the closet, or some of the time climb up onto it and fall asleep, to dream about cream puffs, or the whistle of the tamale man on the corner at night as they went home, or her brother, or the house in Glen Ellyn. Late in the afternoon, if time allowed, there might be another excursion. This one would be to the bakery department of The Fair, where every third day Lulu Dunham would buy a supply of sweet rolls, to take back to the room on Prairie Avenue, and the cream puffs that relieved the afternoon of its monotony. From the subterranean kitchens of the department store, trays rose to the bakery department on dumbwaiters. The child watched with fascination the cakes and cookies and jelly rolls and ladyfingers and gingerbread and warm loaves of white and brown bread and piles of poppyseed rolls and frosted cinnamon buns. These were a delight to the eye, but to the taste there was never a substitute for the cream-filled puffs, made by German bakers who had not yet heard of substitutes for eggs and milk and butter.

Sometimes the customers continued to fill the waiting room long after the department store had closed. The child would grow tired and fretful and sleep again and nibble with distaste at a sandwich quickly thrust at her by her harassed aunt. She would wonder what her brother was doing in the room where they all lived, and sometimes she would cry, not loudly but to herself, feeling a loneliness all around her in spite of her aunt's efforts to fill the void left by her mother's death, by the removal from the house in Glen Ellyn and her separation from the many children and relatives, loved or not, and the absence of her father, who had begun the wanderings that would lead him eventually to the small town in Iowa where he would meet and wed the second mother of his children.

The trip home at night brought a new lift to the day. At that period there were a few isolated communities of Negroes on the North Side of the City and a few on the West Side, but most of the more than half a million dark-skinned inhabitants were relegated to the South Side, where Lulu Dunham lived. All through the late spring and summer Katherine Dunham accompanied her aunt on the elevated train to the downtown beauty parlor and back again at night. The morning trains were crowded, and often by the Thirty-first Street stop there were no seats left; but at night the two were almost alone in the straw-seated coach. The smell of hot iron rails breezed in through the open windows, and when the wind blew from the left, it brought fresh lake and deep-water fish odors, and when it blew from the right, the stench of dried blood and singeing hog bristles from the stockyards. The child would look sleepily into the lamp-lighted, dingy back rooms of tenement rooming houses and flats, then fall asleep against her nodding aunt. By the time she was fully awake, she would be scrambling through the automatic sliding doors of the train and stumbling down the dim wooden staircase plastered with advertisements.

At the bottom of the steps there was a new world. The train rumbled away overhead to lose itself in the far South Side, and the impact of Negro sounds and smells hit the child with such force that she nearly melted with fear, clinging close to her Aunt Lulu and drawing as far away as she could from the dark stares and sullen laughter and bold flaunting, the dust and litter of the pavement, the weariness and sickness. The blind man stayed at his post at the bottom of the dirty wooden steps, unmindful of cigarette butts and greasy papers and spittle and torn "El" tickets that gathered faster than the sweeper with his broom and dustpan could get rid of them. As they passed by, he turned his eyes, thick with an opalescent film, in their direction, calling on the Lord and shaking the few coins that lined the bottom of a battered tin cup. Aunt Lulu always dropped pennies into the cup, but she turned away from the other blind man, who sat beside the open cart where pigs' feet and chitterlings were on display, and who played a guitar and darted his head from side to side, hardly bothering to conceal the fact that he could see through his dark glasses.

They passed a stall where newspapers were sold, along with spotty, half-rotten fruit and withered greens and shriveled potatoes and onions and turnips. Next to this was a plate-glass window marked MADAME WALKER in bold script. A fly-specked window card leaned against a dingy half-curtain, its base garnished with tin cans filled with the famous discovery for rendering unruly hair manageable. The proprietress of the hairdressing salon was a friend of Lulu Dunham's and would wave her smoking irons as the two passed on the way home, and then yank her inquisitive customer's head back into place by a lock of hair without breaking the rhythm of the sizzling pullers. Smoke filtered through the screen door into the street, and the click of the irons, as they were placed on the small gas flame or as they closed on a patch of hair—woolly at the start, patent-leather smooth at the finish—followed the child and her aunt around the corner and blended into the whistle of the tamale man.

One time the tamale man had not been at his stand in the middle of the block under the gas lamppost. Aunt Lulu waited for him, hanging out of the upstairs window of their one room until she heard the whistle from the steam kettle and the sad sing-song, starting long and drawn out, then ending in a sharp upbeat, cut off into a tone as near a yodel as anything. "Ta-m-a-a-a-a——leh!" he sang as he trundled down the middle of the dimly lit street. "Ta-ma-leh, tamaleh, tamaleh, ta-m-a-a-a-a——leh! Come git ya tamaleh! Come git 'em whilst dey hot!"

And Aunt Lulu, tired and sleepy but not wanting to disappoint her niece, had called out of the window, "Tamale man. Oh, tamale man. Wait just a minute!"

And he had stopped in the middle of the street and looked up at them, and when they were all the way down the three flights of stairs and out in the middle of the street panting and with their nickels ready, he had said, "But I ain't got no mo' t'males tonight, baby. They all gone! Folks up there whuppin' up a breeze tonight. Hog maws an' black-eye peas done give out, call on ol' tamale man. Treat ol' tamale man mighty nice. Y'all be back tomorry night, honey chile—tamale man gonna be back, have plenty. Night now, y'all."

And he had pushed his cart down the street, shamelessly calling out the wares that he didn't have, stopping now and then to chat with a disappointed customer, then melting away into the night while they climbed the steps and went to bed without supper.

But the other times he was there, and if they were very late, he would let them know that the boy had already been down to buy his tamale, and they would buy only two. He stood in the street leaning against the lamppost, and the flickering light shone on his shiny black bald pate, ringed with a few gray bristles, and on the pale blue cart which was decorated with angels and hearts and flowers in red and yellow and had the words HOT TAMALES painted on either side in red. An alcohol burner kept the two deep kettles hot, as well as the small kettle at the front end which whistled all the time as steam came out of its thin spout. When he saw Aunt Lulu and her niece approaching, he would lift off a wooden cover, reach way down into the steaming inside of one of the kettles, and pretend to be talking to the tamales, looking for the fattest ones. He would squeeze their spotty corn-shuck coverings and, satisfied that he had the pick of the lot, reach for a pair of rusty scissors that hung from his waist on top of his canvas apron, and snip off the tip that had been tied with shredded corn husk. The child always hated to see the tip thrown away, because it had bits of corn-meal mush clinging to it, and she was very hungry by this time. With mouth watering she would wait until they had reached the bedroom on the third floor, until Aunt Lulu brought the bottle of milk from the community pantry down the hall and poured a glass for her and for her brother. In her greed for food at this hour, she scarcely noticed her brother, who would be on the floor or in the bed or at the single table at the window, drawing pictures or doing his homework.

During the summer months he was in school also, because he had started late and wanted to be up to and ahead of his class, but the girl was happy not to have to go to school. She liked the vagabond life of her Aunt Lulu's beauty parlor, the sights and sounds of the Fair Building, the trip back home at night, and, above all, the hot tamale. After the milk and the tamales they all washed their hands in the hall bathroom and put out the gaslight and undressed and climbed into the one bed. Lulu Dunham always intended to buy a small cot for her niece, but never quite managed the down payment; and besides, the room was already too crowded with the bed, the dresser, the table, and the two chairs which were always full of odd bits of clothing they never found the time to hang up.

*

Sometimes on Sundays they went visiting among the numerous friends that Lulu Dunham effortlessly gathered around her. The gray skirt and sweater were still considered dress-up clothing, though in the spring and summer weather the hood with its yarn roses had been put aside. For her birthday in June her Aunt Lulu took her into the basement of The Fair and, from a table spilling over with remnants of children's clothing, selected a pink gingham dress, size six. It reached the four-year-old's shoe tops, but she was overjoyed to be free of the wool skirt and threw her arms around her aunt's neck, and kissed her over and over all the way home on the elevated. The girl wore the pink dress all summer and, if the evenings were cool, carried the sweater. During the very hot weather that descended on the City in blasts like waves of heat from an oven door, sleeping three in the bed became miserable, and Aunt Lulu made herself a pallet on the floor, leaving the bed to the two children. There were no screens at the windows, and flies came in during the day and mosquitoes at night. People on all sides of their limestone house were now sleeping on the burned-out, dried-up grass plots that might once have been front yards. They slept on blankets or dirty sheets or newspapers, and sometimes when the girl and her Aunt Lulu left the house, they would still be lying asleep, faces covered with newspapers to ward off the sun and flies, men and women and children, half clothed, sprawled into uncouth night postures, dreaming of a land they had left too readily, and fretting in their uneasy sleep at single trouble behind exchanged for double trouble ahead.

The people they visited on Sundays were sometimes relatives of relatives on Albert Dunham's side. Dark-skinned people with the feel of Tennessee land in their rough hands and a softness of voice and candor of glance that set them apart from the predatory evil that blossomed in the streets and doorways on every side. One such distant relative lived in an imposing tenement garrison ironically named Mecca Flats. Four floors of rat-infested, cockroach-dominated cubicles rose from a paved courtyard to a roof festooned with wash, which often blew free and tangled itself into the debris of broken furniture and old bedsprings brought up from some sweltering enclosure for the hot nights, or piled into the corners of skylights to add to the drifts of dusty newspapers, rusty nails, pigeon feathers, and cigarette butts. Between roof and courtyard a hundred doorways opened and shut and slammed from morning till early the following morning and on Saturday nights all the way around the clock without stopping.

It was here, in a two-room flat scrubbed so clean as to seem apart from the rest of the building, that the two children first saw their Uncle Arthur, senior to their father Albert, and their grandfather John Dunham. These members of the family were in conference with a distant relation who had already seen enough of the promised land to know that the grass where he had come from was greener. The children hung over the wooden railing that fenced in the narrow gallery running around the four sides of Mecca Flats. From the third floor the drop onto pavement and ashcans was dizzying; above them, the clothes flapped out against the blue sky. Casbahlike sounds issued from the recesses, and phonographs that had been wound over and over again for days without stopping scratched out the risqué witticisms of Bert Williams and the suggestive lyrics of the blues shouter Ma Rainey. On Sunday mornings the court was littered with broken bottles, and the tops of the trashcans were everywhere but on the trashcans, and the cans themselves were as likely as not turned over and their contents scattered right and left by rats that didn't bother to hide, because even the stray cats were full of chewed-over neckbones and sucked out pigs' knuckles and stray bits of bacon rind and corncobs left with a few overlooked grains.

Once Marie and Earley Clark rode to the City in a shiny new automobile and took them all for their first automobile ride. It was a short one, but to them an unparalleled adventure. They circled the neighborhood between Twenty-ninth and Thirty-fifth streets, and between Indiana Avenue and Ellis Avenue. Aunt Lulu pointed out to the children the houses in the area that had been the property of Fanny June Dunham, missing no opportunity to bring home the fact that it would rightfully now belong to the two children had the "other" side of the family not plundered it from the mother as she lay on her deathbed. This meant little to the girl, except to widen a gulf she already felt between herself and the people who had lived in the house in Glen Ellyn, memory of which was fast receding as experiences in the City multiplied.

When the new automobile stopped in front of the brownstone house where Earley and Marie Clark's son roomed with his wife, the girl asked permission to sit in the car and wait for them. Earley Clark gave her brother two pennies to buy candy at the corner store, and as she waited for him, she climbed back and forth over the shiny leather seats and hoped that people would pass by and see her. But there was no one else on the street, and the afternoon seemed unusually quiet, even for Sunday. She wondered what kept her brother, and her feeling of well-being began to give way to the old melancholy and loneliness of the last days in Glen Ellyn. She wondered what would happen if she were asleep now instead of awake, and if the automobile should turn out not to be real, and if her Aunt Lulu and Aunt Marie and Uncle Earley had disappeared forever into the brownstone house, and if her brother had gone away to leave her in the empty street, never to come back.

As she reflected on these things, becoming less and less overtly active, but more and more agitated inside, she heard the sound of angry voices in the street behind her: the scream of a woman who said things she couldn't understand, and the shout and answer of two men who danced, as she watched through the small window in the back of the automobile, into the middle of the street, arms rigidly extended, hands gripped to wrists, facing each other and twisting and bobbing left to right like principals in a turkey trot. A woman with hair in small braids standing on end, holding ineffectively the two sides of a soiled Mother Hubbard that didn't quite meet across a stomach that hung over the uncovered juncture of her limbs, circled them with the purposeless agitation of a freshly beheaded chicken. One of the men held something that flashed in the hand he held up high, the wrist of which was in the tight grip of his partner. He freed his hand, the arm fell quickly, and the dance ended.

The man whose back had been turned to her walked with jerking, stilted steps to the sidewalk on the side of the street where the child sat in the automobile, and started in her direction, the other man following, still holding in front of him the shiny object, which wasn't a knife because it bent backward and away from his fist. She became suddenly terrified, without knowing why. All of the violence that she had seen in the faces of the streets between the elevated station and her Aunt Lulu's bedroom crowded against her, and she drew as far back into the front seat as she could, rigid, wanting to cry out, but so taken by dread that her mouth dried and her heart moved up into her throat. The man reached the automobile in a series of zigzags across the sidewalk. He wavered at the open window of the automobile, trying to say something, but it was hard because his lower lip couldn't reach his upper lip. His face was neatly separated into two parts from his ear right through the slit of his mouth, making a mouth several times longer than it should be. Pink flesh showed, and a row of white teeth. He seemed to be trying to say something like "He'p, he'p," but while he paused, bright red welled over the pink and drenched the white teeth and began to stream down his chin and onto his clothing and the running board and the sidewalk.

He looked into the eyes of the fear-congealed child, decided that here was no help, and turned away into the street again, where he staggered toward the crossing at the corner, leaving blood spatters in a steady trail on the pavement, from which heat rose shimmering in the afternoon sun. The other man stalked at a distance behind, and the woman sat drunkenly on the steps of the building in front of which the spectacle had taken place.

The silence was so sharp that it hurt, and the child dared not disturb it by moving. She saw her brother turn the corner, a paper bag in his hand. He looked at the man following the man, rather than at the man himself, and then at the ground, and then started running toward his sister. When she saw him, she knew that none of it would have happened if he hadn't left her alone. She breathed again, and her heart dropped back into place, and she began to cry, trying to smooth out the skirt of the pink dress which was damp and knotted without her knowing when or how it came about. She didn't remember any of the rest of the day—not what the candy was like or if she ate it, or when her Aunt Lulu and Uncle Earley and Aunt Marie joined her and her brother, or who poured water on the blood that was on the running board, or how they arrived again at the room, or when she went to bed. She just cried and, when she wasn't crying, buried her face in Aunt Lulu's warm brown neck and tried to shut out the eyes of the man who needed someone to help him when no one would and whose eyes had looked into hers and had seen that she was afraid.

During the summer that Katherine Dunham was four, major changes began to take place in the City's population. What had been a slow infiltration of dark blood became an unforeseen, unwanted transfusion; and this mass exodus of Negroes from south to north had disturbing and permanent consequences on the relationship of the races, profoundly affecting the treatment of dark-skinned citizens by white.

What the child felt and remarked upon, even at four, was the change in attitudes closely affecting her own life, like the embarrassment of the clerks of The Fair's cafeteria, even though her Aunt Lulu was not asking to be seated in the restaurant, and the looks of animosity from the early arriving patrons. She saw an expression of surprise on her aunt's face one day when a man in a dark blue suit walked up to them and said something in a low voice, just as they reached the girl at the cash register. Her aunt abruptly left the money and the tray, took her by the hand, and walked out of the cafeteria, past the girl who always gave them extra-large servings and the boy who smiled as he handed trays to them. Her face was a mask that her niece had never seen before.

There were other alterations in her daily life that somehow seemed to tie in with the crowded elevated trains and the embarrassment of formerly friendly acquaintances and the uncouthness of dark strangers, past whom her Aunt Lulu always hurried her as though she would be contaminated by looking. The most memorable of these alterations was the closing of the beauty parlor in the Fair Building.

Because Lulu Dunham was herself good of heart and instinctively retiring, it was difficult for her to be suspicious, unkind or ungenerous. Having been an embarrassment to others embarrassed her; her humiliation at being asked to give up carry-out privileges at the cafeteria gnawed at her pride, not so much because she felt the injustice of the act as because she had looked upon the tensions arising from the influx of southern Negroes as disagreeable but a thing essentially apart from her own life. And she scarcely had time to digest that unpleasant episode when a new problem presented itself in the expiration of her lease in the Fair Building, which she had annually extended without trouble but which this year not tears nor reminders of verbal agreements nor appeal to faithful and influential customers could help renew.

As the child sat in the closet tracing from her brother's spelling book, she heard her aunt talking on the telephone to people who seemed to be very important, shyly putting her troubles before them. One day one of the friendliest of the ladies cared for by Lulu Dunham came into the beauty parlor, not for a shampoo and a marcel wave and a manicure, but to deliver information.

"I'm sorry, Lulu. I really am. I talked to the manager *myself*, and I just couldn't believe it. An old friend of mine, and all that. Hmph! He'd better not ask *me* for any more favors! I told him that you were different and couldn't be responsible for everybody with the same color of skin! He just wouldn't listen . . ."

Lulu Dunham thanked the woman and said that she would go to her house after this for the manicuring and shampooing and marcel waving, just as soon as the furnishings were sold and the shop closed; that she could do it every bit as well, and it would be ever so much more convenient for the customers, and perhaps it had all happened for the best anyway because the Lord knew best and it wasn't good to question His decisions. The woman dabbed at her eyes with a handkerchief, and Lulu Dunham, to hide shame and panic, wrote in her big appointment book, just as though nothing had happened, that the woman would be coming to the beauty parlor the following Saturday afternoon as usual.

By this time it was fall and school had started, and the child's brother had to give up classes in order to stay in the room with her while her Aunt Lulu packed up and sold things and sorted out what implements she would need to do her work going to people's houses, as she had years ago before she opened her own place. Something in her spirit seemed less certain, and she wondered aloud, as though the children could answer her, where their father was and why she hadn't heard from him, except for a postcard or two and a money order or two for small amounts, during all the months that had gone by since the last days in Glen Ellyn.

The problem of what to do with the small girl became a serious one. She could not accompany her aunt on trips to and from the far North Side, where most of the clients who remained faithful to Lulu Dunham lived. She was too young for kindergarten, there was no money for either a paid nursery or an attendant, and it did not seem right that she should spend the long days alone in the front bedroom, even if she promised not to wander up and down the hallways and into the street. And so began a round of juggling back and forth, of asking a few hours from a friend and a day from a relative, of keeping the boy home from school now and then, of dropping the two children off at an inexpensive movie where they might sit through one installment of a serial over and over, to the graphic accompaniment of an upright piano in the pit at the bottom of the flickering screen, until their aunt came feeling her way down the darkness of the aisle to find them, with relief, and take them home.

Most of Lulu Dunham's acquaintances lived, as she did, in one room; more and more often, as the district took on further its ghettolike aspects, a bed that was vacated in the morning would be taken over by someone who worked at night and slept by day, or someone who just sat up or roamed the streets all night. The relatives who had enjoyed two rooms in Mecca Flats were now overrun with boarders, whom they had taken in so as to be able to pay rent that had doubled and tripled and quadrupled as landlords watched the morning papers for the latest figures on the new arrivals from the South, who rode into the City by boxcar, bus, and coach train and straggled into the South Side on foot, by streetcar, or in the five-cent taxicabs that swarmed around the most likely rail stations like flies over a stream of molasses. The fall went by in this way, but after a dismal attempt at creating a cheerful Christmas, Lulu Dunham decided to incorporate the household bequeathed her into that of a relative who had recently moved to the City from Ohio. By this consolidation a much needed kitchen and space for a second bed were gained.

Aunt Clara Dunham and her daughter Irene had come to the City with enough of the family savings to tide them over for a month or two, in the hope of establishing themselves in some branch of the theatrical profession. With the help of Uncle Arthur Dunham, a vocal coach and choral director of no small reputation who had encouraged them in the venture, they had assembled a group of other hopeful amateurs and proceeded to rehearse a program that included a musical dramatization of *Minnehaha,* scenes from one of the Williams and Walker shows, and a cantata arrangement of the "Blue Danube."

Aunt Lulu's move into the flat on Vincennes Avenue that Clara and Irene Dunham had rented did not really solve the problem of what to do with the child. Sometimes the place was overrun with twenty or thirty people, all busily rehearsing. At other times it might be suddenly silent and empty, and Katherine Dunham would be left alone, with a neighbor to look in on her at random or perhaps the old woman from the flat downstairs, who stopped in once a day to putter around in the kitchen, cooking things for herself and mumbling as she washed out the one pan afterward.

The production never seemed quite ready, although the rehearsals went on and on; and after objections from other tenants, these were shifted from the flat itself to the basement of the building.

The child discovered the basement one day when she had tired of sitting in the window looking out at falling snow. She undid the chain of the door and began by exploring the hallway, but spent little time there because garbage cans were in front of most of the doors and the odors were offensive. Then, descending a flight of steps that led down past the street entrance, she began hearing the voices of the chorus and followed the sound farther down and in through another door.

She crouched in a corner, out of sight, while grownups milled around in a kind of excitement that could only mean they were at last to have a chance to perform in public—perhaps on the stage of the Monogram after the last vaudeville show. Aunt Clara held her head tilted back as she sang, and her eyes were closed; brown makeup covered the freckles that usually stood out on her lightish skin. Cousin Irene, small for her seventeen years because of a spinal deformity, was dressed up in a brown cotton Indian dress with a ragged hemline representing fringe, and a single feather was held in back of her head by a brown ribbon, and she too was in full war paint—ready to play the role of an adult or a child redskin. This meant that *Minnehaha* would be on the program. But before Katherine Dunham could see the Indian choir go into action, she was discovered and sent back upstairs because the basement was too damp and chill; and she was always catching cold and always underfoot, though she didn't intend to be.

Minnehaha was not a success; the Indian dresses and feathers were put away; and Clara Dunham eventually packed up and returned with her daughter to Ohio. The turn, as far as the child was concerned, was not for the better. Still, memories of that winter in Clara Dunham's flat on Vincennes Avenue stayed with her and may have inspired in some small way her own eventual choice of a theatrical career.

After Clara and Irene Dunham were gone, Uncle Arthur moved into the flat, and later there were roomers; but even so—though Aunt Lulu spent most of her time going to and from the North Side—there still didn't seem to be a way for her to help John Dunham, who had returned to Tennessee ill with what might be his last illness, nor was there enough money to pay the rent and feed and clothe her brother's two children.

Uncle Arthur set out to try his luck as a choral leader in California, and Aunt Lulu moved again, this time into an unheated two-room basement flat on Indiana Avenue near Twenty-ninth Street, shared with a woman who claimed relationship but whom the children found completely unsympathetic.

Winters in the City were as bitterly cold as the summers were stifling hot. This winter stood out in the memory of the child as the coldest in all history. It was also the winter when her age was advanced by a year and a half so that she would be taken into the first grade of the neighborhood school, which did not have a kindergarten.

Over the gray skirt and sweater she wore a heavy blue coat, cut by Aunt Clara from an overcoat of her own to somewhere near the child's size. She wore the hood and button shoes and two gray mittens when she went to school the first day, but only one the second day because she began right then her lifelong habit of glove misplacing. Snow hadn't fallen for some time because it was too cold to snow. The two or three inches that coated the ground were left over from weeks before and were now so hard-packed that they would have seemed like an extra paving over the sidewalk and street if there hadn't been the slightest give underfoot, just enough to crunch and squeak from the impact of shoes and wagon wheels, and set one's teeth on edge. Exhaled breath hung suspended for seconds before dissolving, and the sharp sting of the air made breathing unpleasant and brought tears to the child's eyes as she trudged beside her Aunt Lulu, rehearsing her new age in case anyone asked her and desperately reciting her address in case she should lose her way home.

Patiently Lulu Dunham explained to her that she would go out to play in the morning after lessons and that she should wrap up warmly. Then there would be another recess to eat the sandwich that was in her pocket. Then she would play inside, and when the bell rang and all the children put their coats on again, it would be time to go home. She should follow Indiana Avenue, making only one turn at Twenty-ninth Street, and not try to wait for her brother, because he was older and his classes were in another building and finished later. But, above all, she must behave very well, because it had not been easy to persuade the principal to take her into the school so late after the winter term had started.

As they approached the school, the child thought more of the intense cold and her fright at the unknown than of the instructions that her Aunt Lulu continued to give her right up to the door. The morning was a nightmare to her. At recess time she was assigned as partner the only leftover child in the class—a boy who smelled of smoked fish and who wiped his dripping nose with the hand in which he clutched hers. She stood alone during the fifteen-minute recess, and her feet and hands began to ache with the cold. At lunch time when the teacher asked her where her lunch was, she said that she didn't have any. She watched the others at their desks as they unwrapped hard-boiled eggs and sausages and bananas. Her recess partner produced an oily package of smoked whitefish from the pocket of his overcoat in the cloakroom. She was hungry, but the strange conglomeration of food and people, together with her panic, made her feel sick and want to cry. Most of the children went home for lunch, so the teacher didn't bother to stay with those remaining. When they finished with their lunches, they threw things at each other. They had nothing to say to the new pupil, and she was glad, because she would have burst into tears at the first approach.

The child's aunt had not known there was a second recess, in the afternoon. So when the children were led to the cloakroom to put on their coats and mufflers for the few minutes in the play yard, Katherine Dunham, free at last and forgetting her fear of being unable to find her way to the Twenty-ninth Street flat, buttoned herself into her overcoat, tied the strings of her gray hood under her chin, and, leaving one mitten somewhere between the cloakroom and the street, made her way out into Indiana Avenue—only to become lost. An hour later her brother, on his way home from his own classes, found her standing on the corner, face blue with cold, looking for him. She stumbled along beside him, her feet numb in her button shoes, the mittenless hand curled in the pocket of her overcoat.

They tried school for three days more but gave up because she repeatedly lost her way, and her brother always had to circle the block looking for her.

The woman into whose flat Lulu Dunham had moved was perhaps thirty-five years of age, wiry, brown, and with a crown of fuzzy hair that she wore in an imitation pompadour over a small, weasel-like face. Just where she fitted into the hierarchy of relations the girl was never certain, but presumably she was kin to Clara Dunham. Lulu Dunham referred to her as "second cousin," and thus the child remembered her. She unfortunately lacked Clara Dunham's pleasant nature, but shared with her a mothlike devotion to footlights; and, although totally without talent, she proceeded to make every effort to break into the primitive theatrical pattern that was just beginning to take shape on the South Side of the City, its chief outlet being some form of the basement and parlor rehearsals that had so recently disappointed Clara and Arthur Dunham. She let nothing stand in the way of ambition, and—by serving as usher at the Monogram Theatre on State Street at odd hours, pinching pennies from the already tightened food budget, and just generally scrounging—she managed to see innumerable vaudeville shows and so deluded herself into believing that she had already achieved her theatrical goal. One of her favorite economy measures was to "freshen" stale bread by steaming it in a sieve placed on top of an open teakettle on the gasplate. Many times this would be the day's only meal until Aunt Lulu returned with a paper sack full of cold meats and sweet rolls bought at the corner on the North Side where she took the streetcar before boarding the South Side elevated. She would be too exhausted and often too downcast to ask much about the day, and the children would spare her their problems, partly because the second cousin had a nasty temper and shook or pinched them when she was displeased, and partly out of compassion for their aunt, who had taken on much more than she had bargained for.

After the abortive attempt to enter the child in first grade, Aunt Lulu reached an agreement that on certain days the boy would be kept home from school to act as nursemaid, but that on other days the child would be in the cousin's charge, wherever she went. The aunt felt it unwise to leave the child alone with a lighted stove—unaware of the fact that the fire might very well be allowed to die down in the small coalburner shortly after her departure and not be rebuilt until just before her return: the money she left for coal could pay the entrance fee to the Grand or the Monogram. It was by means of such machinations that Katherine Dunham was first initiated into the cult whose preliminary rituals she had only glimpsed in the rehearsals conducted in her Aunt Clara's flat.

The Grand and the Monogram theaters had ceased to compete with each other because of the inpouring torrent from the South: they were so pressed for space that each generously encouraged patronage of the other. The fact that both houses were run by the same management may also have had something to do with this magnanimity. The entrance fee at the Grand was slightly higher than at the Monogram, which—having no history of past glories before the decline of the neighborhood—allocated what funds might have gone into improved sanitation and creature comforts to securing the best entertainment that could be offered.

The unknowing would not have given the nondescript assembly that gathered to wait in the littered vestibule, muddy with trash and dirt ground into melted snow, credit for enough discrimination to appreciate the subtle distinctions that made the stage show at the Monogram superior to that at the Grand. But the management had learned, at the expense of wrecked seats and fistfights and performers forcibly ejected from the stage, that the seasoned act, the perennial joke disguised only enough to give the impression of newness while retaining the comfort of familiarity, the bawdy song full of double meanings sung in a folk code language, were what the audience wanted. Those waiting in the vestibule for seats would make insulting remarks to each person who opened the street door on either side of the glassed-in ticket cage, cursed at the cold knife of air that entered with them, and spat noisily, as though thereby casting out physical discomfort. In this setting the child made her first acquaintance with the residuum of the minstrel era and with forerunners of the Broadway revue.

Cole and Johnson, Buck and Bubbles, Bessie Smith, Ida Cox, Ethel Waters, Florence Mills, and a score of others were only nebulous entities to her, and it was hard for her to distinguish those that she heard about from her stage-struck relatives from those that she stared at once inside the theater. Most of the time she would have to sit on the second cousin's lap, and after about an hour she would fall asleep, her dreams uncomfortable because of the stale air, the fetid breath on either side, the raucous laughter, the comments hurled at the stage and bounced back in kind to the delight of the squealing, squirming audience; the banging of an out-of-tune piano punctuated the guttural rasp of the blues.

Day after day during the coldest part of the winter, a thin, yellow-green sun rose from the slate-colored lake, loitered for a few hours, then couldn't seem to sink quickly enough into the ugly, battened-down, sprawling West Side. These few days the schools closed, and the brother and sister sat often at the window in the basement, watching the subtle shrinkage of people and animals in their efforts to combat the cold. Housewives who had known no more than mild frost faced a first City winter unable to believe in the cruelty of nature. Their earnings, which at first had seemed so munificent, no longer met their requirements, and coal needed by the binful was bought first in buckets, then in tin cooking pans and paper bags. Shoes, comfortably worn thin or lacy with razor slits for the accommodation of corns and bunions, had to be bound in layers of newspaper and rags until new ones could be bought sometime later on. Babies cried for long stretches of time, then grew quiet and died. Old people, picking over trashcans outside the better-off homes, looked very curious in their layers of cast-off clothing, with their feet bound and their heads tied in rags and a gnarled black finger sticking out here and there from several pairs of ragged yarn gloves worn one on top of the other. They bent deep into the trashcans, looking for anything usable but chiefly for cast-off clothing.

One such old man used to pass by at just about the time of the prematurely setting sun. Crouched against the window, the children could hear from the next block the dismal sound of wagon wheels crunching on the fine, dry, tightly packed snow. The bony horse pulling the wagon represented the last measure of misery. The children peered through the clear spots that the boy had scraped and the girl had licked in the ice-coated window, and marveled that the old horse could stay afoot, even though its hoofs were wrapped around with rags. The steam spurted from its straining nostrils in gasps, but each day by some miracle it would make the rounds of the neighborhood, pulling the wagon that seemed on the point of disintegrating and dropping into the soiled snow its content of precious fuel.

The old man sat huddled on the seat of the wagon, inert until at a signal all his own he would thrust his head from the bundle of rags and carpets and mufflers, with which he feebly defied the cold, and quaver into the thin air, penetrating somehow the bleak, clamped tenement houses, "Co-o-o-o-ul man! . . . Co-o-o-o-ul ma-a-a-an!" A rickety sash window would open, and a kerchiefed woman would lean out to attract the attention of the old man and would signal him to wait for her. The scrawny black face would bob up and down in acknowledgment, and the stiff old body would drop the slack reins and clamber down from the seat. Sometimes a child would come into the street and stand trembling in the merciless chill while the old man filled a bucket or pan or paper sack with lumps of coal.

The girl at the window was very sad because she thought that the old man was saying, "Po' ol' man," and for many years she thought of him as saying that and could hear his mournful plaint in her sleep. "Poor old man," she would murmur over and over to herself, wishing that she could help. "Poor, poor, poor old man."

Into this setting Fanny June Weir descended on the coldest day of all. She arrived by taxicab and kept the vehicle waiting while she swept into the basement flat, identified herself to the second cousin, and silenced her with one withering glance at the unwashed kitchen where the woman and the two children sat drawn up before the lighted gas oven. The children had not seen her since the afternoon in the front parlor of the house in Glen Ellyn; with her faint odor of perfume that reminded the girl of her dead mother, this half sister was for her like some fairy godmother come to visit the babes lost in the woods and equip them with wings to fly to places of warmth and good food and pretty clothes. Her brother, however, was not given to random enthusiasms, and when they were told to gather their few belongings and leave without even waiting for Aunt Lulu's approval, he protested.

His protest was labeled ingratitude by Fanny June Weir who, for all her good intentions and honest concern, was quick-tempered and a firm believer in adult authority. She also felt no little animosity toward her stepfather's relatives, partly because of her snobbishness about skin color, partly because of the conditions under which they lived. The brother's hesitancy was quickly overridden, and the children were piled into the waiting cab. Before they knew it, they had passed out of neighborhoods familiar to them, beyond the dwellings of the dark elite, into a borderline area of the far South Side where a community of people neither white nor black, but mostly passing for white, had penetrated beyond the barriers set up against their darker brethren.

The child was shy and embarrassed in the Weir household, which seemed to operate by a system of ascending advantages and facetious witticisms. Until she regained her normal modest appetite, her reaction from the recent period of malnutrition was regarded as greed by the children of the family and even by her half sister. Her hair, which had not improved in spite of Lulu Dunham's weekly grooming, occasioned the same kind of ridicule from which she had suffered in Glen Ellyn; and references to color evoked laughter that filled the child with a shame she couldn't identify, but caused her brother to stare into his plate without eating or to leave the room with a look of distaste.

She inherited gratefully certain clothing outgrown by her niece, but the gray sweater and hood and the overcoat made over from Aunt Clara's heavy blue one remained staples in her wardrobe. (In substance they were indestructible, and in size could see her through other seasons.) These she wore when her half sister, one morning a week or so after the flight from Twenty-ninth Street, announced with a show of annoyance that the presence of the two children was demanded in court and that she hoped that they would tell the truth and not make her look foolish for having tried to help them. The boy seemed to know what the affair was about, but his sister was torn between chagrin at being made to dress again in the disreputable gray skirt and excitement at going somewhere, especially an unknown place called "court," though she couldn't imagine what it would be like.

"Court" turned out to be a dark building among other dark buildings cut from great blocks of smoke-layered sandstone and situated in the labyrinthine midtown section which bordered on the City's sluggish river. Polished brass spittoons dotted the hallways, and as they climbed a much-trodden marble staircase to the third floor, the odor of cigar smoke hung in the air. A man in a blue uniform with shiny silver buttons indicated a door, and when they entered, the child, after her first feelings of temerity at unexpectedly commanding the attention of the room which was moderately filled with people, stood as though fastened to her half sister with safety pins, refusing to move forward and down the aisle to the front row of seats.

The entry was at the back of the room, but as the door opened, a few curious people had turned and passed along information that drew attention from the speaker, a man seated on a small platform with a gate in front of it. The child's brother nudged her, and her half sister pushed her, forcibly concealing impatience. But she remained riveted, unable to fit this moment in with the fragmentary past. The man speaking in a low voice, misery in the droop of his shoulders, shame in his downcast eyes, embarrassment in the crossing and uncrossing of one leg over the other, was the man who had told her the tale of Br'er Rabbit and the Tar Baby, who played the guitar alone after the harp was stilled, who held her in his arms so that she could look into the glass-covered box where the still, waxen figure that she didn't recognize lay under a half-blanket of flowers.

At a desk a little above him a man with glasses listened and asked questions from a piece of paper, and she heard her own name and her brother's; before she could bring herself to move, all the members of the family as she knew them were called by name, as though listed on a roll call interspersed with commentary. Then a man wearing a uniform walked forward down the aisle to escort them, and she walked past the stares of the curious and the hurt look of her Aunt Lulu and sat between her brother and her half sister, who moved as far away as possible from the aunt.

When her father finished answering questions, he left his chair, and her half sister rose and walked past him to take his place. They didn't speak or look at each other, and the people in the courtroom craned forward to stare at the handsome woman, who wore her black hair piled into a high pompadour under a small felt hat and held her dark red skirt in one hand as she mounted the steps to the chair, where she spoke with heated authority, saying things that the child couldn't imagine her knowing because she hadn't been there.

Being so young and talkative by nature and wanting to please, the child herself had been the informer. In effect, she had put all of their names in the big black book in which the man who was there to judge right and wrong was writing at that very moment. She was the final lever that turned the screw that was all set to separate family and destroy allegiance and betray trust and to make one color seem ascendant over another. If she had known this, she would have eaten dry hard bread steamed over the kitchen kettle to make it soft, and sat by the open gas oven, and stood in the dank airlessness of the Monogram vestibule forever, and even swallowed her tongue in place of speaking—like her brother, who had grown tall and deep and silent with the tightening of things and had not toadied to exchange confidences to be able to wear new outgrown clothes.

When all the story had been told, the man at the high desk thought a moment and then asked that her brother step forward. He told about going to school and the best things to be remembered; so that she—when she was led forward by the man in the uniform after a whispered admonition from her half sister to tell the truth—could think of nothing but the cream puffs and the hot tamales late at night; in a final burst of inspiration (because she knew that things were going all wrong) she told about the new automobile and going to visit relatives and sitting in the car alone and the man who stopped and looked at her with blood all over his face. She told about the bread steamed over a kettle again, too, because the man asked her if this was so, and she had been told to tell the truth. Then she looked at her Aunt Lulu and saw a handkerchief in her hand and her hand trembling and her mouth, too, and tears on her cheeks; and at her father, who was looking far away and searching for something, like a young boy punished and trying to understand why, the way she had seen him when he came down the steps from the closed room in Glen Ellyn and went into the parlor and leaned his head in his hands and then took the guitar and began to play it; and at her brother, who looked at her with horror and a kind of emotion that she didn't understand but didn't like because it shut her out and made her feel left alone with only closed doors all around; and at her half sister, who was smiling because everything was all decided. And she felt sick and full of a forlorn desperation such as she had never known before.

She was ushered from the chair, and before anyone could

stop her—while the man at the desk was reading a decision—she turned to the left instead of to the right and fell upon Aunt Lulu and sobbed and sobbed and couldn't be torn away, even when it was all over and people were leaving the room and her father tried to take her in his arms. She fought at him and at her brother and half sister and a kind strange lady who came forward from one of the back seats and tried also to calm her, while people as they left turned back for another glimpse of the drama unfolding.

Aunt Lulu said, "Now, Baby, don't cry so—Aunt Lulu understands—everything will be all right," and her father muttered to no one in particular, "She acts as though she's never seen me before," and her brother ground out between his teeth, over and over, so that only she could hear, "Silly! Why did you do it? Stupid silly!"

They pulled her away and smoothed her gray sweater and tied the woolen roses together under her chin and wiped her nose, which badly needed a handkerchief, and then they were on the way home, with her half sister stonily silent because her brother had been unhelpful and ungrateful, which meant that he would rather be where he had been, with all of its terrible drawbacks, than where he was designated to be from now on until the father, to the satisfaction of the court, proved his ability to provide for both children. But they could not relieve the child of her guilt; and, having thus had her first taste of sin, she learned that there is no absolution in innocence; and that even unwitting collaboration is at least stupidity, which has no place in uprightness; and that betrayal of the trust of others and pride of self is more guilt-engendering than just plain willful sinning; and that loving very hard means caring too much to do injuries that will be written in a big black book and will not be undone with all the tears in the world or until the end of time.

Through the rest of the winter they were warm and well fed, but a heaviness stayed with the child that let her know, without knowing the words, that innocence was gone and that from now on she would have to accept responsibility for her actions. She began to observe more and to follow her brother and watch him, because he seemed to be unerringly, incorruptibly sure of himself at all times, which was not easy in such a setting, where everyone was faultlessly witty all the time and where good looks (meaning almost white skin and hair not only supple, but some of the time blond) were the rule rather than the exception. People came and went, some of them relations on her mother's side. An aunt of her mother's named Ida treated her well on her rare visits; and there were children to play with, but she felt herself apart from them and didn't try very hard to belong.

Spring came early as though to compensate for the harsh winter. One balmy evening Aunt Lulu stopped by for the two children, following some plan previously agreed upon, and there was again the familiar neighborhood, the hot tamale late at night, and the room, all three in the same bed as before. For one night the child was transported back, before all of the troubles and winter cold, before the man with his face cut open, before the coal man who sang his dirge of self-pity into the winter air. She was tall enough now to look into the dresser mirror and watch while her hair was lovingly brushed and braided, and she didn't feel ashamed of it or of her color. Only she didn't look directly into Aunt Lulu's eyes, even though she kissed her and clung to her when they parted the next morning back again at her half sister's flat. Then Aunt Lulu had to leave, because she was making her first trial trip on a special train which was just starting between the City and the West Coast, and she was to be allowed to have her own beauty parlor again, this time on the train; she was to be called "beautician" and would be quite apart from those who performed personal services and had not regular salaries but only what people wanted to give them. She kissed the child and promised to take her one day on the train if all worked out as it should. Then she was gone.

Little was heard from Albert Dunham until the following winter, when he wrote from Iowa that he had met and married a schoolteacher named Annette Poindexter and that he was bringing her back to the City. Fanny Weir had to release the children; so on a cold midwinter day Katherine Dunham and her brother rode again through the borderline area where it was already uncomfortable to trespass if one had dark skin; past the mansions that had belonged to white people but were now stripped of all previous glory and turned over to fat black and brown and light-colored politicians and doctors and schoolteachers and government employees; and finally to the dingy streets of folk poverty where Aunt Lulu had always lived. They stayed there in the two rooms this time, awaiting the arrival of their new mother. They couldn't imagine what to expect and could hardly sleep the night they were told that she would arrive the following day.

They stayed up late talking, wondering what she would look like and be like. To the child, "mother" meant only the one who was no longer there, and she had never expected another. In some unformulated way she expected the reappearance of that one, as on the night when she had come downstairs from the closed room and they had drunk milk together in the darkened kitchen.

Early the following morning they crept to the room where Aunt Lulu, taking time off from her trip between the City and California for this special occasion, had slept, and where they knew the new mother would now be with their father. The door was closed, and Aunt Lulu was still asleep on the cot that she had put in the kitchen the night before. Their next visit was to the clothes closet in the hallway, the only one in the small flat. There were unopened suitcases and a cloak and a long tan wool skirt hanging apart from the other clothes. On the floor was a pair of black patent-leather shoes with high suede tops; the linings were red satin and softer than anything the child could imagine. She put them on and was looking down at her feet—admiring herself and promising herself that she would have some just like them—when her brother came and stood by the closet door.

"She wants to see you," he said. Then he added as an afterthought, "She seems nice, but she isn't very pretty."

Four
The Buggy Ride

*

The horse was named Lady Fern, and in the days when she was hitched to a fine light sulky and raced at the county fairs at Aurora and Elgin and Kankakee and Plainfield, she had been distinguished by her fetlocks, evenly marked snow white against the brown satin of her coat, and by the proud, high step with which she took her starting pace and held it around the track, year after year passing her opponents until time won out and she was reluctantly retired with honors.

She missed the roomy barns and broad oak-shaded pastures of Plainfield, and the workouts on frosty or dewy mornings before the sun was up, when the grass smelled its best and all of the night scents were still there. On such mornings a light saddle or training blanket would replace the shaft of the sulky, and she would trot several times around the track circling the meadow, stretching and prancing and warming her muscles before the stable boy pitted her against one of the saddle horses, on whom she looked down because in her estimation trotting a sulky was far more a gentleman's sport than the simple display of brawn and wind and endurance.

Most of all she missed the races themselves. She had her own private wooden horsecar, drawn by a team of wagon horses and padded so that her shiny coat would not be injured if one of the bad-smelling horseless machines passed by and frightened her into an indiscreet movement. She always made a display of descending the plank from her van, partly because she was genuinely nervous, partly because of a sense of showmanship in front of the admiring audience that gathered whenever their favorites were brought to the fairground stables. Year after year she was either first or second or third in the trotting races that were in those days the featured attractions of the county fair, her position depending more on her rapport with the driver of the sulky than on her form, which was unquestionable, or on endurance, which—she argued bitterly to herself when she finally realized that she was to be put up for auction at one of these same fairs—she defied any yearling to match even though she had now passed her ninth birthday.

The man who made the final bid at the auction pleased her because he seemed to know all about horses and had a touch at once authoritative and considerate. He seemed to realize what her emotions would be at this crucial moment of her life and, when the bargain was made, openly showed his pride in owning such a fine specimen. He led her to another part of the fairground, where a smithy was in operation and where used buggies and surreys and sulkies were on display. What he selected was durable but not flashy, and the horse was pleased to recognize the sulky as one drawn by her several seasons before. She didn't like being harnessed to a buggy, however, and all of the long trip from the fair to the Town, which she had never seen before, she tried by side steps and feints and head tossing to drive home the fact that this was an unaccustomed task and far below her station. And had the short dark-complexioned man not made it clear to her then and there who was in charge, she might have switched around, buggy and all, and bolted back past the fairground to the meadow of her former owner. As it was, she was held well in hand and accepted her new lot. So in the end they rounded the corner of a street she later heard referred to as Bluff Street and came to a halt before a store whose open door emitted the odor of gasoline, the same odor emitted by the horseless carriages —because the store was a clothescleaning establishment, called West Side Cleaners and Dyers, and was owned and operated by her new owner, Albert M. Dunham.

A woman came out of the shop as they halted, and a boy who looked at Lady Fern speculatively, and a young child who seemed afraid but curious. They walked all around her at a distance and admired her. Later the man and the boy drove down the street and back again, then into a yard beside the wooden building where the store was, and the father showed the boy how to unhitch the harness and wipe her off and lead her to a stall set up in a tin shed in the yard and later, when she had cooled off a little, to give her water and food. The boy was dutiful but lacked the enthusiasm for her that the man had; his touch was not unfriendly, but neither was it the touch of someone who knew all about horses and how to talk to them and get the best out of them, so in consequence she felt nervous with the boy and remained so throughout her association with the West Side Cleaners and Dyers.

In Katherine Dunham, feelings about Lady Fern were very mixed. She admired her shining coat and the way she always held her head high and stepped proudly, even when the buggy gave way to the bulky green wagon with the name of the shop and its owner painted in bold letters on either side.

What distressed the child was Lady Fern's unpredictability: one minute she would pass an automobile unalarmed and, at another, jerk so violently to one side that the suits and dresses hanging from the rod in back would be thrown to the floor in disarray. The flaring nostrils and impatient head and rolling eyes also disturbed the child, and although she admired the sheer strength and beauty of the satin-covered muscles, she was terrified by their potential power for destruction.

She kept her distance from the horse but found through her a renewed bond with her father, who no longer seemed to have time to tell the children about the exploits of Br'er Rabbit and Br'er Fox. He made her his Sunday-morning companion on stolen trips to a stretch of tar-covered thoroughfare called Black Road, where, under the pretext of exercising Lady Fern or ordering hay or fodder at a granary on the outskirts of the Town, he would test the mare against the nags, trotters, or hacks that circulated in that area, driven by farmers or amateur, would-be touts looking for an easy bet.

There was little comment or exchange between these men and the dark young man with the child sitting primly beside him in the sulky. In these environs he was stranger than a stranger, but admiration for the spirited and apparently blooded animal that he turned in show-off circles in the hitching yard of the wholesale supply market and the unspoken challenge as he trotted her, reined in just far enough to make their racing instincts function, overcame their instinctive mistrust of outsiders. The challenge would be taken up, and bets placed among the loungers under the maple tree split down the middle by last summer's tornado.

Then tobacco juice would be spat in confirmation of the transaction, and Albert Dunham would turn the sulky into Black Road, and, little by little, give Lady Fern more headway. If his opponent moved dangerously ahead, he would slap the reins over her back and coax and make clucking horse-talk sounds. Finally, if it looked as though she mightn't win, he would take the whip from the side bracket of the sulky and use it until Lady Fern pulled out of danger.

When the serious part of the racing began, the child would have to step down from the sulky and wait under a mulberry tree where the men didn't congregate and watch the road as long as she could see the contestants. There would be a stir among the waiting men when they were in sight again, and she felt proud of Lady Fern, who invariably came in ahead. The mare would be breathing heavily now and snorting and chewing the foam-covered bit, with creamy sweat lathered under and around the leather attachments fitting her into the traces.

The most frightening-looking thing of all was the tar on the faces of the men who raced their horses against the sulky. On the hottest days the sun would melt the tar into a shiny coating which clung to the rubber tires of horse and motor vehicle alike, to the hoofs of the horses, and to the shoes of pedestrians; and fast-moving wheels and hoofs flung up a shower of liquid pitch which left a decoration of black splotches and hair-fine streaks, as though some mad painter had shaken a giant brush in their direction.

On her father the tar was not so distinguishable, except where it had spattered his white shirt, so that he remained dignified beside their ridiculousness. On the way home he would start to wipe the stuff off, but the evidence was there, all over the horse and the sulky and himself. They would pull into the side yard of the shop, and he would try to repair the damage—but not until after he had dried and curried and watered and fed the mare, talking to her because it took a long time for her to calm down after so much excitement.

When the family went on Sunday picnics, they would hitch the horse to a fringed surrey, with seats in front and back covered with dark blue tufted felt. All through the summer Lady Fern would be driven along the pleasant dirt roads, which branched off from the highways and led through fields and orchards, past farmhouses, down tree-shaded lanes, to one of the many clear streams that crisscrossed the country between the Desplaines, the Kankakee, and the Illinois rivers. After lunch beneath the shade of some tree, Albert Dunham and the new mother would nap, while the children went wading or fished with lengths of cotton string baited with grubs or angleworms. Then in the late afternoon there would be a peaceful return to Bluff Street.

The child remembered with special vividness one Sunday when, searching aimlessly for a place to picnic, the family happened on what they later learned was the source of the Illinois River. After miles of dusty road and hot sun the father turned Lady Fern into a rutted path made by wagon wheels, hoping to arrive at what seemed to be a secluded woodland at the bottom of a pasture. The woodland proved to be a fringe of willow trees bent over a marshy swamp and shielding from view the skeleton of a decaying river boat. What there had been of a hold had long ago been claimed by the ooze in which she rested, so that a rotting gangplank from the bank slanted upward only slightly to reach the gallery that sagged in front of what must have been the main deck. A rusted iron ladder led up to the captain's bridge, the floor of which caved into the single room of the main deck where the child, supported by her brother as she clung to the ladder, could see the rat-ravaged cushions littering the floor beside the benches along the walls that they had once covered.

Beneath the willows the family spread their lunch. As they ate, they deciphered the faded name *Betsy Ann* shaded into the prow like a half-obliterated charcoal drawing. Prey to the uneasy enchantment of their surroundings, they spoke in lowered voices, speculating on the vessel's origin and the means by which it had arrived here high above a body of water that they could glimpse, through trees on the other side of the marsh, in a valleylike depression far below.

After the remnants of the picnic had been packed away, the father decided to follow the wagon tracks farther instead of turning back immediately toward the Town. The reward was breathtaking. A dead end brought into full view the water in the valley below the derelict boat. From the top of a cliff the child could see the broad, tranquil pool that was the river's source, serenely welling from a tangle of berry and ivy and cocklebur brush. As she watched, the setting sun flooded the valley with orange and red, tinting the watercourses that stole silently from the source, later to become rapid waterways, and ultimately rivers.

The child felt as though she were standing on the edge of the world, in the shadow of invisible glaciers drowned in a silence so intense that it hurt. The sight was beyond her comprehension and therefore disquieting; her only comfort lay in the nearness of her family, brought into an affectionate, instinctive communion with one another on rare occasions such as this. Her brother mused into the scene below, and in the dying rays of the sun his face, so often inscrutable, turned gentle. Her father held the hand of the new mother—a gesture of affection that the child seldom saw again. All of this reassured her, and when they climbed back into the surrey, the specter of the *Betsy Ann* had melted again into the willow grove.

Country Sundays like this one seemed especially festive occasions that first summer because for an interval after their arrival in the Town the family was nomadic, sleeping and eating in the rear of the shop part of the time, part of the time living as boarders in the homes of strangers who had managed to measure up to the strict standards set by Annette Dunham. Their longest stay was in the house of a devout churchgoing widow named Rebecca Brown, who lived on the outskirts of the Town, but in a section well built up and easily accessible by trolley car. The children were charmed by the approach to the elm-shaded avenue that gave the street its name. A sharp turn from a wooden bridge led down stone steps into a heavily wooded park, and a path ran beside the wide stone wall which held a creek within bounds in the spring when snow melted or rains were unduly heavy.

The boy was soon busy every spare moment learning the trade into which his father hoped one day to launch him, so that the child was often left in the care of Rebecca Brown, who had been widowed only shortly before their arrival. She was a pillar of the African Methodist Episcopal Church, locally named Brown's Chapel. For some twenty years she had faithfully served as stewardess and lent her rich contralto to the choir; between times she baked bread and cleaned house for those rich enough to afford her services. When she agreed to share her cottage with the Dunhams, it was partly with a plan for retirement in view, partly because of her immediate affection for the two children. The girl became her constant companion, and, besides revealing to her the secret of the golden loaves that issued from the coalburner in the kitchen, Rebecca Brown taught her to knit and to forage in the woods of the park for tender young dandelion greens and helped her decipher the volumes in the dining-room bookcase, most of which were popular contemporary religious works with flamboyant illustrations of Bible texts.

Actually the child much preferred looking over the contents of a cabinet in which were odd bits of cut glass and blown Venetian glass and here and there a fine piece of Wedgwood, chipped where it would not show to the casual observer. But she was happiest in the park with the old woman, where the two of them, supplied with market baskets, spent many Saturday mornings—while the bread was rising for the second time—bending back maidenhair fern and searching under buttercups and violets for the tenderest of the young dandelion greens. She was sad when Annette Dunham finally decided to move the family to the rear of the West Side Cleaners and Dyers.

Later the child realized that Rebecca Brown, who had a will of her own, had refused to assume the position of satellite to Annette Dunham; she had held her head high and said No whenever she felt like it, in spite of having darker skin and doing "house service," and had shown her displeasure because the children were being reared churchless and like heathen, and had run her part of the house, which after all she owned outright, as she pleased. And all of this, along with the child's affection for Rebecca Brown, Annette Dunham had found irksome.

The shop on Bluff Street, at the bottom of the Western Avenue hill, was the smaller portion of a building leased to an elderly man who ran a carpet-cleaning establishment, the office of which adjoined Albert Dunham's dry-cleaning business. The child stood inarticulate at her first introduction to the proprietor because his name was Crandall, which evoked all sorts of misty terrors and shadowy apprehensions as she recollected the beings who in her childhood fancy had lurked in the halltree of the house in Glen Ellyn.

In a few days industriously spent, the mother had fitted green and brown checkered linoleum into the window shelf and hung dark green alpaca curtains on a drawstring one third of the height of the window, which made it a showcase and at the same time sheltered the sewing machine, at which she spent much of the day mending and stitching, from the view of passers-by. The rest of the front room was given over to a roll-top desk on the left of the entrance, at which the mother worked on a meticulously kept set of ledgers, and on the right of the entrance to a curtained-off space where finished clothing hung ready for delivery.

Behind a partition of plywood and plasterboard, papered and then calcimined a pale yellow to match the ceiling, the father constructed two durable pressing tables and overhead racks for unfinished clothing. A fat-bellied stove with isinglass windows burned trash during the summer and would provide the only heating, aside from the heavy pressing irons, for the coming winter.

In the front room, after the lights were out and the last pedestrians gone from Bluff Street, the mother and father would set up a double cot. The children slept in the back room, the boy on a daybed, the sister on a cot. Through the summer this was placed next to the daybed, but when cooler weather came it was moved beneath one of the pressing tables. Meals, simple but substantial, were prepared on a gasplate in a vestibule behind the shop, which connected the smaller part of the building with Mr. Crandall's carpet shop. On one side of the vestibule were two toilets, in constant disrepair, hidden behind swinging doors.

From the moment he set eyes on the premises Albert Dunham had been obsessed by the desire to oust Mr. Crandall and come into possession of the entire building. His wildest dreams were of total ownership; his more practical ones, simply of becoming sole tenant, absorbing Mr. Crandall's carpet-cleaning business, and installing his family in the barnlike rooms of the second floor.

By the early spring of his first year in the Town, his more practical dreams had been realized.

Diagonally across the street from the West Side Cleaners and Dyers, a man named Rube had ensured the future of his thriving saloon after the coming of Prohibition by enlarging a small basement storeroom into a contraband warehouse, with a gaming room in front as a decoy in case federal instead of local authorities should come in to inspect the place.

The child felt the stir of excitement and listened to discussions about the new laws, but it was the people more than these mysteries that really caught her interest. To her "Rube's Saloon" meant a skinny parchment-colored man with an enormous stomach which her father had said would one day be his finish if he didn't stop drinking beer. His name was Tommy, and though he was taciturn and hardly ever spoke when he brought clothes to the shop to be pressed while he waited, the fascination of his distended stomach was too strong for her, and she would stand near him, trying to make conversation and following him to the curb when he left. Her father said that Tommy had dropsy and that the swelling was because his stomach was full of water. She wanted badly to discuss this phenomenon and, most of all, to touch the stomach and see if it was as hard as it looked; but she was discouraged by her own reticence and by Tommy's almost sullen lack of interest in anything that did not have to do with the profession of bartending, which he had followed as far back as anyone on Bluff Street could remember. Prohibition was perhaps as responsible for the sudden decline of the former bartender as his dropsical condition: some said he never recovered from the closing of the bar, which was his pride and joy, and that running errands for the Rube family and the men who went to and from the City, sometimes arriving in the middle of the night in big black limousines, proved to be too poor a substitute for his former duties. When her father remarked that poor Tommy had wasted away and how thin he was, the girl was puzzled because she saw only the huge stomach which swelled above the spindly legs. Once in a while she wondered about his coloring, which was pale gray over brown—skin, hair, and eyes. Her mother said that Tommy was a mulatto and that he stayed with the Rubes because they knew something about him and could make things very disagreeable if he left. One day she heard that Tommy had died and she was sorry that she had not asked him to let her feel the balloon that was his stomach.

From the cot under the pressing table the child learned to recognize customers who stopped by the shop after closing hours by their shoes and trousers more than by their voices. Businessmen on their way home found the father a pleasant and informative conversationalist, particularly because at such an early age he had been proprietor of his own establishment in the City and after that had traveled so extensively in areas known to them only by name. Old Man Crandall was a frequent late visitor, and many nights, as the weather turned colder and the back room of the shop with its heated pressing irons and later its steam pressing machine became a comfortable refuge, she would lie in her snug retreat—unpleasant only because of the fumes of gasoline escaping from clothes hanging on the racks and mingling with the steam of the irons which her father planted rhythmically on wet pressing cloths—and, fighting sleep, listen to political talk and Bluff Street gossip. Looking at the tattered trouser cuffs and at the cracked shoes that crossed and uncrossed before her eyes as Old Man Crandall leaned against the table opposite her, she learned piecemeal about the people who would be their neighbors for years to come, and especially about goings-on across the street in and around Rube's Saloon, and about the building in which the family now lived.

This had originally been equipped for various entertainments, some of them illegal. As a front, two large dance halls had been outfitted, one where the carpet cleaner now had his roomy office, the other occupying two thirds of the second floor. There were several secret stairways through subterranean recesses, and a side door led from the ground-floor room to a flight of wide steps going up to an inner hallway. To the left of the hallway two wide, flimsy doors opened onto the larger of the dance halls, which was sixty or seventy feet long and thirty feet wide, and up the steps and into this room the old man dragged his dusty carpets for cleaning. The front part of the building had housed other, more suspect diversions. A large front room had definitely, according to Mr. Crandall, been a gambling room; the other rooms—one in front over the office of the cleaning shop, one behind the gambling room, and one next to that —had served even shadier purposes. It was this apartment that Albert Dunham coveted as living quarters for his family.

The illegal activities had continued for a while after Old Man Crandall took over the bottom floor for his business.

Then there had arisen uneasy competition with the men responsible for the alterations going on in the basement of Rube's Saloon. Bluff Street turned from one faction to the other, not wanting to miss any excitement. One night shortly before the advent of the Dunham family, several men were seen crossing the street from Rube's, all with overcoats on and with their hands in their pockets, though it was already spring. They walked up the steps and into the gambling room, and there (as the child gathered from conversations between her father and Old Man Crandall) they had quietly dispersed a small-time poker game. But it was on that same night, apparently, that the Greek in charge of the establishment had been shot; later there were one or two fights and accidents at the dances, and within a short time the building had been vacated, to stand with the upstairs in disuse until Mr. Crandall decided to expand his carpet-cleaning business into the upper rear regions.

The child had hardly entered her first semester at the new school before she began to complain of pains in her knees and of sore throats, and during the winter she spent more time out of school than in, often with an abnormally high temperature. Her tonsils were severely infected, and were undoubtedly the source of the rheumatic pain as well as of the sore throat. A doctor newly arrived in the Town was consulted and prescribed bed and some powders that relieved the swelling in her throat and reduced the temperature for a time. But a few days later she would be home from school early again, her forehead flaming and her voice a painful croak. Then the cot would be pulled into the front office and a screen placed in front of it, so she could escape to some degree the naphtha odor she had grown to loathe. Sometimes she would cry silently just because of the fumes, and her temperature would rise, and the distracted mother would telephone again for Dr. Williams.

The extra-thick lenses of the doctor's glasses fascinated the child; so did the patina of his brown skull—bald and polished as a piece of saddle leather—which gleamed in the light as he bent forward with his ear to her chest or tilted his head to look at the thermometer. His eyes were kindly, and his laughter was infectious, starting with a hearty "Haw, haw" and simmering down and back into a liquid gurgle. She also liked him because he was the first to address her as "young lady," in a way that gave great dignity to her years.

His patients at that time were still few, and the Dunhams promised to be not only loyal clients, but good friends. After a few visits he brought along his wife, a quiet, birdlike woman, who had taught in rural schools, as Annette Dunham had, and who knew the area of southern Illinois from which Annette Dunham's family came. Before long the child was as devoted to Mrs. Williams as to her husband, and the friendship between the two families that started in the back room of the cleaning shop was to last a lifetime.

Often during the late night or early morning hours the child would stir in her sleep and be awakened by the sound of heavy motor vehicles stopping or starting with a grinding of brakes and gears; and she learned to distinguish another sound, which her brother identified for her as a motorboat on the canal. She could hear voices, too, and the sound of crates being loaded and unloaded.

One night she was startled by an authoritative knocking on the front door; it was followed by a sharp rapping on the front window and then by a rattling of the locked door. She wondered why her father was so slow answering; then she heard a whispered consultation with her mother, who was not at all in favor of unlocking the door. But the knocking and rapping and rattling continued, and finally her father pulled trousers over his pajamas, opened the door as far as the safety chain would permit, and demanded an explanation.

Two men had an overcoat that they wanted spots taken

out of immediately. Her father protested vehemently the hour and the intrusion and tried to close the door; but something obstructed him, then low words were spoken, then she heard the door close and the chain released. The door opened again, and her father took the coat from the men. It seemed most urgent that it be ready for them within the hour, with no traces left of the spots.

Her father turned the light on in the back room, rather crossly told his son to go back to sleep, refused assistance from his wife, and lit the pressing iron in preparation for the finished job. The child could see his legs move from table to sink, and she heard him ripping pieces from the bag of spotting cloths hanging above the pressing board. She heard him untwist the corks from bottles and buried her nose in the covers at the sting of acids. When he dropped crumpled cloths onto the floor beside the table, she saw that they were smudged with red and wondered why paint had to be removed from an overcoat at this hour of the night. The next morning she heard her father tell her mother emphatically that if it hadn't been for the children, who might have been awakened by further argument, he would never have consented to play a part in covering up the dirty work, whatever it was, that was going on across the street. Her mother looked worried and said that they should take their bloodstains somewhere else.

After that the only disturbances in the night were the sounds of loading and unloading barrels and crates of bottles, and of trucks and an occasional motorboat. And presently these sounds became more discreet, after a series of complaints from conservative townsfolk who had found out what was happening.

For several weeks before the move was made from the back room of the shop to the flat above, there was a bustle of scrubbing, painting, plastering, papering, calcimining, and fumigating, which the father carried on with the aid of the boy after school and of his wife into the late hours of the night after the shop was closed. One of the father's aspirations was being realized; for the mother, being within sight of her dream of proper housing and having the family of four together under one roof made the extra work a joy rather than a burden. A base-burner was installed in the former gambling room; and although there was as yet no electricity, gas fixtures with frosted globes gave the lemon-yellow calcimined walls and white ceilings and woodwork of the large front room a charm that partly made up for the crooked doorframes, slanting floors, and cracked plaster.

The room directly above the office became the bedroom of the parents. Behind that a kitchen was installed, and behind the living room, a dining room. This, which must have been an inner office before, had no windows and no lighting fixture. Its outer door opened onto the inner hallway, which in turn led to the carpet room. Behind the kitchen was a room of equal size which became the bathroom. A storeroom to the right of the living room completed the floor plan.

Since the only heat was the base-burner in the living room, the winter task of the child, besides cleaning lamp chimneys and refilling the bases with kerosene, was to trim the wicks of the oil stove that was carried from one room to another and to keep this also in fuel. To the boy went the chore of cleaning out ashes and banking at night and rebuilding in the day the fire in the hungry stove which, no matter how much it was fed, could never thoroughly warm the flat.

With the new living quarters the family began to take on a more cohesive form. A few pieces of furniture salvaged from Glen Ellyn appeared from a storage warehouse in the City, and the child recognized with a somewhat diffident pleasure a writing desk, with curved legs and a gold and yellow design on the front which opened out into a shelf, and a matching bookcase. The light-oak residence of the

"Crandalls," who still lurked in her memory, took its place in the darkest corner of the inner hallway; and as Fu Manchu and Tarzan's apes replaced the "Crandalls" in her private mythology of evil, she learned to circle it when entering or leaving the front room alone or to avoid it entirely by entering the flat through the dining room.

The appearance of these familiar objects had the ill effect on her of setting in motion a train of nostalgic reveries. She tried hard to pick up the family life where it had left off, her favorite flights of fancy being into the period before the room at the top of the flight of stairs in the Glen Ellyn house had been closed. Intending no infidelity toward her present mother, she found herself struggling to recall the first. She compared their physical aspects, innocently at first and then with guilt. She saw her present mother bent over the sewing machine in the half-curtained window of the shop, worrying about seams and alterations, and thought of the other one seated at the harp in the Sunday evening lampglow, her face pale and lovely, highlights on the shining pompadour of her black hair.

Annette Dunham, as the son had said, was not very pretty. A pair of good, frankly pleasant brown eyes under quizzically raised eyebrows were her greatest asset. High cheekbones showed her Choctaw inheritance; full lips, her Negroid. Her moderate jawline, rounded cheeks, and dark brown wavy hair, were evidence of Caucasian ancestry, and so was her light, though not exactly fair, skin. Her feet and hands were well made, and even in old age she would take inordinate pride in a size-six shoe, quadruple-A, with an even narrower heel. She remained slender, upright, and neatly proportioned until the day of her death, forty years after her entry into the children's lives.

The child finally gave up expecting the reappearance of her first mother and settled into a deep regard for the second, who, though fiercely loyal to the children and as full of mother love as a human being can be, lacked the capacity to show affection with the kiss, the touch, the fondling that the girl in particular missed. In the beginning she regretted that the new mother was not ravishingly beautiful like some of the movie heroines she had seen, and that she did not wear makeup or brilliantly colored clothing; gradually she grew to appreciate the quiet good taste with which Annette Dunham dressed herself and her daughter and the conservatism that evoked the respect of all with whom she came in contact. The indomitable willfulness, the inflexible hewing to the line of her own choosing, the insistence upon first consideration or none, the sense of obeisance due her from all and sundry that turned later to a demand for recognition of her self-appointed position as martyr—all of these were to be met with later by the young girl and then the woman and, when weighed, found still to the credit of the second mother.

Lady Fern's inadequacies for the task that was put upon her came not from her years or lack of stamina, but from the simple fact that the father visualized her in dual and triple roles. His needs were for a work animal, but his esthetic sensibilities had dictated the purchase of a high-strung racing mare. And during the summer that followed the move to the flat above the shop, it became an obsession with him to justify the high cost of her food and upkeep by training her for saddle use for his son. He envisaged part-time and light deliveries by this method to supplement those by the motor truck that he felt he must acquire before the summer was over. He was not looking upon the shift from harness to saddle as diversion for the boy: by the first summer vacation he had made it clear to his wife and to the boy himself that in the scheme of things as he saw it there was no leisure for the male members of the family and very little for the female. In any event, the saddle was purchased, and the boy would have to learn to ride.

Albert Dunham, Jr., had seen clearly, during the first

days of the new business, that the pattern of his life had already been firmly plotted by his father. The lectures on inheritance, descent, family obligations, and responsibilities, and the evaluations of brains and business over learning, were not lost on him as they were on his sister. He realized that his father's life revolved around the continuance of the business he had established and that his own scholarly inclinations represented a challenge to parental authority.

The son was obedient not because he respected this authority, but in order to avoid conflict. He returned from school and drove the horse on the rounds of deliveries through the cold winter evenings and often into the night. After the evening meal he studied assiduously, even feverishly, as though to make up for the narrowing-down of time. Grudgingly, and often because of the mother's intervention, he was permitted to study at night. But then there were thinly veiled comments on the amount of fuel burned for heating and lighting when so much more could be learned by simple application to the business—a priceless opportunity for a boy to have right at hand. Had the father dared make the boy driver of the delivery truck the instant he bought it, he probably would not have thought of the saddle. As it was, the boy before long made some of the deliveries with brown-paper packages of cleaned and pressed clothing neatly folded across the bow of the saddle, while the father might be somewhere in the same vicinity, driving the second-hand Ford delivery truck, which he had painted bottle green and lettered with the name of the shop and its proprietor.

Between the boy and the horse there was a mutual mistrust, in no way diminished because it was also his duty to feed her. After the truck had been acquired, she was exiled to a deserted stable a block down Bluff Street, just north of the hill. Here the boy continued to feed and water her, often at the end of an exhausting day when he could well have been asleep. On these excursions he would carry a book as well as a lantern because it was his habit to read while the horse munched her feed and then to water and blanket her for the night.

One night he was sent to the stable later than usual. It was bitter cold, with one fall of snow tightly packed on the ground and another drifting from low clouds. Well past midnight Annette Dunham woke in alarm to find the gaslight still burning in the living room, roused her husband, and insisted that he look for the boy. He went grudgingly into the bleak night. As he approached the barn, he saw the light of the lantern through the door cracks and inside found his son sound asleep, book in hand and the bucket of oats, which he had been about to pass into the stall, spilled in the hay at his feet. The hungry mare was pawing the floor of her stall impatiently and nuzzling her empty trough. The food so near her was unattainable because the boy sat on the other side of the barrier and slept so soundly that her fretfulness had no effect whatever. It was not until his father descended upon him, furious at the waste, outraged at the offense to the horse, and chagrined at being routed from his bed, that he was aware of his whereabouts.

The boy was not unaccustomed to his father's rages. The combination of self-aggrandizement and serious business and family responsibilities had begun to engender patterns of anger, intolerance, and physical violence that were later to have serious consequences. How much of this had to do with longing for the life past and bitterness at the defeat of his earliest dreams would be hard to say; and although he appreciated his second wife as helpmate and as foster mother to his children, he nevertheless had begun to chafe at her intrusions into his running of the business and at her constant championing of the son, who in her eyes could do no wrong. The oats scattered irretrievably in the hay and mud on the floor of the stall made his anger explode: the boy returned to the flat shivering with cold and pain and resentment and bearing marks from his father's belt strap, which became Albert Dunham's favored instrument of punishment for both children.

The antipathy between the boy and the horse reached its culmination within a few months. One spring day, as though seizing a long-awaited opportunity, Lady Fern felt the reins slacken on a return trip from one of the deliveries, reared with a sudden side swerve, threw the boy onto the hard pavement of Raynor Avenue, and triumphantly galloped her way back to the Bluff Street barn. Someone informed the father, and he set out in the delivery wagon to search for his son. Meanwhile a motorist, relieved at having by a miracle missed running over the inert figure in the middle of the road, had revived the boy with a glass of water and driven him to the shop. By the time Albert Dunham returned after a fruitless search, his son was installed in his parents' bedroom, and Dr. Williams was probing, cleaning, salving, and bandaging a skinless area on his right side, where he had been dragged along the pavement before the horse had galloped away.

In spite of the father's lightly tossing off the accident as something that would help toughen the boy for manhood, Annette Dunham forbade further use of the saddle and insisted that their own bedroom be given up to him during his convalescence. Thus began a pattern of rivalry in which the father gradually felt himself pushed into second place in favor of his son. Assigned the role of nurse, the girl delighted in helping Dr. Williams change bandages and in carrying meal trays to the patient. Her constant attendance on her brother did nothing to assuage the jealousy the father felt toward the son; and the breach between them widened.

Five
The Canal

*

Albert Dunham had built singlehanded the corrugated tin shed where the delivery truck was now sheltered. To this he added a smaller limestone warehouse just high enough to stand in comfortably, but with a doorless entrance so low that he himself had to bend to enter. Inside the warehouse, which was called "the tumbler room" or just "out back," he stored gasoline in iron drums and passed clothes through a wood-lined cylindrical tumbler, electrically operated, and after that into a flat, open-topped, circular drying tub. The floor was dirt, and winter and summer pools of black oil sat in the saturated, hard-packed earth. The electrically operated machinery was an important addition to the expanding business, and because he could not quite foresee getting around to installing a door with adequate bolts, the father began to talk about acquiring a watchdog. Closer to his true reason may have been the fact that Lady Fern's days were numbered and that his need to dominate some dumb animal remained constant.

The mother acquiesced, and the father began inquiries among his customers for a dog that would fill his customary requirements of breeding and intelligence. The child was overjoyed at the prospect; she imagined happy promenades with a playful but faithful puppy and even dared hope that it might be allowed to sleep on cool evenings at the foot of the living-room davenport, which she now shared with her brother. But when one day her father led home the dog of his choice, straining at a heavy leash clasped to a brass-studded collar, her hopes were shattered. The creature answered to the name of Rex and was grayish in color and uglier than any animal that she had ever seen. Because of the black, foreshortened muzzle, the powerful chest, and the bowed legs, her father boasted that it was mostly English bulldog. It was only half grown, but already belligerent: through red, mucus-rimmed eyes it glared balefully at each member of the family, and when the father patted it on the head and said, "There, there, Rex," it raised a slobbering upper lip, disclosed canine teeth as sharp as stilettos, and emitted a warning growl.

The breaking-in of Rex was slow and laborious. He did not recognize the man as master, as Lady Fern had done, but accepted every overture ungraciously, growling and snarling at master and stranger alike. He was attached to a heavy chain, near the opening in the base of the building. The chain was shortened in daytime so that father and son and other helpers could pass unmolested to and from the tumbler room; at night, though, it was lengthened, and anyone approaching the rear entrance to the carpet shop or the windows of the garage or the doorway of the tumbler room ran the risk of a savage onslaught. But periods without food and water did much to subdue the animal, and a leather strap cut from an old harness did the rest.

The feeding of the dog was a constant irritant to mother and daughter. The father would, it seemed to them, choose a time when all burners of the kitchen stove were needed, and appropriate the pot or boiler that had been taken from the cupboard the moment before or just scoured and put away. Then he would produce bones, joints, and meat ends scavenged from friendly butchers on his delivery rounds and boil them even though they might be well on the way to decay; he added scraps of dry bread, onions, and seasoning until the pot simmered with a scummy stew, which had to sit on the burner and cool before being scraped into the dog's tin serving dish. Her feeling for the dog being what it was, the child could not help resenting the ritual that meant a delayed evening meal or an extra pot to scour. She found the food revolting to look at and would soak the pot later in hot water and soap powder, as though the slobbering jowls had fed directly from it.

Rex was only the first in a succession of watchdogs, all bearing the same name and each more vicious than his predecessor.

During all the time they lived on Bluff Street, the Dunhams had direct contact with very few of their neighbors. On the far edge of the side yard a family named McGuire lived in an unpainted three-room wooden house, with a back porch on the yard and a small front stoop with steps leading down to the street. The child saw into the house on only one or two fleeting occasions, because her mother took an immediate aversion to the McGuires, referring to them, along with the McCarthys across the street, as "shanty" Irish. At times terrible sounds of dissension came from the McGuire house, and when finally an older daughter found work and moved away, Katherine Dunham's mother said that was much better; perhaps there would be less trouble in the family, and the older girl would be able to move her mother from the miserable little house, which in fact she eventually managed to do. As for the McCarthys, they were more a clan than a family, coming and going from other parts of the Town, sometimes as many as ten or twelve living at the same time in the narrow, two-story, ramshackle house backed up against the canal. The McCarthy children were of all ages. An older girl was very pretty, and the boys ranged from small, sturdy roughnecks to swaggering young men with affairs of their own which took them frequently to the City and gave them ready access to Rube's basement.

Halfway down the block on the same side of the street as the cleaning shop was a dark gray, rather ornate stone building, in which lived many of the transients of the street, whom the child would never know. She was strictly forbidden to make new acquaintances but was allowed on this section of the street to wander alone as far as the door of Reimer's soda pop factory. On sweltering summer days she would stand inside Reimer's door enjoying the cool, damp air and the mixed synthetic odors which filled the cement room; and now and then Mrs. Reimer would happen down from the apartment over the factory and offer the child her choice of a drink from one of the tin tubs where bottles were kept ice cold.

Across the street from the shop, Old Lady McGrath fought a losing battle to run a grocery store in which the stock depleted by the few sales was never replenished, until finally the remaining items were auctioned off to creditors and the premises turned into a hardware store. She also fought a losing battle to rid herself of a tapeworm, to which she attributed a voracious appetite and an outsized abdomen. She was a clean, neat old Irish woman, and the child was allowed to visit now and then the bare room that Mrs. McGrath kept dusted and polished so that, when "They" came to take her away, there would be no suggestion that the last of the McGraths had been "shanty." "They" came not long after the grocery store had failed, because there was no money for the rent, and a nurse sent by the City decided that the tapeworm could best be dealt with in a hospital. So there was an end to the informative discussions about the tapeworm, and, too, to Mrs. McGrath's unsurpassable jams and jellies, the latter of such lucidity that it was a pleasure to hold them to the light and imagine that the simple jelly glass was a solid, priceless ruby or garnet or topaz or amethyst.

The family to which the mother raised no social objections was that of Henry Simon. He had inherited the grocery store two doors down from the West Side Cleaners, and the red brick building that went with it, from his rugged German father, who had brought to the new world little money but a strong body and a Teutonic determination. Henry Simon ran the combination grocery and meat market with his spinster sister, Mary; now and then there would be a token visit from his wife or her sister, who stayed most of the time in the cheerful flat above the store tending the three Simon boys or visited relatives on the west side of the Town, where it was Margaret Simon's nagging ambition to live. To whatever extent the ever-watchful street would permit, the two families became friendly. Bobby Simon was near the age of the boy; Art Simon, the age of the girl. And when the Dunham family had first moved to Bluff Street, Henry Simon, Jr., was a happy, brown-eyed infant. Once or more a day the child would visit the store on errands for her mother or father. She enjoyed the rows of gunny sacks filled with dried beans and peas and, when no one was watching, indulged in the sensuous pleasure of scooping up handfuls of kidney beans, lentils, black-eyed peas, and lima beans and letting them trickle slowly through her fingers back into the open sack. Cookies were in square tin boxes with colored pictures of the contents pasted on the outside; glass pharmacists' jars filled with fruit drops, mints, licorice balls, and gum drops stood on top of a showcase that displayed an assortment of needles, pins, safety pins, threads, yarns, knitting wools, and tape measures. Meandering to the meat department at the back of the shop, customers stopped to examine fresh bread wrapped in waxed paper and trays of fresh bakery rolls. Rows of canned and bottled goods led to a wired-in cage where Mary Simon sat on a high stool and computed figures. Now and then she slid off the stool and went to a shelf to look at a price mark or wait on a customer. The child, fascinated as always by physical nonconformity, waited for this moment in order to see the thick sole on a specially built shoe that Mary Simon wore to make up for the shortness of one leg.

Henry Simon was a great practical joker, and he and the child were good friends until one day there was an incident that almost destroyed the relationship between the two families. Albert Dunham, always ready to display any knowledge reminiscent of his former life, enjoyed addressing his neighbor in the language he had learned from the master tailors when he was an apprentice and often, as he pointed out a sirloin or porterhouse steak, would carry on with Henry Simon a rapid banter in German. The child listened and yearned to belong to this exclusive linguistic society. One day, while waiting for an order to be trimmed and wrapped, she urged Henry Simon to teach her a sentence in German so that she could surprise her father. She refused to take No for an answer, and he finally said to her, "All right, I'll teach you. Just go back and say, '*Mein Arsch und dein Gesicht sind Zwillinge!*'"

And he wrapped the meat in brown paper, shoved it across the counter, and moved on to the next customer with a grin. At her cash register his sister looked around sharply as she heard the German words, then shook her head, rang up forty-eight cents, and gave the child change from a dollar. Repeating the foreign words over and over, the child hopped and skipped her way back to the shop. Ignoring her mother she hurried to the back room, where her father was discussing the future of Negro business in America with a customer. She stood first on one foot, then the other, until he finally took notice and said, "What is it, Katherine? Why are you standing there? Why don't you put the meat in the icebox?"

"*Mein Arsch und dein Gesicht sind Zwillinge,*" she said proudly.

The pressing iron stopped in midair, and her father's jaw fell open. She repeated the phrase. When her father's mouth closed and he put the iron on its stand and a rising anger replaced the surprise in his face, she began to waver and said lamely, "Mr. Simon told me that. He was teaching me German. I thought——"

But her father had grabbed his hat and brushed past her, walking right over the unfinished explanation and paying no attention to his wife, who said, "Al, where are you going?"

The child knew where he would be going and, though she couldn't translate what she had said, supposed that it was something better not to be said, at least not to her father. As she sadly put the meat for dinner in the icebox at the top of the upstairs hall, she prepared herself for the worst. Once her father had had his way with Henry Simon, she knew she would be next. Of late he had been indulging in more frequent and more lasting displays of anger, and her only uncertainty was whether she would be punished immediately or later, by hand or by leather strap, and if she would ever find out what she had said that was so sinful.

"Katherine," her mother would say, "is going to be a doctor, I'm *sure!*"

Illnesses, cachets, bandages, pills, and potions fascinated the child. One Christmas, she had received a nurse's kit, equipped with a uniform and numerous bottles, rolls of lint, splints, ointments, and a book of first-aid instruction. Her brother came upon a nest of newborn mice one day and managed to save one for her. She cared for it devotedly, dressing in uniform when attempting to feed it milk and water from an eyedropper; but after three days the mouse died. When she discovered it, pathetically curled into a tiny knot in one corner of the wire cage built by her brother, she wept, more from frustration than loss. She was sure that she would find another but, instead, became interested in curing a sickly kitten which had found its way into the side yard. After one day the cat was ousted by her mother, who detested cats, and a small sparrow took its place. But the mouse cage was loosely constructed, and the sparrow soon took flight.

After that the child became engrossed in the home manufacture of cosmetics and, with the encouragement of the doctor's wife, Mrs. Williams, grated and mashed beet roots, hoping that by mixing the juice with petroleum jelly she might concoct a new and marketable form of face rouge. Some afternoons she would visit the doctor's wife, and the experiments would be carried on in the kitchen of the upstairs flat across from the First Baptist Church. Mrs. Williams sent for all the sample medicines and cosmetics offered in newspapers and magazines, and the child's greatest delight was to open a small package and find, enveloped in tissue or corrugated paper, a jar or pot or bottle or tin containing a minute quantity of cold cream or aids for biliousness or ointments for burns and sprains. She and Mrs. Williams planned to amass a quantity of medicines and dispose of them to the doctor's patients; but they found after a time that the amount of money spent for return postage ended any hope of profit.

Then the mother discovered that the daughter really wanted to be an explorer and that she and Mrs. Williams, surrounded by maps and illustrated adventure stories gleaned from the *Saturday Evening Post* and the *Ladies' Home Journal* and the Sunday newspaper supplements, were already charting a path into the depths of Africa. Mrs. Williams invariably saw herself as a missionary, but the child was alternately explorer, big-game hunter, shipwrecked castaway, and physician to a tribe of powerful but friendly aborigines. This dream the mother refused to take seriously, as no "respectable" young lady could conceivably find herself in such outlandish situations.

Curiosity about people and their ways of living and a yearning for adventure led the girl to scale the cliff in back of the Bluff Street establishment; clinging to vines and treacherous rocks, she would skirt its summit to where it ended in a wild grape arbor just before tapering off at the Jefferson Street hill. The playground of a Catholic girls' school occupied part of the area, and she would look through the iron fence rails at girls in uniform going through drills or playing baseball under the supervision of black-robed, white-hooded nuns. At this point she had to inch her way along the cliff top, holding to the iron bars, until she found herself in the overgrown back yard of an old woman with whom she had promptly made friends.

The old woman had a daughter named Bobby, who had left home years before to go into "show business"; and one day she invited the child into the shuttered, musty, red brick, former mansion, which was empty now, with all the rooms locked except the kitchen and the living room. The kitchen had frayed linoleum on the floor and wooden sinks with faucets turning green and a wood-burning stove; in the oversized living room were an unused fireplace, numerous pieces of furniture covered with shiny horsehair, floor lamps whose silk shades had a heavy beaded fringe, and a vast assortment of trunks. From the oldest one, with brass bands on top of a torn leather covering and large nail studs dotting the top, the woman extracted a worn scrapbook. She talked about her daughter, but she showed the child pictures of herself when she was touring a theatrical circuit—pointing to a yellowed clipping of a plump lady in tights and laced shoes and calling her Bobby. She dug further into the contents of the trunk and found an old beaded bag and a green ostrich-feather boa and some long, yellowed kid gloves, which she presented to the child. In spite of the heat, the child wore the scarf and gloves and carried the bag on her descent from the cliff. When her mother asked her how she had come by them, she was vague, not wanting to implicate the old woman because she never quite knew what was acceptable conduct and what was not; but, under pressure and close to tears, she revealed the identity of the donor. Fortunately the old woman was known to the parents and approved of. Cliff climbing, however, was not, and for this the child was reprimanded.

The part of Bluff Street extending north beyond Western Avenue was like another town, almost another country to the child. The houses were two-story shacks, mostly unpainted, set close to one another and separated from the sidewalk by only a few feet of dusty earth. The street ended at the impressive waterworks, where the water flowing from the City and a number of intervening towns and hamlets was diverted and channeled into either the river or the canal.

Her brother sometimes took her to see the waterworks, and one day they dared follow a workman's path to the lower level, where the roar of water passing from level to level and chamber to chamber fascinated the child, repelling and attracting her at the same time. The keeper of this maelstrom emerged from a cement hut and waved them away with his cane, and after that they saw it only from the bridge. The foaming, churning water called and beckoned to the child, suggesting vague far places, like the Africa that she and Mrs. Williams planned to conquer; but its ruthless churning filled her with a loneliness and a sense of futility that she tried to fathom but couldn't.

Just as alluring was the near-by district, forbidden to the child, that was called Mexican Town. On hot summer days small children played on the doorsteps and in the streets, naked except for shifts that hardly reached their olive-brown bottoms. Women lounged out of windows and spoke to each other in a language far more mellifluous than German, and once a man sat in a window playing a guitar and singing something that was sad and happy at the same time. Most of the men were thin and had pockmarks on their faces. The women were plump and insinuatingly friendly and seemed to spend a large part of their time brushing their long black hair and nursing large-eyed babies. The child was curious to know what they were saying about her as she passed—as brown as they were, neat in her freshly pressed summer dresses, with her unruly hair in two braids, a ribbon bow at the end of each.

One day she descended alone to the embankment beside the turbulent water and discovered a path that for a short distance followed the sluggish canal. On the nearly motionless surface of the water floated bits of trash escaped from the jaws of the locks, turning slowly as though gathering energy to move onward. The sulphurous odor rising from the water no longer bothered the child, and she squatted on the wall, dreamily poking at the debris with a long stick which she had picked up on her walk. She imagined herself finding a bottle with a map of pirate treasure or perhaps just some loose bills blown over the bridge and into the canal—enough to buy ice-cream cones and Coca-Cola for the rest of the summer. After a while she noticed near the wall a number of small, elongated, semitransparent, cream-colored rubber tubes. It seemed incredible to her that anyone would throw away perfectly good balloons; she fished them out with the stick and laid them on the wall. Since her brother had warned her against touching anything from the stagnant water of the canal, she gingerly hung them along the stick with the aid of a twig and clambered up into the street to take them home to be sterilized by boiling.

As she marched through the Mexican district, holding the stick far in front of her in order not to stain her dress with the dripping water, she knew she was arousing an unusual degree of interest—astonished silence, looks of disbelief, perplexity on the verge of laughter. By the time she reached the intersection of Western Avenue and Bluff Street, she had gathered a following of black-eyed urchins, who solemnly escorted her to the line of separation. She safely passed by the shop window, where her mother sat with bent head at the sewing machine, but at the door to the upstairs flat she met her brother, whose mouth fell open when his eyes traveled to the end of the stick.

"Look," she said proudly. "I found these in the canal!" She stopped, misinterpreting his look of horror. "Oh, I didn't blow them up yet. I didn't touch them. I'm going to take them upstairs and sterilize them."

"Put them down," her brother said. "This minute!"

She looked at him defiantly. "They're mine," she said. "I found them down by the canal."

Her father appeared around the side of the building, hurrying to the shop with a suit fresh from the tumbler. At her words he stopped short. "The canal," he said. "Did I hear you say the canal? How many times have your mother and I told you about going across the street?"

"It wasn't across the street," she said, as though the geographic distance altered the direction. "It was down by the locks."

That only made matters worse, she realized as soon as she said it. But she was trying at one and the same time to work up a defense for her disobedience and to hold on to the stick, which her brother was attempting to wrest from her without attracting her father's attention. There dawned upon her the realization that this sort of behavior was entirely uncharacteristic of her brother and that if he was so set on taking the stick away from her, she must again have violated some rule of conduct without knowing it. She decided that it would be best to give in to her brother and try to mollify her father, who, being busy, would waste little time on explanations. She gave up the stick and watched her brother walk disgustedly with it to the garbage can at the back of the yard. Then she began her explanation of a short walk to see the locks because it was so hot, and of leaning over the bridge where it was so cool because the water coming through the locks cooled the air, and so forth and so on, while her father just looked at her and then said, "Go upstairs and I'll see to you later!"

"Later" meant a whipping with the strap. Sitting on the sofa in the living room, waiting for the punishment, she was grateful to her brother. She had planned to forage later for the balloons, but respect for her brother's judgment and the punishment later that evening made the risk seem not worth taking.

The fretful summer ended, and the girl's second year at Beale School began, and she looked forward to making friends other than the Simon boys, who were often at their grandparents' house on the West Side or visiting playmates from the Catholic school they attended, or Helen Byfield, a new arrival on Bluff Street, who spent much of her time calling on and entertaining friends with her mother, a young and attractive widow.

The school, a red brick, ivy-covered building, was set far back from the street in a courtyard, which began as a tree-shaded grass plot and turned into a gravel playground. Roller skates over her shoulder, the child climbed the hill from Bluff Street at the five-minute warning bell, which tolled from the school tower, and arrived just in time to take her seat in the fifth-grade classroom. Her first class this term was in singing, and she found herself looking forward to it not so much for the music as for the pleasure she derived from the poetry—sometimes just the sound of the words themselves, sometimes the story they told. "Every evening by the water, walked the Sultan's lovely daughter, every evening by the fountain where the waters white were plashing." How clever of the anonymous poet to have written "plashing" instead of the ordinary "splashing," and how clever of *her* to know what "plashing" meant!

Her marks were good in composition or reading or spelling or music, poor in arithmetic, good in physical education, and erratic in conduct and deportment; down again in history and the best in her class in cooking and sewing. The black marks in conduct seemed to come from divided interests, whispering in study periods, loitering on the way to and from classes, and a periodic inarticulateness which was interpreted as stubbornness.

The truth of the matter was that the girl was extremely unhappy. She alternately basked in the reflected glory of her brother, who had preceded her at the school with a flawless record of scholarship and deportment, and of her father, who was by then well known in that area of the Town as the proprietor of the cleaning establishment; or she would withdraw into a loneliness that stemmed purely and simply from a lack of adequate companionship. An unwritten, unspoken code allowed the children of the school to be friendly to a certain point and then forbade further communication, so that the effect was like a continuous series of effervescent sentences begun but interrupted midway for no apparent reason and petering out into silence. Her recess periods were happy when she had opportunity to excel in sports, but if it were one of those times when girls and boys gathered in separate little groups, looking for an opportunity to assert their "belongingness" as over and against the unbelongingness of someone else, she felt at first bewilderment, then panic, then despair.

So she resorted to a common device of the imaginative and self-willed when faced with social ostracism: she formed, with two or three other girls who had not won total acceptance, a secret society, called "The Eagle Eye," which was relentlessly exclusive and totalitarian, which demanded oaths of allegiance and secrecy and special insignia, and which, in short, was as fascistic in structure and intention as anything the distracted teachers had ever had to cope with.

Of course she was president of the organization. She begged of her mother a piece of dark red satin, removed from a fur coat that was being relined, and a box of raveled bead fringe from an altered evening dress. From these scraps she made headbands that closed with snap fasteners and had a beaded eye in the center of the forehead which stared starkly at the playground mistress during recess and haunted teachers and principal. None of them could fail to see the headband hastily whipped into place at the sound of the four-o'clock bell or to note the cluster of small girls gathered around their dark leader, who outlined the after-school project for the day. This might be to explore the Bluff Street cliffs, sprawl on a grassy plot in the schoolyard and look at pictures in a book of American Indian mythology which the child had received for Christmas from her brother, or sit on the steps of the school for a half-hour to add more beads to their headbands from the box that she carried to school.

The Eagle Eye Society helped to restore the girl's self-confidence, but was doomed to be short-lived. Much of the glamour was removed when the beaded headbands were forbidden by the principal. By degrees the membership dwindled. But, having experienced a brief victory, the girl became reconciled for the present to the idea of casual and passing friendships.

A candy and notions store, diagonally across Western Avenue from the school, gave rise to a second temptation, disastrous in its ultimate results. A pretext for going into the store was provided by an assortment of pencils, rulers, erasers, paste, water colors, tablets, and notebooks, but of course all the children were really drawn by the bright yellow marshmallow bananas, the marshmallow ice-cream cones, the licorice sticks, and similar confections irresistible to the young. The girl herself liked best those assorted gumdrops known vulgarly as "nigger babies" but considerately and officially as "jujubes." She liked the name "jujube" because it relieved her of the embarrassment of just pointing and because it reminded her of the candies Br'er Rabbit took with him when he went courting his lady friend. The most expensive kind were hard and shiny and sharply flavored and lasted indefinitely because they had to be sucked; and it occurred to the girl that she could win popularity by distributing them freely to her schoolmates.

Her mother did not approve of the idea of personal spending money for a girl of her age and could not understand her constant requests for pennies and nickels. Whatever she did receive for some rare special service or what she could divert into her own pockets from savings on school supplies, she immediately spent on jujubes. Then she began bolstering her resources in less innocuous ways. She first tried returning from Simon's grocery store with a little less change than she had been given, but her mother's careful calculations and Mary Simon's faultless reckoning at the cash register discouraged this method. She turned next to two hidden stores of small change that she knew about. One was a drawer in the desk of the front room of the shop, in which all odd small items removed from clothing before it went into the gasoline tumblers were deposited to await claim by a customer or be returned with the finished garment, but opportunities to pilfer from this drawer were infrequent, and she soon abandoned it as a source of revenue. The other source was a hoard of petty cash saved by the mother from the weekly household budget and put to one side, under the shelf lining of the kitchen cabinet, to be spent for some item of clothing for one of the children that the husband would not have approved of, or to be contributed toward the upkeep of her mother, who was living on the charity of several sons and daughters. The first time the child removed two five-cent pieces from this hoard, she felt miserably ashamed because she knew by what ingenuity and enterprise her mother had managed to put aside this store and that she might very well be depriving herself of a new hair ribbon or a Saturday motion picture, or her brother of something he had to have for school. This constant need for small sums of money was forever creating difficulties between the father and mother, and there would be more trouble and accusations and unkind words and even threats.

Once the girl had come upon her parents by accident and had been shocked by the violence of their emotions, though it was not hard for her to see that her father was all attack and her mother all defense. (It took her a long while to understand that her mother was not altogether innocent of aggravating these attacks.) The mother had asked for money for some household improvement, and from the father there were angry words which finally turned ugly. Then the mother said things about what she had had before she married him; she said that if he didn't throw money away on dogs and second-hand machinery, maybe she would have enough to take care of the house and send the children to school properly dressed. When he told her that she would drive any man insane, she began to cry. It was the first time the child had seen her cry or seen her father so terrible, unless she was being punished; and somehow this seemed worse.

They saw her then, standing transfixed in the doorway, wondering whether to run to her mother and try to help, but too sick and frightened and aware of the badness of things to move. Her mother said, "Al, not in front of Katherine," and went into the bedroom, and her father said, "Young lady, go about your business and keep out of other people's affairs." He was breathing heavily and looked very black and angry, so she turned and ran down the steps and sat in the old delivery wagon, wishing that her brother would come back in the truck.

She thought of this as she took the two nickels, and again two or three days later when she took a dime and a nickel, and again when she foolishly took a quarter, not really needing it but just to see if she could and to find out what it would feel like to go in the store at the top of the hill and astonish everybody by casually asking for enormous quantities of jujubes. By this time she was becoming a little weary of the whole business, and the strain was beginning to tell in the disdain with which she handed out the candy, often not taking any herself, just watching the eager grubby hands dig into the paper sacks at recess or after school. And at home she felt unhappy and out of place and imagined that everyone was looking at her accusingly.

A few days after she had taken the quarter, she was helping with the evening meal when her mother discovered that she needed some small item from the corner store. She felt under the paper on the shelf; then, a surprised expression on her face, lifted the paper and even removed some of the dishes.

"Why, that's strange," she said, talking to herself. "I was *sure* that I put a twenty-five-cent piece there yesterday. I *know* I did!" Realizing that her daughter was looking at her and having no idea that her interest masked panic and fear and shame, but feeling herself the culprit at having been discovered with this secret store, she hurriedly scooped the remaining pieces of money into her hand and went into the bedroom.

"I left some change there yesterday," she said, as though her daughter should have an explanation. "Never mind. I'll order from Simon's tomorrow. We can make out tonight." And she turned again to the steak frying on the stove.

Sick at heart, the child carried the plates for the evening meal into the dining room and began setting the table. She wanted to tell her mother what she had done; she wanted to be back two weeks ago before this terrible thing had started. She wanted to shut from her mind the look of surprise on her mother's face, the crease in her forehead, the worry in her eyes as she lifted plates and cups and saucers from the shelf and felt farther and farther under the paper. She refused her dinner and went to bed early, pleading a sore throat. Her dreams were so foreboding that she awoke the next morning with the firm resolution never again to touch that which wasn't rightfully hers. The absolution offered by her resolve was fortifying, but she felt tired and spent and old from the experience and wondered when she would ever learn to stay away from things that made her feel so bad.

And then it turned out that she could not so easily free herself of responsibility for her deed. Gazing at the candy display one day after she had bought a new notebook, she noticed that the owner of the store, a rather indifferent, unsympathetic woman, was eyeing her curiously.

"What's the matter?" she asked. "You don't seem to have any more money in the bank. I was just thinking about asking your mother how you came by so much spending change."

The child looked at her, feeling blood mount to her face. A look of understanding passed between them; the woman smiled at the rage and hatred she saw in the girl's eyes, and the child sickened at the victory she saw in the woman's smirk. She turned and ran from the store and from then on went several blocks out of her way for her school supplies.

Her brother, too, besieged her defenses, but more gently. He saved the half-dollar a week that the mother insisted he be paid for work after hours, and carefully hoarded tips customers gave him on his delivery rounds, in preparation for the dream known at this time only to himself and his mother. He had heard of the University in the City and had set his heart on going there, knowing all the time that it would mean a permanent rupture with his father and that he would have to pay his own way. His hiding place was under the paper in a drawer of the dining-room buffet, in which he had been allowed two drawers for his personal use.

Often in the hour after dinner when the mother and father had returned to the shop, leaving the children to wash and dry dishes and put the kitchen in order, the brother and sister lay side by side on the living-room floor, looking at forbidden adventure magazines and science-fiction books. These were the happiest moments of the day for the child. By now the rising and setting of the sun would have been meaningless if her brother had not shared them with her, and his approval or disapproval by word or glance carried far more weight than her mother's scolding or her father's leather strap. To amuse and humor her and in recognition of her loneliness, he would frequently share enthusiasms that he had long outgrown. One of these dreams concerned a trip to the moon, inspired by a science-fiction magazine that invited readers to fill in an application stating their qualifications and availability for enlistment in such a venture. For the sum of one dollar, a map of the moon with photographs of its present inhabitants would be supplied, along with a pattern for the special clothing that would be needed. The child begged her brother to send in the dollar. He was reluctant to part with his savings, but his sister's recent moodiness had disturbed him, and he thought that making the uniform might serve as an amusement for her. He made her promise to keep the plan a deep secret and, sighing, closed the dining-room door while he went to his hiding place for the money.

He stayed away for some time and, when he returned to the living room, he was more upset than she had ever seen him. He looked at her for a long time without saying anything, as though examining the innermost recesses of her mind, and at last said, wearily, "What did you do with it?"

"With what?" she asked in genuine astonishment.

"With the dollar bill," he said. "I had two, because I changed the dimes and quarters into dollars just yesterday and put them there. Why did you do it?" He spoke quietly, almost gently, as though he would like very much to fathom what went on in her troubled mind and to help if he could before it was too late.

"I didn't take it," she said. "I didn't. I wouldn't." She almost said that she wouldn't steal from *him,* but that would have been an admission of her other thefts. "I *didn't!*"

She began to cry over the hopelessness of everything and the terrible damage to their relationship if he believed that any of the things she might do to someone else she could do to him, the only person in the whole world who really knew her or cared about her loneliness.

"You did before," he said, "from me and from mother. To buy candy." He thought awhile, looking deeply into her misery. "But this was so much. You couldn't have bought candy with all of that. Why did you do it?"

Before she could continue her protests, they heard the downstairs shop door close and a moment later the opening of the street door to the upstairs flat. This was their warning to scramble into the kitchen and busy themselves with dishwashing. It was her turn to dry, and she wiped her tears with the cloth before bending over the plates that her brother was piling unrinsed on the draining board. Her father stood in the doorway, breathing hard from his climb. He looked from one to the other and then at the disarray of dishes and at the kettle boiling furiously on the stove.

"What's taken you so long?" he asked the boy, looking at him strangely. "I thought you wanted to study so badly. You waste time up here, and still you have too much to do to help downstairs! I suppose you think you're too good to work like everybody else."

Neither child spoke, although they knew their silence would further enrage the father.

"I'm talking to you!" The father's voice thickened. "Are you going to answer me or do I have to take a strap to make you talk?"

"We were looking at magazines," the girl said, hoping to appease him.

"You speak when you're spoken to," he advised her, "or I'll take care of you at the same time!"

The brother turned the gas off under the teakettle and poured hot water over the soapy dishes.

"We were looking at magazines for a few minutes," he said. "I forgot to put the water on before dinner, and it wasn't hot enough to wash the dishes. I'll study afterward." He spoke so calmly and honestly that the father, even in his anger, could find no justification for the punishment he needed to administer for his own catharsis. He grunted and went across into the living room, where he was confronted by the magazines. Here was proof of their innocence, but it damned them at the same time because all this was prohibited reading. They heard him ripping the bindings and then the opening of the stove door and roar of the flames as the moon-conquering project went up in its own smoke.

This whole sequence of events had a dénouement that was at once a nightmare and an anticlimax. During the summer Annette Dunham had admitted to her small circle of intimates a family named Baxter, for reasons that had mostly to do with the snobbery to which she often fell victim. Although Mr. and Mrs. Baxter had certain vulgarities of manner and dress and speech, they were house servants for one of the founding families of the Town and were light in skin color. And their fifteen-year-old daughter Emily, even lighter than her mother, seemed a suitable companion-chaperone for the child, whom she sometimes accompanied to a park or a movie. Eventually the child was even allowed to visit Emily Baxter at her home. She had her own room in the apartment over the garage where her father tended the automobiles and sharpened the lawn mowers of the big limestone house in front. After lunch the two girls spent the afternoon in this room, going through boxes hidden at the back of drawers and behind suitcases in the closet. To the child it seemed strange to hoard in secret all sorts of things that she imagined would not be disapproved of, especially because Mrs. Baxter was apparently so easy-going. There were boxes and boxes of ten-cent-store powders of all shades, unopened powderpuffs in shiny transparent glass papers, small tin pots of cream rouge, and gaily-colored cardboard squares with small lipsticks or little flasks of perfume attached to them by elastic. There were unused handkerchiefs and scarves and a collection of rings, earrings, and bracelets, all bearing the stamp of one or the other of the ten-cent stores in the Town. Wide-eyed, the child paraded before the dresser mirror, adorned with as many of the baubles as she could wear at one time, and then happily accepted a pin with her name spelled almost correctly in twisted gold letters like handwriting, on the condition that she wouldn't wear it until she reached home.

During the winter months, guided by the elder girl, the child began a deception that bothered her simply because she did not want to add further wrongdoing to her record. Sometimes on the occasional Saturday afternoons when Emily Baxter took her to a movie, they did not return directly to Bluff Street afterward but would loiter at the counters of Woolworth's or Kresge's, lovingly fondling cosmetics, smelling samples of perfumes, and unscrewing jar tops to stick their noses close to the cold cream inside. And they almost always ended up at the jewelry counter. Urged on by her companion, the child became inordinately fond of a fine imitation gold bangle on which hung three small, delicate hearts of the same metal, and she dreamed of being given it on her birthday or at Christmas or hoped some unexpected windfall would enable her to buy it.

Emily Baxter liked a similar bracelet, and the child was surprised to see her wearing it one evening at Annette Dunham's club meeting. Some precautionary flicker in the older girl's eyes kept her from exclaiming about it; but she was envious and felt cross that she could not be wearing the bracelet with the hearts, which she already looked upon as her own and which she found much prettier. That Saturday as the two girls left the Princess Theatre, Emily Baxter seemed unusually eager to go "shopping." They passed through the store, smelling perfumes and opening jars and saying, "We're just looking," when clerks turned toward them expectantly. At the jewelry counter they lingered longer than usual, and the child began to feel fretful. She also felt conspicuous because a man passed them several times, apparently interested in what they might buy. When they left the store, it was cold and snowy and she was anxious to get home. At the corner of Bluff Street and Western Avenue the older girl decided to separate from her charge.

"I'm late," she said. "Don't forget to tell your mother that we saw the beginning again."

"I won't," the child said spitefully. "I'll tell her that you wouldn't leave the store and that you take me there all the time. And I'll tell her that you left me here at the corner, and she won't like it a bit. She'll tell your mother!"

To her surprise, the older girl was not angry or upset or argumentative, as she expected. "It's not really telling a lie," she said. "Besides, here is the bracelet you wanted. You can have it if you don't say what you just said you would. Why do you want to spoil everything, anyway?" But even though she chided, she smiled; and the child, overcome with gratitude, saw it as a friendly smile and trudged the short block through the snow, happily shaking the bracelet on her arm and listening to the fairy jingle of the tiny hearts.

Her mother was busy and paid little attention to her lateness, nor did she notice the bracelet. On this night the West Side Cleaners was open late, besieged by telephone calls and annoyed customers waiting impatiently for garments, the delivery of which fell entirely to the boy so that his father could stand the full evening at the hand iron. The doors were closed because of the cold, and the air in the shop was heavy with the smell of acetic acid and scorched canvas pressing cloths.

As much as the child disliked these odors, she preferred being here to being alone in the upstairs flat, from which she fled as rapidly as she could after she had washed the supper dishes. When she re-entered the shop, she noticed a man talking with her mother, who sat with a suit jacket across her knees and several buttons lined up on the sewing machine. Her mother looked at her but right through her, and her hands were trembling as she kept trying to thread a fine needle. The man looked at the child, too, and nodded his head as she walked past. She didn't think that she knew him, but he seemed to know her, and as she leaned against the warm pad of the pressing machine, she wondered if it was the new insurance man or the man to talk about installing electric lights upstairs, as her father was always promising to do.

She heard the man say, "I'm very sorry, Mrs. Dunham, but that's the way it is. It happens all the time. In your case, because it's the first time we won't do anything about it. Just thought you'd better know. Could turn out to be pretty serious the next time . . ."

"I don't believe it," her mother was saying over and over, and her voice trembled, and she talked some of the time while the thread was in her mouth and she was trying to bite it off. "A child who has *everything* that her father and I can give her. There must be some mistake. It just couldn't have been Katherine!"

The man rose with a sigh. The girl eased her way to where she could see him as he said goodbye to her mother, who still sat fingering the thread and shaking her head, trying to make what he had said not true. The man's hair was dark on the edges and white where it was parted, and his dark-blue suit was pressed but very shiny. The cuffs of his overcoat sleeves were a little frayed, and he looked tired, as though he had been on his feet all day, and pale, as though he seldom went outside, and unhappy, as though the story that he had just told was one repeated over and over, and as though he had lived and relived the same scene until he wanted no more of it.

"I've been to see the Baxter girl," he said. "I went there first because, frankly, I hold her to blame. But—well, there you are. Good night, Mrs. Dunham." And he opened the door of the shop and went out, shoulders drooping, head lowered against the cold wind.

Her mother sat for a long time after he had gone, with her hands in her lap. Then she threaded the needle with no trouble and started sewing on a button. By now the child was genuinely concerned. Whatever it was, she wanted it to be over and finished before her father returned, because while punishment from her mother was often quick and stinging, it was never prolonged or cruel like the strap lashes of her father in one of his worst moods. She moved to lean in the doorway between the two rooms and cleared her throat.

Finally her mother said, "Katherine, let me see the bracelet that you are wearing."

She moved to her mother and extended her arm, glad for the respite. "Emily gave it to me," she said. "We stopped after the Princess today, and she bought it for me."

Her mother looked at her pityingly. "Don't lie, Katherine," she said. "Don't make it worse by lying!" Her voice broke and tears spilled onto the jacket. She brushed them away angrily, dropped the needle, took the child by the shoulder, and shook her until both hair ribbons fell to the floor.

"Why did you do it?" she said. "Why did you have to go and disgrace your father and me by stealing? Why? Why?" And she was still shaking the child, who was too stunned to answer, when the father opened the back door and entered with his arms full of half-dried clothing, which he deposited on the pressing table before he went into the front office. He looked for a moment and then turned and went back to the pressing table. Finally the child struggled loose and backed across the room to the opposite wall. Huddled into the corner of the desk as though to ward off a second attack, she shook her head violently from side to side until she had regained her breath and equilibrium.

"I didn't do it," she said. "I didn't steal anything. She gave it to me. Ask her. Emily Baxter gave me the bracelet!"

Her mother spoke evenly and deliberately, and she could hear the silence in the next room as her father stopped hanging up clothes to listen. She was more afraid of the silence than of her mother and felt the growing desperateness of her situation; she prayed for a customer to come in or for the phone to ring so that she could get herself together and try and figure out what had suddenly happened to her and what to do to ward off the chaos that seemed inevitable.

"The man who was in here was a detective from the ten-cent store, Katherine," her mother said, "and he saw you this afternoon and lots of other afternoons. He didn't want to say anything until he was sure, but this time he saw you. He saw you take the bracelet. Go upstairs until I can speak to your father."

The walls and ceiling seemed to close on the child. Her father stepped to the door of the front room and hitched his trousers up as he always did when he was getting ready to undo his belt to use it for a whipping. Her panic drove her from the corner. She threw herself on her mother's neck, half screaming, half crying. She fought for something to hold on to, but her mother pushed both hands away and turned her face and held her at arm's length. Her voice was harsh and unnatural.

"All of this isn't doing any good, you know," she said, "and if you keep on telling lies it will only be worse."

"Let me talk to her," the child sobbed. "Let me just talk to her on the telephone, and she'll tell you the truth. She bought it for me. She said it was a present if I didn't say we stopped all the time to look at things. Please, please, Mother, don't let him; I didn't!" While she said these things and at the height of her panic, she thought about the money under the shelf in the kitchen and that she would never be free from that crime. Then there had been her brother's unfounded suspicions. And now this. She would gladly have gone to prison and done her atonement. The close air of the shop, and shock and fear and frustration, and the terrors of the shadowy creaking flat upstairs, and her mother looking at her as though she didn't know her, and her father standing waiting, ready to loosen his belt—all converged and she wanted to die. Slowly her mother turned to the telephone and asked for the number. Mrs. Baxter answered and was not cordial at all and didn't want to call her daughter to the phone. The mother was firm and then passed the telephone to her daughter. Her knees weaker than water, the child walked to the desk and spoke.

"Emily," she said, "please tell my mother about the bracelet."

There was a silence, and then the girl answered. "I don't know what you're talking about."

The child thought that she could not be hearing correctly. "The bracelet," she said, "the one you gave me today. A man said I stole it, and I told my mother how you bought it and gave it to me. Tell her Emily! She's right here!"

There was an ominous silence on the other end of the phone. Then she heard the voice again, strange, cold, indifferent. "I don't know what you're talking about. What bracelet? Maybe you did." Then the click of the telephone as it was put in place at the other end of the line.

The only sound in the shop was the muted hissing of the steam dying in the pipes of the pressing machine. Then the door opened and her brother came in, stamping snow off his feet, his face blue with cold. The child held the receiver limply at her side and turned to her mother.

"Call her again," she said. "She hung up. She said she didn't give it to me. She must've not understood. Please call her again, Mother. You ask her." But she said it hopelessly.

Her mother turned to her father. "I can hardly believe it," she said, "that this could happen to us."

Her father said, "Go upstairs, young lady."

She turned to her brother, who seemed to be listening to something else, far away, which made him very sad. "I didn't do it." She choked on the words, and her throat hurt, and she felt suddenly hot, as she did when she stayed home from school with the old winter sickness. As she passed her brother, she looked imploringly at him, for the first time not ashamed of her tears before him, not ashamed to be weak and acting like a girl. He said nothing but followed her with his eyes, giving her what courage he could.

Upstairs she sat on the sofa and waited. When she was lucky, she did not have to take her clothes off. But this time she knew she wouldn't be lucky. The crime that she hadn't committed was too monstrous. She sighed and, without waiting to be told, undressed and put on her flannel pajamas. To stop her shivering she wrapped herself in the Indian blanket thrown across the back of the sofa and, her fever mounting, waited for her father's steps in the hallway.

Late that night she woke her brother and put his hands on the raw welts on her arms and back and legs. They were bigger than usual and hot and sore to the touch. Her brother turned on the flashlight to look at the marks and was very much impressed, so she felt better and went to sleep.

In the dining room of the flat two water colors hung, one on either pale yellow calcimined wall. The child was kneeling on a chair one day, studying the picture of a country stream flowing out of a field through clusters of bushes and overhanging willow trees. Her father passed her on his way to the kitchen.

"Your mother drew that," he said.

She looked at him with surprise.

"No!" he said, reading her thoughts. "Your *real* mother!"

Then he went into the kitchen, and she examined the water color with renewed interest. This was something else to know about that strange, faraway, wraithlike person who was becoming harder and harder to recall and who existed in a world and time never spoken of in the new family, except in references that were weapons against the present mother. She was glad to know but uncomfortable that her father had told her, because it seemed like treason. She wondered if Annette Dunham knew and decided that she didn't, because not only was the subject of the first mother strictly taboo, but the few photographs of Fanny June Dunham or of the half sister Fanny that had fallen out of the desk drawer when it was unpacked, were hidden away somewhere out of reach of the children.

On the other wall of the dining room was a rectangular, glass-covered text, floridly enhanced by wreaths of flowers tied with gold ribbons, surely the work of another artist. It read: "A friend is one who knows all about you and loves you just the same." The child read and reread the words. Optimistically she believed that one could have many friends and that they would all be like those suggested by the text. All that would come with growing up and going away from Bluff Street and having a real house and being wise. In this new order of things her brother would not be driving a delivery truck and so could spend more time with her, as he had long ago, and her mother wouldn't look so worried all the time, and her father would be friendly again and tell stories about the Tar Baby on Sunday nights.

Six
The Dust Wheel

*

Immediately behind the flat above the shop was the big barnlike room that had been converted by Old Man Crandall from dance hall to carpet room, and Albert Dunham had acquired it with the rest of the top floor when he took over Crandall's business. Upon entering this barren expanse by way of improvised doors leading from the hallway of the flat, one was at first aware only of rows of windows, velvety opaque from particles beaten out of carpets, and of dust piled into thick padding like a floor covering in a desert tent, with areas brushed clean for carpet scrubbing. Near the doorway a sharp turn to the right disclosed the priceless treasure dominating the loft—the prize for which the family had paid by months of deprivation: the dust wheel, an immense, lustreless jewel suspended in a vaulted and bottomless setting.

Owning it, Albert Dunham felt himself firmly established in the business life of the town. To possess such a costly piece of equipment would have been far beyond the wildest hopes of the tailors' apprentice or the traveling salesman, and he never tired of leading visitors up to its yawning mouth.

When the wheel was not in motion, its lower jaw lay open, resting on the edge of the wooden floor. Between the open slats through which dust poured once it was charged with carpets and set in motion, one had glimpses into the dark vertiginous depths of the pit below. The wheel itself seemed primordial, boundless like the heavens on a dark night when one first becomes aware of the vastness in which the stars hang. A single two-by-four plank held it at rest, propped at an angle between the top of the jaw and the floor. Sometimes, further to impress an unsuspecting visitor, the father would kick the prop out from under, and the wheel, carried by its own momentum, would drop into its mechanical round, grinding, whining, moving slowly but ponderously and murderously, held back by the flapping open gate and by lack of the current that normally propelled it. After a few revolutions it would stop, always with the gate on the back side, and Albert Dunham would have to reach out daringly and, straining, coax the monster back into position and replace the prop. He would grin like a happy schoolboy, while customer or visitor would comment with "My, My's" and tongue cluckings, and his children stood round-eyed, not too near but just near enough to peer down into the blackness below and marvel at their father in this new and exultant aspect.

If he were away too long from the pressing table, Annette Dunham might leave her sewing machine and come running up the front stairs. "Al, Mr. Cummings has phoned *three times!* What on earth are you doing so long?" Then, as though she had just gathered what was taking place from the pleased look on her husband's face and the admiring glances of his audience, she would say, "Oh, pshaw! Are you at that dust wheel again? Why don't you let it *alone* for a while? There's too much to be done downstairs to take time to fiddle with *that* thing!" She would then turn to go back to the shop, and the demonstration would be over. But as time went on, she interrupted less frequently, aware of his growing resentment at her intrusion into these celebrations of dreams fulfilled.

As for the children of the neighborhood, when the wheel

was loaded to its capacity with rugs and carpets, when the open jaw had been securely fastened by a number of tough bolts and the switch thrown that would start small cogs to revolving large ones by means of a system of patched and spliced leather belts hooked up to a constantly defaulting, amateur electrical system—then, like flies at the edge of a jam pot, they would approach as close as they dared and crane their necks through clouds of choking dust to follow the revolutions of the wheel, loosed now like some lumbering pachyderm, carrying its weight with rumbling protest to the top of its orbit and dropping it at the last possible moment allowed by gravity. And as the grimy cargo hit bottom with a terrifying thud, it released the particles that made up the padding of the carpet room, that curtained the windows with a film as heavy as closed blinds, and that filtered into the flat, thus firmly establishing the seignory of the dust wheel, of which the flat seemed but a small and insignificant fief.

At first as fascinated by the wheel as the neighborhood youngsters, the girl later learned to fear and despise its vacant, staring, Cyclopean waiting and its dumb response to the throwing of the switch. And she came to hate its domination of the household. Often dinners would be serenaded by the groaning and keening of ungreased wood against spliced, straining belts; and sometimes, when a strap too worn to bear more strain had broken and the wheel suddenly stopped, silence seemed louder than sound, and her father would shove his chair back and leap from the table—in the early years indulgently, but later with a muttered curse.

Sometimes the brother, too, would have to leave in the middle of the meal in order to wriggle his child's body through the narrow aperture that the father would effect by removing the prop, tilting the opening slightly backward, and then fighting to hold the wheel from succumbing to gravity. After clinging perilously to the edge of the floor, the boy would drop into the dungeon below the wheel and, groping in the dim light that filtered from the windows above or from a flashlight, he would tread his way like an undersea explorer, choosing with care where to step so as to avoid sinking hip deep or farther into unexpected loosely packed pockets of dust. Down below in this awesome enclosure the full evil of the wheel seemed to become manifest: jungle beasts, great apes, grinning vampire bats, slow-moving brontosauri, and, worse than all these, the Unknown—the silent, waiting Presence, formless and without definition but ready to take over at the slightest faltering of courage. This Something—inescapable, deliberate, already set in motion to reach out blindly and without reason, on orders transmitted by some celestial switchboard operator, to draw unto itself one Albert Millard Dunham, Jr., before his full season—began its motion in these places and these years and under these conditions.

All of these things the sister felt and knew when on one occasion she followed from the dinner table and peered into the depths. That her brother had seen and felt them she knew by his terror, which he somehow managed to control enough to locate the broken strap, splice it, and regain the level above, but which was apparent to her because so much of the time she breathed the same air that he breathed. Once again on floor level he would always turn his face from his father so as not to expose his fear, and on the occasion when she was present he scowled ferociously at her, wiping his moist and trembling upper lip with the blackened back of his hand.

Father and son would return to the table, dust-covered, victors for the moment but defeated in essence, because time and wear and the development of more efficient mechanisms were destined to win out over hope and wish and will and the most ardent and well-meaning desire for advancement and improvement. The father would sit in black, impatient, anger-filled silence, eating whatever was left on his plate. At these times and others like them, no one dared talk, even to ask for a second serving. The wheel continued to hurl the imprisoned carpets, and dust continued its seepage through the walls, unseen but ubiquitous.

The girl grew to associate the disintegration of the dust wheel with the disintegration of the family. Bringing more security of one kind, it robbed them of another. Gone were summer Saturday afternoons with the father stealing a moment here and there to take a hand at churning the freezer, brimming with heavy fresh cream and crushed ripe strawberries. Fewer too were Sundays like those of the first years on Bluff Street, and fewer the family trips to Bush Park to drink mineral water as the early evening shadows made a fairyland of the rocky, moss-covered boskage around the springs. Instead, the entire family bent to the will of the dust wheel and the incoming orders of carpets.

To the daughter, this expansion of the business was a milestone in the passage of her childhood. To the mother, the carpets were always alien. Clothing she could understand and deal with, but in these early years the carpets, upon removal from the wheel, were scrubbed by hand, and they seemed to her endlessly time-consuming. Furthermore, she considered that their weight frequently was too great for the boy to manage singlehanded on his deliveries; but after once suggesting this to the father, she dared not again face his rage at what he felt to be unnecessary pampering of the boy. The father's ambition to enter every branch of dry cleaning and certain sub-branches of wet cleaning sometimes drove him to accept larger or more pressing orders than he could handle, and often it was the sharp eye of his wife that would detect an article not quite ready to be delivered. At the risk of incurring his anger, she would telephone and calm the most impatient customer; and back up into the shadowy room the unfinished carpet would go, to be rescrubbed or thoroughly aired and sent out on a later delivery.

As long as the dust wheel churned from early morning until late at night, the wads of crumpled notes in Albert Dunham's pockets increased, and there were notable alterations for the better in both flat and shop. In the flat, electricity replaced gaslight. The yellow calcimined walls of the sitting room were papered. Two changes were made in delivery trucks, but the replacements were invariably only slightly newer and more brightly painted replicas of the discarded ones. A few weeks, or perhaps as much as two or three months of service for the shop, and it was hard to distinguish the last arrival from its predecessors, now backed into corners against the building and cluttering the yard. Always the father hoped that a fabulous offer would turn up, that, with patience and shrewd bargaining and luck, the sale or trade of one or two of the junked trucks would lead to purchase of the latest model. But the hulks remained until they were rotted and rusted and were only hauled away, years later, when they were completely choking the side lot.

The wheel also grudgingly gave the girl some of the coveted clothing that she envied so on other girls of her class at school. And help was added in the shop below, so that there were summer vacations away from the Town. Once the girl went alone; once the mother and two children went; but the father could not or would not risk even one night away from his thriving establishment.

The first summer after RUGS AND CARPETS was proudly lettered by the father himself under WEST SIDE CLEANERS AND DYERS, the mother received a letter from a brother asking that the daughter be allowed to visit him and his childless wife for the summer. The daughter had often heard tales of the dashing Uncle Ed and of Aunt Alice, whose reputation seemed to rest on her remarkable size and her culinary skill. She had heard, too, of Delavan, Wisconsin, which her mother had described as a sort of sylvan paradise. And it was firmly impressed upon her—most frequently within the father's hearing—that the position occupied by Edward Poindexter and his wife was unique not only in the state of Wisconsin, but anywhere in the United States.

Edward Poindexter, abetted by some of the ingratiating charm that also characterized Albert Dunham, had left Alton, Illinois, at the very first sign of a change in race relations, and after various meanderings arrived in Los Angeles, where he had shared for a time a practice in chiropractic with his younger brother, Will. Then he had left Will, made his way to firmer and cooler ground, and found his true calling in the genteel, snobbish little lake resort of Delavan. There he met and wooed Alice, chief cook for one of the wealthiest and therefore most genteel of the permanent residents. A family accustomed to periodic excursions to Europe, they were versed in all of those fine shades of decorum between master and servant that often distinguish the newly rich from landed aristocracy. Proof of their inherent gentility lay in the sumptuous wedding gifts they bestowed on their former servant and in their patronage of the business her husband had established.

For the chiropractic now developed into a highly personal and specialized beauty salon, catering to the whims and vanities of debutantes, visiting vacationers, and bored housewives. Soon, aided by his aristocratic patrons, "Dr. Ed" became a "must" for all women who would gain what they never had possessed in pulchritude or regain what time and circumstance had ungraciously withdrawn.

The girl, when she arrived quaking after a trip by boat and train, was immediately put at ease by her dashing uncle. She fell wholly and completely in love with him and felt only a small regret that her Aunt Alice seemed incapable of joining them on their excursions into beauty lore and did not appreciate their experiments in concocting creams, packs, liquids, emollients, pimple removers, mole banishers, tints for fingernails and toenails, bleaches to produce pallor, and stimulants to produce high color.

Mornings she would walk with her Uncle Ed, who might easily have been mistaken for an East Indian or a Pacific Islander, from the flat above an antique shop on one side of the town to the shop in the small central business district. They often took a pleasant detour along an avenue shaded by elms and oaks and pines, past the villas of wealthy residents who, when summer came, generally fled to Europe before the annual invasion of schoolteachers, office workers, and anonymous city dwellers. So most of these houses were shuttered now, and only their well-kept lawns suggested that they had not been abandoned permanently. The child looked with wonder and excitement at the turrets and balconies that she could see through gaps in closely clipped hedges or wrought-iron gates. Although the houses seemed frightening in their emptiness, they fascinated her, so that she had to force herself to look away from the staring, blind windows in order to enjoy beds of roses and late-blooming peonies, velvet borders of pansies and nasturtiums, ponds of full-blown lilies, and hydrangea bushes heavy with blossom. The avenue itself was filled with the fresh odor of lake breeze and melting pine and spicy phlox and roses.

One day as they walked along, in no hurry to be at the beauty shop, a fine limousine passed them slowly, as though time in no way entered into its owner's scheme of life. Her uncle told her he was the richest man in Wisconsin and perhaps in a number of neighboring states, too. He sat comfortably back in the limousine, which her uncle said was the only Rolls-Royce that side of the City; he was fat and florid and seemed to look without seeing.

The next day she made her first trip alone from the flat to the shop, and when she reached the end of the avenue of villas, a car pulled noiselessly to the curb beside her, and the same man who had passed the day before leaned from the window. He smiled in a friendly and courtly fashion and said, "And whose pretty little girl are you?"

She was too charmed to name her father's name, and, besides, he really didn't seem to need an answer. He reached through the window. Red hairs curled on the back of a heavily veined hand, a gold cufflink caught bits of sun, and strong, well-manicured fingers held out to her a rose. A single, perfect, very dark red rose. She took the rose and held it, holding her breath, too, and feeling the intense peaceful silence of the morning. Lighter than a fairy, more beautiful than any princess, freer than air, she stood, watching the fat man settle back into the cushions of his limousine and glide out of sight down the avenue behind the straight uniformed back of the chauffeur.

She walked on, suffused with the first real joy that she could remember. A stranger had found her pretty, and he had offered her a flower more lovely than any that she had ever known existed, and at any moment now he would return for her and take her in the limousine far away to some warm and sunny land.

Her uncle was impressed by the flower, and she placed it in a tall vase on top of the glass showcase of beauty products in the waiting room. But she never again saw the gallant stranger, and the rose died, and the feeling of specialness faded, too. She took her place again as her uncle's assistant, fellow alchemist, daring laboratory assistant, delving deeper and with far more professional equipment into the experiments started long ago on Saturday afternoon visits to Mrs. Williams, the doctor's wife.

Edward Poindexter, though a self-taught beautician, must have been possessed of some of that uncanny instinct that characterized two branches of his triple ancestry, the African and the American Indian. The creams he compounded in the back room of his beauty parlor under the watchful eye of his niece were mostly the product of sheer inspiration, but inspiration aided by bits of information and observation filched from feathered and buckskinned braves during his wanderings from Illinois to the great West, as he earned his living touting for a Choctaw medicine show; from books and correspondence courses in chemistry; and from the customers themselves, always eager when smothered in one cream to tell about the wonders of another or to recall some cosmetic tried or heard of at some other resort. And though his hands by themselves were what might have been designated as "healing," he still delighted in all kinds and shapes and sizes of mechanical manipulators. Rows of metal objects in glass cases in the middle room, the sanctum sanctorum, were as meticulously laid out and as artistically arranged as a display of jade in an Oriental museum.

It was a special privilege when an indulgent customer would allow the child to witness the secrets of regeneration. The customer would be stretched out in the leather-cushioned reclining chair in the room which was a cool, dimly lit refuge from the shimmering midsummer pavement outside. Covered modestly to the chin in snow-white scented linen sheets—wedding gifts from Aunt Alice's patrons and laundered daily by her—they would sigh and yawn and stretch under the covers, while Dr. Ed, spotless in white coat, sprayed his own mixture of toilet water on brown palms and finger tips. The girl never tired of examining her uncle's hands during the sacred stagesetting seconds when, spread open, they were held motionless, near but not touching the recumbent votary. This, he explained to her, was the most important part of the treatment, because without the transference of life fluids from body to body, the magic contact could not be made, and any amount of skill or technique would be worthless.

Dr. Ed's clients also appreciated these special gifts of his. Semicomatose under the touch of his brown fingers, they opened up like heavy wax flowers and spilled, in soft whispers through heady creams and lotions, their own innermost secrets and those of their closest intimates. At times, suddenly aware through packs and hot towels of the unaccustomed presence of the child, they would roll their eyes in her direction as if to say, "Well of course, there's much much more, but of course I can't tell you just *now*. Remind me next Wednesday, will you Dr. Ed? You simply wouldn't *believe!*"

The girl would look questioningly at her uncle for some sign that she should leave the room, but often, glad of a respite from town gossip, he would indicate by a slight shake of the head that she should remain. And so she would watch from a stool in a corner and sometimes imagine that she was a real accredited assistant. She would be utterly absorbed in the patting, pressing, molding, manipulating, smoothing and coaxing of cheeks, chins, and foreheads. Her uncle seemed to concentrate all his efforts on trying to charm lines of cupidity, boredom, anxiety, frustration, and the simple passage of time from their wearer, and in the full hour that he allotted to each customer he would transform the withered into the burgeoning, the arid into the florescent. They would enter life-weary, put-upon, and frequently irritable, but they would depart on wings of radiance, ready to face the harsh sunlight of a garden party or an afternoon at the beach or even to toy with the thought of a new conquest.

Dr. Ed was also an accomplished chiropodist, and as his customers lay swathed in layers of demulcents, he would draw a low stool to the foot of the reclining couch and, gently lifting the extended foot, decorously remove shoe and stocking and go through a routine of soaking, massaging, paring, filing, pumicing, balming, and finally dusting with scented talcum—which would elicit from the shrouded figure earthy expressions of ecstasy, made inarticulate by the swatches of cotton soaked in witch hazel which Dr. Ed, whether for cosmetic purposes or in self-defense, had at this stage of the treatment placed firmly over the mouths and eyes of his ladies. While these cotton pads were in place, uncle and niece could freely exchange glances, eye rollings, nostril flarings, lip pursings, and shoulder shruggings.

When at times the sounds of sensual appreciation issuing from beneath the wet cotton became extravagant, the girl could no longer contain herself and, hands to mouth, would run giggling into the waiting room or the laboratory.

For all of this the resort clientele paid handsomely, and Ed and Alice Poindexter seemed on the brink of affluence. The apartment above the antique shop was well furnished, and the food was of a richness that seemed excessive compared with the well-set but modest table of the Dunham household. The atmosphere was generally cheerful, but the girl, in spite of all her Aunt Alice's overtures, never felt quite at ease with her. Sometimes uncle and niece would arrive at the flat later than they had realized. They would find the buxom Alice not at all jovial, as she had been in the morning and as the girl had been led to believe all fat people were, but scowling, muttering, angry at the ruination of some culinary work of art, and not trying to hide her jealousy of the deep and tender bond between her husband and his niece by marriage. The hearty laughter, along with jokes and gossip of the day, would be put aside for the evening, and the meal would be eaten in stiff silence, the two culprits scarcely looking at each other, until finally Dr. Ed's warm good humor would win over Alice's offended pride, and again the flat would seem cheerful.

But on one occasion the girl was not forgiven.

Annette Dunham did not pride herself on being a good cook. These laurels she let fall willingly to her husband, bragging in front of company about Mr. Dunham's hotcakes, corn bread, fried rabbit, and roast stuffed fowl of any kind. She did, however, reserve to herself full credit for two specialties: as a very special treat, a Sunday or a party dessert would be one of her chocolate cream or lemon cream pies—inch deep, creamy to just the proper consistency, and topped with blobs of toast-colored meringue. And about her refusal to use cornstarch, her intense dislike of it, Annette Dunham was vehemently verbal.

One day in anticipation of her niece's imminent departure, Alice Poindexter announced that she was preparing a delicious surprise for the evening meal and that furthermore her husband and the girl must be punctual because, this being Thursday, it was servants' day off at her former employer's, and she had invited the cook who had replaced her to dinner. So they sat down to a meal more sumptuous than ever, served on handworked table linen, on the best English chinaware, and conveyed from plate to mouth by silverware usually kept under lock and key. This was the only occasion during the weeks of the girl's stay that they had had a guest, and her aunt's efforts to impress the tall, bony brown woman who had succeeded her gave Katherine Dunham complex feelings of pride, embarrassment, and tenderness.

The real *pièce de résistance* was to be the dessert. The lemon pie that Aunt Alice carried proudly into the dining room was an architectural triumph, a mountain of spun gold surrounded by a fluted border of crust sculptured in terra cotta. The heavy silver pie knife slid voluptuously through the stiff, frothy mound and buried itself inches deep in firm yellow filling. Small flakes fell away from the perfect crust, but the marvel was the upright, solid firmness of that filling, deeper by at least two inches than any that the girl had seen before. Jealousy struggled for a moment with appetite as she thought of her mother's comparatively modest creations. Then she cut with her fork through the tender meringue, down through the yellow solidity beneath, into the yielding crust. She placed a large forkful in her mouth. There were whinnied ooh's and ah's from the angular guest and nods and sounds of approbation from her uncle. But once the fork had passed *her* lips she could only hold the lump in her mouth and look with startled anguish from one to the other. The strongest taste was unmistakably that of cornstarch.

Startled, Alice stared at her niece, and the smug triumph froze on her oily round face. Woman and girl looked at each other across the table. The girl noticed for the first time a spray of fine raised dots under her aunt's smallish eyes, and in a sharp moment of clarity she saw that they were really little pig's eyes, and that three tightly spiraled hairs grew from beneath her chin, and that the knot that she always wore twisted on the back of her head didn't match the front hair in either color or texture.

The eyes sparkled meanly, demanding an explanation. The girl forced herself to swallow. Her mouth drew up in the center and her nostrils curled at the aftertaste.

"It is made with cornstarch," she said. "We don't eat things made with cornstarch. My mother thinks it's lazy and poor white trash." She knew that she was saying more than she should, but feeling herself already damned, she felt also the need of self-justification.

Ed Poindexter cleared his throat and heartily ate his piece of pie. The dinner guest whinnied again and made nervous sucking noises, licking a mustache of meringue from her upper lip, and then dabbed at her mouth with pecking motions. Alice Poindexter seemed to swell to twice her normal size, and the spots under her eyes stood out darkly. Her voice quivered, barely able to force its way out from under her tremendous bosom.

"Eat your pie!" she said. "Don't tell me about Annette Poindexter's cooking! Just *eat that pie!*" Pent-up resentment against the Poindexter family and all the venom held in check under her jolly fat exterior against the niece who had so readily found a place in the escapist, romantic world of her husband, froze the maiden name of Annette Dunham, so that it hung suspended in the charged air.

"I can't. I don't like cornstarch. At home we never——" The impact of the murderous bulk in front of her stopped the sentence. She went on bravely, lower lip quivering, "And, besides, my mother's name is Annette Poindexter *Dunham!*"

Her uncle looked at her, pleading. For his sake she pared off another bit and put it in her mouth. But it refused to go down. A lump of tasteless glue, it stuck in her mouth until without warning her gorge rose, and it was only by madly sprinting to the bathroom that she was saved the embarrassment of depositing her full meal in the center of the table.

She stayed in her room, quaking, knowing that something would happen when the door closed on the guest, but not knowing what it would be. She heard her uncle accompany the guest to the sidewalk below. She heard his slow, timorous mounting of the stairs, and the scraping of dishes, the slamming of oven and icebox, and the rush of hot water in suds. She wanted a drink of water but she dared not leave the room. She wanted to read but was afraid that that would seem too frivolous a gesture in view of the gravity of her offense. She wanted to help with the dishes but was terrified of the presence in the kitchen.

She heard footsteps approaching her room. Her aunt stood in the open doorway and switched on the ceiling light. In its harsh glare she looked ill, and the child's impulse was to offer assistance. Then she saw that the illness was of a different kind, deep and gnawing inside. Blazing with hatred, Alice Poindexter struck the child full in the face as she half stood, putting behind the blow all of the muscle that had for many years stirred and beaten and whipped, and mixed pastries and dressings, and washed and starched and ironed Ed Poindexter's uniforms and shirts and scented office sheets. The girl fell backward onto the bed, stunned. When she sat up again, her aunt had gone. She started to cry, but there were no tears, only dry gasps. In the harsh glare of the ceiling light she saw a red print swelling on her face. After a while the tears came. She shut the door and, weeping convulsively, undressed and went to bed. She felt pure, correct, and completely justified in her actions. She also felt some pride in having defended her mother; in having, being a Dunham and in no way directly related, defended the Poindexters against unworthy detractors.

The following morning preparations were made for her return to her family. They were made slowly, however, because the red welt was reluctant to subside, and it was not until three days later that she left. Her uncle accompanied her to the City, and there she was met by her mother and brother.

She had arrived in Delavan thin almost to the point of frailty; but, except for the lemon pie, she had devoured Alice Poindexter's food with gusto, and during her weeks of comparative inactivity, free of roller skating and bicycling and tree climbing, she had put on so many pounds that her mother exclaimed, "Good gracious! I hardly knew you!" and her brother wryly made fun of her.

In the Dunham household the incident of the lemon pie took its place among a few other cherished anecdotes with which the mother tried to cling to the fleeting stuff of childhood. She would cover up any ugliness with these recollections and sometimes, when an awkward silence or painful tension would strain the air between herself and her grown daughter, she would say, looking far back at the wispy little girl who had returned from a summer vacation tanned and plump, "Katherine, do you remember the summer that you went to visit Aunt Alice and how *awful* you acted about the lemon pie? My, my! Why, Alice was the best cook in Wisconsin, and *I* never claimed to cook at all. It was always your father who did the *really* good cooking. But you wouldn't *touch* that lemon pie. Had cornstarch in it. I never *could* understand people who put cornstarch in lemon pie. Only poor white folks. And Lord knows *Alice* ought to have known better. Only catered for the very best right up till she married your Uncle Ed . . ."

There was, of course, reproof for bad behavior as reported by the indignant Alice. But there was on Annette Dunham's part, even while the episode was fresh and certainly as it mellowed with the years, a deep sense of pride that the child had proved a stanch defender of family mores and discrimination as laid out by her mother.

During the early spring following the vacation at Lake Delavan, Annette Dunham decided to revisit the deserted mining town of Buxton, where Albert Dunham had courted and wedded her and where her sister Mayme and Mayme's husband William Humbles still lived on the dwindling capital they had salvaged when, overnight, the flourishing hamlet became a silent, unyielding skeleton set in the cornfields of middle Iowa. After a certain amount of persuasion the father consented to part with the son, yielding to the argument that the boy had not yet been allowed any summer vacation and that he seemed thinner and more withdrawn into himself that year than ever before.

By early July plans were complete, and one hot summer's day the children watched, from the open windows of their train, the Town and then the City glide by. They slept through the wide prairies of Illinois and awoke to look out on the tall corn and the long grass of Iowa. At Dubuque they waited hours for a connecting train; when it arrived, it discharged few passengers and received fewer. Cinders were thick on the red plush seats, and the engine panted asthmatically as it traversed country given over exclusively to farmland, with here and there a stop hardly worth the name painted in faded letters on the station signs.

Buxton proved to be a junction more dejected than any of the others. A thin, wiry man, with skin the color of ivory and the texture of leather, stood alone on the platform. He swept off a tremendous pearl hat, wide-brimmed and high-crowned, which the children at once recognized as kindred to that worn by their motion-picture idol, William S. Hart. A blue denim shirt, a flowing tie, a buckskin jacket, and tight-fitting overalls tucked into boots with pointed toes and raised heels, increased his resemblance to their hero. His eyes were a brilliant blue, and the girl noticed that the center of his head was bald and that the hair circling it was very fair, streaked with silver, and without the slightest curl or crimp.

"Why didn't she *say* that he was *white?*" she thought, feeling betrayed and annoyed, but not knowing just why.

In a full, adventurous life Will Humbles had made the most of his fair skin and blue eyes, working his way into positions that probably would have been closed to him if his mixed ancestry had been more apparent. In the mines he had moved rapidly from laborer to foreman and he had bought farmland not customarily sold to men of darker skin. He had always used this advantage to its fullest in business matters, but in his private life he had remained faithful to the Negro strain. His aged mulatto mother and a number of full-grown mulatto sons and daughters by the full-blooded Negro woman who had been Will's first wife, lived on the farm adjoining his, which he had bought for them. Years after the death of the first wife he had met Mayme Humbles, who had joined her sister Annette in applying for a teaching post in the out-of-the-way mining town and who, left alone when Annette married Albert Dunham, was more than willing to marry Will Humbles.

The girl felt friendly toward the single, quiet main street, deep in its Midwestern siesta. The ocean of gently waving corn beyond the town excited her, and the barren shafts of the deserted mines seemed sad but at the same time morbidly attractive. Here and there, where there were no mine shafts, she could see the roofs of barns and farmhouses buried in knolls of elm, oak, willow, and hazelnut trees. Surrounding the farms were orchards of pear and apple trees already heavy with fruit. There were cool inviting grape arbors, and a stream that they crossed not far from the railroad stop, and hares which darted under the wagon wheels to safety in the thick undergrowth which protected the fields from the summer dust. She sat happily squeezed into the front seat of the jaunty wagon and admired the skill with which her uncle drove the two impatient bays. As they threaded the dusty roads leading into open country and Will Humbles' farmland, the mother and uncle talked of the changes that had taken place during the time since the mother's departure and the "running dry" of the mines, which had occurred almost simultaneously.

Buxton had been created solely because of the coal mines, which served the town, the farmers surrounding the town, and the state. When the mines ran dry, the exploiters and contractors and traffickers and simple diggers were unbelieving, unprepared, and deeply aggrieved, as though the owners, along with nature, had betrayed them. The generosity of the earth had been short-lived; the owners withdrew to search for virgin fields, and the overseers and laborers who were itinerant turned to the Far West. But the home wanters, the root seekers who had invested their earnings in farmland without knowing how to farm, were hard hit, and so were the already established farmers who had abandoned their husbandry to work in the mines. These men were bitter at what had happened and looked on it as a conspiracy.

Will Humbles had always loved the land and open spaces, but in the Far West and the Southwest. He had known horses in corrals or on the open range and cattle without fences or barns, only branding marks. Moving from West to Middle West, he had married and sired and moved again to the West, leaving his family in the city near the mining town. He had returned when they sent word of the discovery of coal. His wife had died, his children were grown, and at fifty or so he felt a need for roots. He learned about barns, he learned about corn, but he never learned to love them. He had earned his living in the mines, and he had enjoyed a certain amount of free time for his real love, horses. The scale of things was different from his former life, however, and instead of riding a Texas range, he had to content himself with the fields and lanes and sparse woodlands between his farm and the town.

Mayme Humbles was constantly dazzled by her dashing husband, but she had inherited the dull and wearisome and never-ending side of farm life. She scarcely had time to admire him as he put the white charger through its paces under the huge oak tree in the yard in front of the frame house. Hens had to be fed and cows milked; cream had to be skimmed and churned into butter; cheese had to be squeezed from the whey left over. Fruit had to be picked from the trees in season, and preserved and canned and sealed with melted wax in Ball jars, and stored in the cool, musty basement. She felt a great relief that butchering was by common consent done at the adjoining farm, under the supervision of the ailing but active grandmother.

The tall, raw-boned, gray-eyed, crinkly-haired sons of Will Humbles by his former marriage tilled the land and accepted with laconic indifference their father's new wife and the visit of her relatives. They seldom visited Will Humbles' farm and seemed, when the girl tried to recall them later, a gaunt, cheerless, zombi family, almost all of them the same copper color as the ailing matriarch who controlled them and who seemed their closest tie with their father. Periodically one of the sons would lead a pig or a sow or a calf or heifer across the fields to the butchering grounds of his own farm. The girl stayed away from the barns and pens at such times, but when the brothers drove into town with a part of their spoils and passed in front of the house, she might see the quivering, black-clotted segments dangling out from under a blood-spattered canvas; and she would refuse to eat meat that night for dinner. She felt the same way about the plump hens that went into her Aunt Mayme's stews on Sunday and the younger, cackling, silly fryers that turned into golden fritters.

So after the first few days her play was confined to the

front yard and to the fields and woods and to the yards and fields of friends and acquaintances of Annette Dunham and Mayme Humbles. Some of them were familiar to her because she had seen them in the Poindexter family album, always on display on the living-room table in the Bluff Street flat. Often her mother had pored fondly over the treasured prints pasted into the earlier pages, pointing out serious wedding photographs, poses held still for minutes before a hooded cameraman. Grandfather and Grandmother Poindexter side by side: a stern-looking, bearded, aquiline-nosed giant and a solemn, high-cheekboned bride, smooth hair parted Choctaw-style in the middle. Then followed some of the twelve children, those who had reached adulthood: gray-eyed, fair-haired Uncle Will Poindexter; Beth, the shadow of early death already showing at sixteen; copper-colored Uncle Fred, sire of five children miraculously begotten after fifteen years of fruitless marriage; Gertrude, fairest of all the Poindexter girls, dead in childbirth, accompanying her stillborn son to the family plot in the Alton cemetery. There were also groups of smiling ladies at the edge of the small river, surrounded by picnic baskets and sunshades; and numerous school classes, groups of children and fellow teachers. These happy companions ranged in age from eighteen to the indefinite, but they were always referred to by each other as "girls."

Later, in other summers far removed, the girl wondered if the people she had met in Buxton had all faded in her memory into farmyard sun dust and fried chicken and early autumn chill because of some lack in her, or if they had moved through the world leaving no print, no substantial memory with anybody.

And yet it was a very social summer. After the lean first winter in the City and the subsequent uncertain years in the new Town, Annette Dunham had decided to experience again the carefree gaiety of her widowhood. She may, too, have experienced some foreboding, have felt that these might very well be her last carefree days and this the last summer sun filtering into a deepening autumn, which already hinted at the darkness that would beset her troubled household.

So there were breakfasts and luncheons and late afternoon dinners, and always there was fried chicken. The girl began to take note, as they drove to some shaded lawn or garden or dust-dried front porch, whether or not she could smell hot fat frying in the kitchen or an odor of steaming feathers, indicating that the chosen fowl had only just been dispatched. Once they arrived in time to see the sprightly grandmother of one of the "girls" wildly chasing an elusive, desperate Rock Island Red around and around the back yard, finally cornering it near the pigsty in the folds of her flapping gingham dress. In her embarrassment and exasperation the old lady twisted the neck of the fowl on the spot.

When it arrived at table an hour or so later, the girl pleaded that she was already full; for she had purposely allowed her plate to be heaped again and again with servings of fried corn, candied sweet potatoes, ham hocks boiled with giant green beans, sliced tomatoes, home-cured ham baked with brown sugar and whole cloves, hot biscuits brought to the table with pale yellow sweet butter oozing from between golden top and bottom, garden lettuce, radishes, cucumbers, and green onions. Besides, she must save space for peach cobbler and the custard ice cream that even now would be turning in a freezer in the spring house.

There were picnics at the river, and, spread out Monet-fashion by its fern-fringed banks, the gaily chatting "girls" would unfold hampers filled with good food—corn pudding still warm in covered casseroles, mashed turnips, turnip tops or mustard tops or beet tops, and now and then, by some rare circumstance, a "mess" of beloved dandelion greens. The banks of the river would echo with laughter at anecdotes, yarns, recollections, mimicries (at which Aunt Mayme excelled), and grow hushed and pregnant with listening as conversation drifted into gossip.

The only young companions the girl later remembered were Marion Carter, as tomboyishly inclined as she, and Marion's younger sister, who could scarcely walk, and toddled behind them and seemed a burden. Much of the time her brother would accompany them to these sylvan banquets, though he sought every excuse to be exempted from indoor sessions. While the "girls" chattered, the three older children would wander into the woods, wading in shallow parts of the river, exploring hollow tree trunks, peering into caves, losing each other for the thrill of hiding and seeking, playing at being lost, playing at fright. Except when exploring, the brother would be a bystander at the antics of his sister and her playmate, chewing a blade of grass or a fresh twig, whittling the end of a stick or lying on a knoll and staring across the narrow stream at far fields and fences. When the sun was low in the sky, and the woods were shadows stretched out to darken the quietly moving stream, he would lead them back to the riverbank.

The summer passed unruffled for the most part, and the two children experienced a joy in belonging to the mother that they had not known so fully before. Once or twice, when she thought of it at all, the girl was mildly surprised at the blandness with which her mother's friends ignored chronology. On one occasion a visitor remarked, between forkfuls of strawberry pie, on the resemblance in feature between mother and daughter. The girl, in a flash of annoyance for which she later felt ashamed, looked at her mother for denial. There were nods of assent among the other guests, and Annette Dunham, with just the right measure of coquettish modesty, acknowledged the statement as a compliment, even remarking on how many times this resemblance had been brought to her attention before.

*

With the last lingering days of summer, as the leaves began to turn, Annette Dunham took leave of her friends, knowing that most of the farewells were forever. Before departing, however, she extracted from her sister Mayme a solemn promise to withdraw from the exhausted mining town and come with Will Humbles to live in the community where she herself had already started to take root. Will could find an outlet for his restless energy in the steel mills, and the gain from selling house and barns and stock and land would buy a modest residence. But the deciding issue was the lack of a church in Buxton and the fact that Mayme was deeply religious. Although, at that time, the Dunham family had not yet joined the African Methodist Episcopal Church, Annette Dunham gave her sister a glowing description of Brown's Chapel and its young, enthusiastic pastor.

When the girl heard of the decision, she wondered to what degree her uncle had been consulted and how complex the persuasions of her aunt had been. She wondered if he left the lonely spaces of the cornfields knowing that steel mills are not coal mines and that his life had run dry like the veins of coal, so that resistance was no longer interesting. In any case, Will and Mayme Humbles moved to the Town the following spring.

Before leaving for home, the girl went alone late one afternoon to pay her respects to Uncle Will's old mother. She found her huddled under a grape arbor, wrapped in woolens against the evening dew. Her fine-spun woolly hair turned iridescent in the afternoon haze, and her wizened brown face seemed gentler and more youthful than the girl had remembered it. Her lightish, film-covered eyes peered at her visitor, and she took the hand offered timidly by the girl in one of hers.

"Come here, child," she said. She leaned forward urgently, speaking in a low voice, as though she feared that one of the gigantic brothers or their solid mulatto wives would hear and interfere. "Girl," she said, "so you're Will's new little girl."

Continuing to hold the child's hand, she reached into a pocket buried under the woolens and took out a polished wooden snuffbox, which she opened deftly with one hand. Her bare gums, stained brown as she exposed them in replacing a worn-out wad of the stuff with a fresh one, seemed not at all repulsive to the girl, but clean and sculptured. She did not bother to correct the old lady's genealogy.

"Child," Will Humbles' mother continued, "them don't like for the truth to be known. Them don't like for me to tell folks. This old lady was a slave, child. A slave. You hear that? And this old lady ain't a bit ashamed, not a bit ashamed about Will Humbles. The old Master did bed me with that child and give me the name of Humbles. Good name it were, and thought of well. Now they 'shamed. But not me. Don't you forget that, girl, and don't you be 'shamed neither!"

One of the brothers entered the grape arbor, stalking down the shady lane, bending a little under the heavy fruit clusters, crunching the fallen leaves under great muddy boots. He saluted his grandmother and looked suspiciously at the child. In the kitchen of the house a lamp was lighted, its yellow glow spreading into the gathering darkness of the arbor.

"You go now, child," said the old woman. "It growing dark. Cornfield's no place for a child at night. Will oughtn't let you run around like that." Slyly, with a sweetly radiant smile, she added, squeezing the child's hand, "We gonna keep a secret, you and me. Ain't we, child?"

The girl nodded many times, and not until she was crossing the field, threading through the ripe-smelling corn, hurrying against the darkness, did she realize that she had not once opened her mouth, not once said the farewell that she had for some reason wanted to make to this old lady above all the other summer acquaintances.

Albert Dunham, Jr., had returned to the Town alone some weeks before the mother and daughter. They arrived to find the shop on Bluff Street at the beginning of a flourishing fall season. A second delivery boy had been added, and another presser besides Mr. Crusoe, the taciturn old man Albert Dunham had been employing since their first Christmas in the Town. The sound of canvas-padded top slamming down onto trousers and skirts and coats, followed by the sharp hiss of steam released under pressure, issued from the open front door of the shop from morning until late evening. Between his passionate scourings of carpets the father still did the fine hand finishings of garments and continued with the important supervision of the gasoline tumblers; the son and his assistant tugged and pulled at heavy folds of grime-covered carpets, hauling them from the delivery truck up the wide stairs past the entrance to the flat and into the busy carpet room behind. The dust wheel creaked and groaned its monotonous round.

The son, about to enter his last year of high school, seemed driven by some inner taskmaster to work with special zeal during these last days of vacation, as if this might be a kind of insurance against the months when he would be cruelly put to it to maintain his position as head of the class and at the same time serve the insatiable dust wheel and his father. But in spite of his long hours in the delivery truck and further hours of skimming gasoline and turning the hand crank of the heavy rotary tubs which had been installed as auxiliary to the mechanically rotated tumblers, a tension between father and son was evident to both mother and daughter immediately upon their return. The flesh coaxed onto the boy's slender frame by the Iowa feasts of corn and fried chicken had already disappeared, and his smile of greeting to the mother and girl seemed forced.

The mother turned to her husband for some explanation, but his black countenance warned her against pushing the issue too far, and she took her place at the sewing machine in the window, puzzled and unquiet.

Annette Dunham, however, was not one to let any important issue pass before she had pursued it to its farthest retreat, and she began questioning acquaintances, all too eager to impart gossip, and also the workers in the shop, whose allegiance was gradually veering over to her side as Albert Dunham, Sr., became more and more arrogant, intolerant, and inclined toward violence. Her most helpful informant turned out to be the new delivery boy.

He was in fact a member of the clan—the son of a senile Confederate Army veteran and Albert Dunham's deceased young sister. His name was Howard Owings and he was sturdy of build like most of the Dunhams; in return for his services, he was to receive food, the privilege of attending school, and the use of a pallet on the floor of the back room of the shop. He must have smarted under the rigid discipline of this uncle who had promised him freedom; he must have sensed an ally in the wife, who seemed to be driven by none of the demons that possessed her husband. In any case, he willingly divulged some choice bits of information, which—though the mother adjusted to them once she had recovered from her first shock and indignation—were to remain graven in the girl's catalogue of disillusion.

A friend of Annette Dunham's had profited by her absence to play hostess to the father on every possible occasion permitted by her own unsuspecting husband. In some way the returned son had found this out, accused his father of infidelity, and so brought down upon himself a savage punishment. Perhaps by way of revenge, he had then begun to visit the woman himself.

Cousin Howard had got wind of all this quite accidentally, on an off-schedule delivery near the sedate Buell Avenue house above whose garage the woman and her husband had a small apartment. Passing the back alleyway behind the drive, he had on that occasion seen his uncle climbing the stairs to the apartment. From then on Howard visited the neighborhood whenever he could, timing his sorties to coincide with his uncle's increasingly frequent, increasingly protracted afternoon absences from the shop. Then he became aware that the son had also begun to visit the apartment, and he had witnessed the dénouement of this drama when the father arrived before the son had left it.

The girl could not know this sequence of happenings in order or fully. Her cousin, smirking and insinuating, made references to long absences of first the father and then the son on trips that took them toward the West Side. He seemed determined to impart to her some knowledge she could not grasp, which she found all the more bewildering because of the mounting tension in the household.

But it was easy for him to impart his knowledge to the mother, who proceeded at once to confront the offender. She invited the unsuspecting woman to stop by the West Side Cleaners at a time when she felt certain that both father and son would be present.

Bursting with the importance of his role, the cousin hurried to the girl and, finger to lips, led her to a vent in the kitchen floor that was kept open in the cold months so that heat might rise from the shop into the flat above. Heart pounding, the girl stealthily slid back the lattice, which had been closed since the beginning of summer, and pressed her face against the opening. Fine hairs of dust blew into her nostrils on the warm air, and the vapors of evaporating benzine made her eyes sting. She could see the top of her father's head: he stood with his arms folded and was leaning against the open board of the steam-pressing machine. She could not see her mother, but she could hear her and wondered what convergence of disasters could cause the quaver, the near tears, the combined hurt and anger that made her words almost unintelligible.

She was at this point repeating again and again, "After all I've done for you I wouldn't have believed it! I simply wouldn't have believed it! I wouldn't have believed it!" At another point she said, "He's only a *child!* How *could* you?" And at another point: "My own husband, and you a married woman yourself. Why, what *wouldn't* you sink to!"

Her mother did almost all the talking, but the girl could hear sobs from where she imagined the guilty woman to be standing, and could feel the black anger that mounted in her father. She learned later that her brother, after calmly admitting the truth of the mother's statement, had turned and walked out into the street and driven off in the delivery wagon. She did not grasp the meaning of what she heard, but she sensed the end of whatever happiness and pleasures they had known as a family.

She rose from her knees after cautiously closing the radiator. As she stood, she heard Annette Dunham issue the final malediction: *"You ought to be run out of town!"* And, in effect, this was what happened. Although there were perfunctory greetings at accidental encounters, and although on more than one occasion the two families exchanged half-hearted hospitalities, it was not long before the woman folded her tent and eased away into anonymity in the City.

Behind the carpet room, dug into the cliff that backed the Bluff Street building, was a small, dirt-floored room, barely large enough to accommodate two hand-cranked tumblers and two drums of solvent, one of them virgin, the other clouded and waiting to be skimmed for future use. The churning of the tubs kept up such a din that to be heard in the cubicle it was necessary to shout or to stop turning the cranks. Here the boy spent a certain part of the day—perhaps the part he liked best. He could be reasonably free from interference as long as he kept to his schedule, and the familiar machines seemed docile and co-operative compared with the fretful horse or undependable delivery trucks.

Here he could feel the stirrings of that quest into metaphysics, combined with the laws of science, which later became his absorbing preoccupation in philosophy. His thin shoulders rose and fell rhythmically. He felt near to the purpose of things; he felt the meaning of useful activity; he felt at peace in this enclosure scratched out of the bowels of the earth, protected by grease-smeared limestone walls, lulled by the monotony of the crank that turned the wheel that turned the wheel that turned the tub, but strong in being master of it all.

A few days after Annette Dunham had denounced Kate Mason, the girl sat on the oil-soaked step to this cavern. Her brother's back was to the door, and either he was unaware of her presence or he chose to ignore it. Sad without knowing why, she examined his shoes, laced ankle-high; his ribbed stockings, seen below knickers that he hoped to exchange for trousers with the opening of school; his back, patient and abstracted in the continuous movement. A surge of love and pity and wanting to belong and all the *Weltschmerz* of early childhood surged over her. She stood up and went to him, but she did not want to interrupt him; the most comfortable way to embrace, to pour out affection, to turn some of her undefined mourning to him and offer her yearning tenderness and her wish to comfort and be comforted, was to rest her cheek on his back, clasping him at the same time around the waist, pressing her body close to his, feeling against her stomach and chest the soothing rising-falling motion of his body, feeling his stomach encircled in the clasp of her hands.

He showed no surprise when she embraced him, but said, "Go away. Go and practice or do the dishes or something."

She paid no attention because she had already practiced her hour and a half at the piano, and he knew very well that there were no dishes to wash. She rose and fell, drifting in a soporific mist, lulled by the sound of cog fitting easily into cog, too welded to her need to pay attention to her brother's repudiation. Suspended in this way, she was unaware of any change until she felt the tightening of the muscles of her brother's stomach and heard the gradual cessation of the hum of the machinery. She turned her head toward the open door and looked directly into the horror-stricken face of her father.

He attacked her first. "Young lady, I thought you were told to stay out of this room!" At a disadvantage, she did not move with her usual agility when expecting punishment. The stinging blow from his open palm burst on her cheek, and flame blinded her so that she stumbled from the room, half crouching, squeezing against the wall to avoid touching her father as he stood aside to let her pass. She did not try to look at him, because tears had already flooded her eyes, but she heard the violence of his breathing and the first blow as he fell in a fury upon his son. Sobbing, she ran across the spongy blanket of the carpet room, heedless of the dust that billowed around her feet and knees in her flight. She wanted to run to her mother, but stopped on the way down the front steps and turned into the flat. There was nothing to tell. She had trespassed in the forbidden room, and this had released in her father some primitive, overwhelming rage. She could not see the cause for such an effect, but perhaps her mother would. She hoped that her brother's punishment would not be so severe as when he had spilled the oats and deprived Lady Fern of her evening meal, and as she bathed her swollen cheek in cold water, she felt vaguely uneasy, guilty, as though she had been to blame in some devious way beyond the minor disobedience of trespassing.

Nothing was said of the incident at supper, but she knew that her mother could not help noticing her swollen cheek; and after the meal, before the joint washing and drying of dishes, brother and sister, alone in the kitchen, compared notes. Raw welts had begun to rise on her brother's back, and his cheek, too, was swollen.

The brother's refusal to cry out or flinch under the cutting blows from the leather strap had always elicited the utmost admiration and respect from the girl; but his stoicism infuriated the father, stimulating him to excesses of passion. "I'll teach you," he would grind out between clenched teeth, panting heavily as his arm rose and fell in the lashing. "I'll teach you to talk back to me! I'll show you what you'll get for your insolence!" And all the while the brother would be biting his lips, looking at his father with unconcealed contempt, uttering not a cry or a word—unmoved, unimpressed, giving every impression of biding his time, of tolerating any extravagance of abuse from the man who was now his sworn enemy, because he knew he would triumph in the end. And he always did. The father, puffing and panting, would hitch up his trousers, rethread his belt, and mutter, "I guess that'll teach you." But with less and less conviction.

The davenport in the front room of the flat opened by means of a series of springs and pulleys into a fairly comfortable double bed, and here the brother and sister had slept for the last several years. On this night the mother went to the storeroom curtained off from one end of the living room, and after some probing extracted a folding cot that had not been in use since the family's move from the rear room of the shop. This she installed in the far corner of the living room opposite the davenport. A few days later the storeroom was emptied and transformed into a sleeping den for the girl. Until that time she slept on the cot, staring into the darkness after the others had gone to bed, trying to understand the nature of her sin.

That summer the girl had passed her eleventh birthday, and with the coming of late autumn the brother would arrive at his fifteenth. She was about to enter her last year at Farragut Grade School, and he to begin his last year at the

Town high school. Conflicts between mother and father became more frequent and uncontrolled; between father and son resentment turned into passionate hatred, and their studied avoidance of each other made reconciliation impossible.

That year the girl wrote a poem that was published in the name of her class in a national magazine and a story about how the tortoise acquired his shell which was published in a children's magazine under her own name. At a Saturday afternoon movie one of the passionately forlorn episodes portrayed by the Gish sisters moved her to tears, and she tried her hand at melodrama. Her mother burned the scrawled sheaves of paper and suggested that, should she continue her literary pursuits, she stick to simple subjects of nature.

Knowledge of her brother's scholastic brilliance had spread among patrons of the shop, and from time to time they congratulated the mother or father on having a son who not only would finish as class valedictorian, but would probably graduate with the highest honors yet awarded by the school. Would he go immediately into the near-by City University, or would he take advantage of the first two college years offered by a newly established junior college in the Town?

The father accepted the compliments with taciturn condescension. The mother was overjoyed and would have swelled with pride had she dared. As it was, she saw in her son's brilliance a new irritant to her pathologically jealous husband; she received the praise modestly and succeeded in diverting much of the mounting venom in her own direction.

During that year Mayme and Will Humbles arrived, trailing in half a boxcar behind them their worldly possessions, in the form of bushel baskets of apples and pears and potatoes, sides of bacon and hams, cardboard boxes of preserved and pickled and jellied fruits and vegetables, and as many of the farmhouse furnishings as they were able to cram into reduced quarters. They also brought cash from the sale of the farm and livestock. With a part of this they bought, in an unpretentious neighborhood not far west of Bluff Street, a small three-room bungalow set closely between two others identical to it. It had a porch in front and in back a yard approximately the size of the hog pen on the Iowa farm.

The girl found herself moving through her life as a stranger, bewildered by the threat of newly discovered passions, deadened at the start of the day by arguments overheard the night before and by the ensuing bad dreams, afraid of what new violence each night might bring. The dust wheel reluctantly doled out its rewards, and the household bettered itself in every way except joy.

Seven
The Room and the Star

*

The girl looked upon the move to the improvised bedroom as a kind of exile, a punishment that may have been just but that to her was bewildering and inexplicable. Stifling hot in summer, bitterly cold in winter, the Room, with its single high window and its heavy damask drapery covering the doorway, became a symbol of unreasoning parental authority. A year had passed before she learned to think of it as a refuge and to welcome the hours when she could lie in seclusion on the narrow iron cot, reading, writing, or looking at the yellow calcimined ceiling and daydreaming ways of escape from the tightening mesh that seemed to be her destiny.

A single iron bed filled the width of the Room, leaving no passage into the small space at either end unless one climbed across it. A row of hooks at the foot served for the girl's wardrobe; at the other end she could, by kneeling on the bed, pull the drawers of a second-hand repainted chest halfway out, and in these drawers she kept other items of clothing as well as books, papers, letters, and the mementos through which she clung to her childhood. Intermittently she wrote to her niece in the City, Helen Weir, the daughter of her half sister Fanny; to her Aunt Lulu, whom she remembered with great fondness from the dark days before Annette Dunham had arrived to take charge of the motherless household; to newly made friends who lived in her mother's birthplace, Alton, Illinois.

The truly wonderful thing about the Room was the Star. Being high and square and single-paned, the window framed the Star and gave it meaning. If the window had been lower or longer, more of the night sky would have been exposed, and the girl might never have formed her attachment to the single bright planet that stayed just above the lower sill when she lay stretched out, or shone full in her face if she was kneeling on the bed. Sometimes she missed the Star, because of the passing of the seasons or because the sky was clouded; but over the years, even in memory, these times mattered little, because the Room was a whole piece of her life, and the Star was the Room. She absorbed from the Star some strange dreamdust of hope and traveled a thousand times into the cold clear heart of its mystery.

One spring night, as she slept with the window open for the first time since the passing of snow and freezing winter winds and cold Easter rain, the Star woke her with a gentle caress. She opened her eyes in peace, filled with the certainty that she would never again feel the isolation or the fear of loneliness which had haunted her since the days of the closed room upstairs in the Glen Ellyn house. The choreography of her inner being stirred at this instant, Dionysus took possession of her, and she rose to her knees and looked full into the silver radiance. Breathlessly she poured into the night the prayer that was to be worded almost identically for the rest of her life.

"Help me, Star," she said. "Help me. Make me strong, give me courage, make me know the right thing to do."

Sometimes she would address the planet as "Dear Star," sometimes later on as "God," but most of the time without a name, just looking at it and asking it or begging it or urging it, and feeling it reach out to her in answer. When everything else seemed unreasoning and unheeding, the Star with its cold unwinking serenity somehow gave her confidence in the presence of some divinity, somewhere in that vast outer space, dispassionately guiding destinies according to a plan so blindingly obvious as to appear obscure. Although sometimes worded a little differently, affected by a changing vocabulary or another climate, the petition in essence remained the same: for strength, for courage, and for further knowledge. If she possessed these, bewilderment would end and the message that the Star was trying to transmit to her would become comprehensible.

There were occasions other than communication with the Star that drew Katherine Dunham to the window of the Room. One night she was awakened by the shriek of sirens as fire engines catapulted from the red brick station halfway between the West Side Cleaners and the Jefferson Street bridge. She rose to her knees, half asleep, and her throat constricted for a moment. She thought of the hazards of the tumbler rooms and the tanks of used and unused gasoline. But a red glow the other side of the canal relieved her of this anxiety.

Then, cutting through the wail of the Bluff Street fire-engine sirens and of others that were approaching from all directions, a new chilling sound penetrated her consciousness. That it was a sound rendered in an extremity of agony and terror there could be no doubt; something else about its quality and volume distinguished it as animal rather than human. The girl thrust her head through the damask curtains and saw her father and brother at the unshaded front windows.

They were both dressing hurriedly, and her mother stood in the door of the bedroom saying, "Al, what is it? Will it reach over here? Are the tanks all right? Should I wake Katherine up? Where is it? Will they put it out?"

Albert Dunham was talking to his son, his voice pitched higher than usual, in excitement tinged with anxiety.

"Fitzsimmon's barn. Better get right over and see which way the wind's blowing. Never know with sparks up that high. Wonder how on earth *that* happened. My, just listen to those horses. Might as well not try and force them out. Never get a horse to go through that kind of fire. Just listen to that!"

Cries now began to fill the street, and men were running here and there recruiting neighbors to cross over the bridge and help the fire brigades or at least to watch and give advice. The women in other windows behaved much as Annette Dunham did. At first all questions, then all admonitions. "Al, do you think you'd better go? Wouldn't it be better to stay here in case? . . . Does Albert have to go? What if . . . just supposing . . ." And as the two of them ran from the room and down the front stairs: "Al, be careful! Don't get too close to that barn. You can't do anything anyway as far gone as it is. Don't let Albert get near it!" Her voice was lost on them, because by then they were well into the street and halfway to the bridge, joining the Simons and the O'Connors and a pasty-faced shirt-sleeved man who came up from the mysterious subterranean gambling rooms beneath Rube's Saloon.

No one thought of putting on lights, because they would have diminished the drama across the canal. Standing in the front room, bathed in fireglow, and breathing air already tainted with smoke and with another kind of stench which made them both cover their nostrils with their nightdresses, the mother and daughter strained to distinguish familiar landmarks in the steadily growing pandemonium on the other side of the canal. . . .

The street parallel to Bluff Street and directly opposite across the bridge was unpaved, and traffic passing from one bridge to the other found the Bluff Street side far more convenient. The opposite street was used for the most part by truck and wagon drivers who loaded or unloaded crates and boxes of assorted supplies, and bales and coils of hemp, and cases of bottles and tins, and drums and barrels of crude oil, and sacks of sugar and coffee at the wooden or limestone warehouses over there. When the mother and daughter had driven or walked across either one of the bridges, they had seen men hauling and lifting and loading and other men backing up or urging forward or wheeling into half circles the great, specially bred Belgian horses, descendants of stock imported when the German and Irish-owned breweries were a more important factor in the Town than the steel mills.

Often these wagons would turn into Bluff Street from one of the bridges and stop to make a delivery at Reimer's pop factory or Simon's grocery store. The great cinnamon-colored stallions, with their heavy rippling platinum manes and tails and fetlocks, fascinated the girl but at the same time terrified her. In the fine days before Prohibition the wagons had passed down the street empty and returned in stately procession loaded with wooden beer kegs stacked into elongated pyramids; when the Eighteenth Amendment closed the breweries, the Belgian horses and the loaders and the draymen were gradually absorbed into the Town's other economies.

As she stood beside her mother at the window, the animal sounds from across the river suddenly made sharp connection with other long-forgotten animal sounds. Sometimes during her early days on the street the girl had sat inside the smithy next to her father's shop, watching the blacksmith prepare the horny soles of Lady Fern's hoofs for the white-hot iron shoes. Although he assured her that Lady Fern felt no discomfort, the girl winced each time the curved blade explored the cavities between the digits. The molten shoe gripped in tongs and curling over the side of the anvil, the steady rhythm of the hammer as it rose and fell and coaxed the iron into shape, the hiss and spurt of steam as the shoe was thrust into a wooden tub of water for tempering, then another heating and the joyous paean of the anvil as the final touches brought the iron into form—this she never tired of watching. The fitting of the shoe she found unpleasant: Lady Fern's foot would draw sharply up as the hot iron touched her thick cuticle, and, gripping her slender shank more closely between his two knees covered by the leather apron, the blacksmith would talk to her gently and soothingly in the special language that horses understand. Yellow smoke would rise and sting the girl's nostrils, and she would turn from where she sat on an overturned bucket or unused anvil and look out through the wide barn doorway until the nails were hammered in, and the blacksmith stroked Lady Fern while she nibbled at pieces of apple that were always somewhere in the ample inside pockets of his apron.

One day at the finish of the shoeing, the girl was about to leave the smithy to find her brother, so that he could lead Lady Fern to the side yard. As she rose from her seat near the door, she heard the ponderous approach of the team of Belgian horses and saw the dray turn into the curb just ahead of Simon's grocery store. The driver slid from his perch and sauntered across the street to Rube's Saloon, stopping long enough to drop an iron disk to the ground and attach it by a double leather thong to the bit of the horse nearest the curb. His companion shuffled to the rear of the wagon and started hauling down potato sacks, dragging them across the sidewalk, and into the cool recesses of the grocery store.

A curse, something that she had never before heard from the blacksmith, caused her to turn sharply again to the dark interior. With no warning Lady Fern had arched her neck convulsively, and the movement had painfully twisted the blacksmith's shoulder as he stood with the reins of her bridle wound around his arm and put the finishing touches to her brown satin coat with a steel currycomb. Low whinnying sounds tore from her throat, and from mane to buttock her glossy hide quivered, until it seemed that she was overcome by some sort of epilepsy. Then the blacksmith, untangled from the reins, began to coax and stroke and soothe her, while she, tail arched straight in the air, braced her rear legs farther apart and pawed the dirt with her forelegs and flared her nostrils and strained to veer toward the open door.

Outside there was a sudden and violent commotion. The nostrils of the two Belgian stallions, yoked together between the double shafts of the dray, had caught the scent of invitation that reached them from the mare inside the smithy. Maddened by her proximity and each infuriated by the challenging presence of the other, they screamed with rage and rose simultaneously upon their hind legs, pawing the air, snapping rivets, splintering shafts, in an effort to be free of their trappings and confront one another in the most ancient and classic of contests. The hitching iron flew into the air like a paperweight and nicked off a piece of the curb when it crashed down again. The violence of the stallions' antagonism as they slashed out with massive iron-shod hoofs and the deadly intent of their passion rooted the girl to the doorsill in terror.

Bobby Simon dashed across the street between gathering spectators to summon the wagoner from Rube's taproom, and the girl saw her father and brother among others who darted forward quickly and backward more quickly, like featherweights shadowboxing to gain the attention of battling giants. Her father managed to snatch a line of reins from under the flashing hoofs and toss it to the helper, who shouted ineffectual and unheeded orders from the driver's seat. The heavy wagon rocked and reeled and gunnysacks of supplies shot out from the back. The driver ran across the street livid with anger, and a stream of curses poured from his mouth as he yanked a whip from the dashboard of the wagon and fell upon the two stallions with a viciousness equaling their own.

Inside the smithy, Lady Fern seemed suddenly and

strangely past her crisis and followed submissively as the blacksmith led her to one of the rear stalls, filled one bucket with cold water which she drank greedily, and doused her with another. Then he covered her with a blanket and ran outside, building anger as he went, because although the Irish of Bluff Street looked upon one another affectionately as "shanty," they felt a healthy superiority to the hard-drinking, brawling, trade-union Irish from the other side of the canal. The blacksmith had heard the curses and seen the fury of the whip, and he looked upon horseflesh as superior to most human flesh. He also felt an uneasy concern for his neighbor, whom he had learned to respect for his knowledge and handling of horses. Red already streaked the blond coat of the older stallion, and the maddened beast fought desperately, distracted between the drayman and the rival stallion. By now Albert Dunham had gained access to the checkrein of the horse nearest the curb, and by force and persuasion and horse talk sought to reduce its frenzy and draw its attention away from the sound of the whip and the smell of anger and back to the familiar feel of harness and collar and traces and straps tightened one by one.

The blacksmith took the whip from the raging drayman and held the hand that was raised to strike him in his steel fingers, which had pumped bellows for more years than the drayman had been alive.

"Ye better check yerself, Paddy," he said in a hard, tight voice. "The likes of ye don't belong this side o' the river, and the likes of ye sh'd be run from the Union fer layin' whip to a dumb beast the way ye just did. Mickey Fitzsimmons 'ud back me up on that, and so would Packy McFarland." He released the drayman's wrist and turned his attention to the quivering beast.

Still cursing and swaying unsteadily on his feet, the drayman circled in front of the horses to the curb where the girl's father was holding the reins of the quieted stallion and stroking its foam-covered mane and chest and shoulder, talking softly all the time. Her father was sweat-soaked, wetter than she had ever seen him. His shirt was pasted to his body, and the darkness of his skin showed in streaks beneath the white shirt; the sleeves were rolled up, and blood trickled down the arm that was holding the bit-reins. As the driver crossed in front of the horses, the stallion closest to the curb snorted and tried to free its head and rose up and struck out at the man with both forefeet. Albert Dunham dragged with all his force and patted the trembling mane reassuringly. The Irishman cursed at the horse and then turned to the man and spat at his feet and cursed again and added something that the girl knew about but had never heard said just so or right out like that or with such insult.

The spectators from Bluff Street shifted from one foot to the other with embarrassment, as though this were a thing they had all hoped would never happen or be brought up. Katherine Dunham saw on her father's face the disbelief that made him for a moment seem as young as the boy who stood beside him, stroking the horse. Then he appeared to grow taller; he passed the bit to his son without turning his head and took a step forward, hands forming into fists, nostrils distending so that from where the girl stood she could see the red of flushed membranes inside. No one seemed to be willing or able to do anything to stop the terrible thing that was happening. She had never seen her father so angry or her brother so drawn and tense and full of hate. For the first time they seemed to be related, father and son alone on a small island of violence.

The Irishman opened his mouth to speak again, but the white hair and calm blue eyes and smoke-grimed face of the blacksmith stood between the two men. The cold edge of the blacksmith's voice cut through the tight silence.

"Paddy O'Rourke," he said, "git up into the wagon and git yer dirty low sneakin' self back across the river where ye belong. And if I *ivver* ketch ye *our* side of the bridge er hear of ye talkin' words like them agin or horse-beatin', *so help me before the Blessed Virgin I'll cut out yer black heart and take it with me up to the state penitentiary on Scott Street.*"

The old man stood in front of the disconcerted drayman like a piece of white-hot steel; his controlled anger had mounted to the breaking point, and he began to tremble as he reached behind to untie the thongs of the leather apron, as though to make good the threat on the spot. Like the loosening of a terrible pressure or the releasing of water that has been dammed to bursting, Henry Simon and the McGuire boys and even Rube, who hardly ever crossed over to the west side of the street, took their cue from the blacksmith and all began to talk at once: "That's right, Paddy, get somebody else to make your deliveries on Bluff Street." "Tell Fitzsimmons we don't need you fellows any more. There's other trucking companies and other trucks." "Come on, Paddy, get a move on." And so on, while the blacksmith tied his apron again with shaking hands, and her father clenched and unclenched his fists, and her brother let go the bitrein and turned away, putting this hate into a neat envelope where he kept filed the ways of men that he would never become reconciled to.

The girl began to cry a little and went into the shop with a terrible lump in her throat, partly because of shock and shattered nerves and relief and partly because she had at that moment fallen in love with the blacksmith and wanted to tie his apron for him because his hands were trembling so. As she entered the shop, where Annette Dunham stood at the small pressing board putting pins into knife pleats in Mrs. McFarland's fine wool skirt, she heard words from her father and the blacksmith's answer.

"Mr. Dunham, I wouldn't waste me time or thought on the likes o' him if I was you. It's the likes o' him has spoiled the name of the Old Country, and the likes o' him that will make trouble wheriver they go. Yer place is Bluff Street, and his place is with his like across the canal. I'll bring ye Lady Fern now, and I do think the lass needs a nice long vacation in the country. Change of climate."

That was the most that she had ever heard the blacksmith speak. Not long afterward he went to live with a daughter on the outskirts of the City, because he felt that he was too old to work at anvils and, besides, there would soon be more automobiles than horses. The barn was closed and the anvils were stilled, and then someone told her father that the smith had died, peacefully and in his sleep as he deserved. The girl grieved for him but, standing in the window while Fitzsimmons' stable burned, she was glad that he was not there, because he would have suffered anguish with the trapped animals, and the horrible death of each one of them would have meant his own agonized death.

There was little to be seen from the window except people milling around in the street below. Tall flames licked into the sky, and billowing smoke drifted sometimes toward them and sometimes away. The sound was the thing to be remembered: people shouting and giving orders, and the sirens of arriving engines and departing ambulances rising over and over and then dying down like stifled groans. But worst of all were the terrible death cries of the horses which, in their fright at the first sign of fire, fell into numb stupidity and refused to be coaxed or beaten or led to safety, but stayed inside the stable, rearing, lashing, screaming, fighting blindly, and striking out for as long as they could see or breathe or rise up against the man-made confinements. As dawn streaked the sky, the fire died down, but ash and smoke shut even the river from view. People began to return to their houses, and the mother and daughter each went to her own bed, sad and chilled at having witnessed the essential helplessness of man and beast.

The father and brother returned with accounts of the horrors first hand: firemen and stablemen caught between fallen rafters or buried under a collapsed hayloft; bodies of fallen horses roasting in the wooden furnace and swelling twice their normal size and then bursting with a gruesome noise and stench. The ambulance arrived too late for Paddy O'Rourke and for Mr. Fitzsimmons, who had rushed to the scene with a raincoat over his long drawers when a night watchman phoned at the start of the fire. There were many injured, and it took days to clear away the wreckage and rubble and charred bodies of the horses. It was better that Mr. Fitzsimmons had died that way, fighting to save what he loved most, hacking away at fallen beams as though possessed, tearing into any obstruction in the path of the ropes of twisting firehose, yanking fiercely and cursing and kicking at hack and Belgian alike as he tried to encourage them to cross the flaming doorways to safety.

As the girl listened from behind the damask curtains, she climbed to her knees and looked for the Star. She wanted to thank it for the safe return of her brother and father, and somewhere in the back of her mind was an unformed wish to thank it for the removal of Paddy O'Rourke from the vicinity of Bluff Street. But early morning had erased the stars, and in a very short while it would be time to comb and brush and wash and breakfast before the long walk to her eight-thirty algebra class.

In the late spring of that year Albert Dunham held a number of conferences in the back of the shop with the secondhand automobile dealer who had been responsible for the replacement of Lady Fern by the truck and for the replacement of the first truck by one slightly larger and with a more important-sounding engine. His wife seemed to know what the conferences were about and to be pleased by whatever was going on—not at all out of sorts at her husband's frequent departures with the dealer, sometimes in the delivery truck, sometimes in an open touring car equipped with a canvas top, which—as the dealer proudly demonstrated—could in a few minutes be extricated, already attached to its frame, from a space behind the rear seat and unfolded to clamp onto the windshield. As a further inducement, in the side pockets of each door were folded windows of transparent isinglass squares set in black canvas frames which could be stretched between roof and doorframe and secured by means of outsize snap fasteners. When these were in place, the occupants were as safe from rain and snow, the dealer assured Mr. Dunham, as they would be in the back part of the delivery truck, and they would be infinitely more fashionable and more comfortable.

One day the father went out with the dealer and returned behind the wheel with the dealer at his side. It was during the first days after the closing of school, and the weather was warm, a forecast of the hot summer. The girl was seated on the curbstone in front of the shop, playing jacks with Helen Byfield, and the two girls had barely time to swing their legs to the sidewalk when, with a shrieking of brakes and grinding of gears, Albert Dunham drew to a halt a few feet from the open door. He was grinning with satisfaction and raced the motor two or three times in final token of ownership. He shook hands with the dealer, then hurried to the shop to call his wife from her sewing machine.

She was smiling as she went to the automobile; the brother drove up in the delivery wagon and climbed out and looked pleased and smiled, too; and it suddenly dawned on the girl that this was a new and wonderful acquisition, and she left her friend and joined the other three in their inspection. Bobby and Art Simon coasted around the corner on their bicycles, came to a stop in front of the grocery store, walked their bicycles over, and joined the family. Much impressed, they stood leaning on their handle bars, each with one foot on the ground.

Art said to Helen Byfield, "Gee, Mr. Dunham's bought a Studebaker. Gee, that makes *two* cars now." And to the father: "Hey, Mr. Dunham, can we look inside?"

And from Bobby, who by now had a healthy interest in automobiles and prided himself on recognizing any model or make from a block away: "How many cylinders, Mr. Dunham? Can I look at the motor, can I?"

The girl invited Helen Byfield to sit with her in the front seat, and the two of them examined the dashboard and slid back and forth over the somewhat used leather upholstery, wishing that they knew how to drive and that Mr. Dunham had left the top down so that everybody passing on Bluff Street would be sure to see them.

As to the letting-down of the top, however, Annette Dunham had very firm ideas of her own. In answer to her daughter's continuous whining and pleading and hinting and sulking, she would reply emphatically, "I should say *not*. You are conspicuous enough already, Katherine, without going around town with the top down, attracting attention like somebody from Collins Street!" The girl knew that a reference to Collins Street clinched all her mother's arguments about immorality. And so she gave up asking for the top to be put down and went to picnics and to Bush Park leaning as far out as she dared.

And whatever chagrin she may have felt was more than compensated for by her mother's wholehearted support of her craving to learn to drive. As long as the delivery truck had been the Dunhams' only motor vehicle, the idea had seemed impractical, but with the new car more or less at her disposal, the mother felt thwarted at having to depend for its use on her husband's good humor or spare time or on her son's availability. She stressed the girl's other aptitudes and her need for some interest that would occasionally take her away from Bluff Street during summer vacation, and her own need for some freedom from the drudgery of the West Side Cleaners. But the decisive argument was that the father would be relieved of the duty of squiring his wife and daughter to services at Brown's Chapel African Methodist Episcopal Church—a duty that he had accepted some time ago, but only grudgingly.

Albert Dunham was a Christian by faith and upbringing, but he did not pretend to be what is known as a "good" Christian. When his first child was born, he had been too deeply immersed in maintaining a foothold in a community where the color of his skin was a handicap to give thought to such formalities as baptism. By the time his second child was born, he had been beset by problems connected with his growing family and his increasingly delicate wife. No one seemed to have any idea how Fanny June Dunham felt about such matters, but in all probability, knowing she might die soon, she was chiefly troubled about her children's physical well-being. So both of them were innocent of any formal religious training, and, had it not been for the intervention of their God-respecting Aunt Mayme, their Sunday nights would doubtless have continued to be given over to moving pictures, musical soirees, and games of whist.

Mayme Humbles, however, attacked these pagan practices with the zeal of the white-robed and anointed, and even the father was swept up in the tide of her righteous indignation.

"Nett Poindexter!" she exclaimed, once she was fully aware of the situation, "the Lord will never forgive you! You're raising these children like heathen. Motion pictures and cardplaying on the Lord's day! Why, I never *heard* of such a thing!"

So Sunday nights at the Princess and Orpheum became a thing of the past, and Sunday drives and picnics were always governed by the time and distance from the weather-beaten wooden edifice that was to rob the girl of so many precious hours of living.

One of the paradoxes about Albert Dunham was that,

while he begrudged his son each moment of freedom from weekday duties for the pursuit of his studies, he made no effort to force him from these studies to attend church services. When the daughter, because she had no other choice, and the mother, because of her aroused sense of duty, and the father, in order to avoid the scathing reprimands of his sister-in-law or because of some special circumstance having to do with politics or business or community status, would take their places in the family pew, the brother would almost invariably profit by the welcome solitude and plunge into the studies that kept him far ahead of his class.

For the girl the new Sunday routine included morning service at eleven o'clock and evening service at eight-fifteen. Added to this was Sunday school, which immediately followed morning service, and a sort of guided youth meeting, called Young People's Christian Endeavor, for the hour preceding evening service. From this schedule tears and expostulations brought no relief. Although she loved her Aunt Mayme dearly, she held her wholly responsible for hours that constituted a large portion of her adolescence and young womanhood—hours spent at church services, rallies, Ladies' Aid meetings, revival meetings, basement suppers to raise funds from the same few who already contributed at every service, funerals, choir rehearsals, and special events. It may have been that the mother, aware of the separation of the girl's path from that of the other Bluff Street children, guided her into Brown's Chapel so that she might have some social contact, however limited, outside of school. Whatever the reasons, during this twelfth summer the bicycle and roller skates gave way to the Studebaker; and softball in the streets and jacks on the curb and rope skipping on the sidewalk in front of the shop and expeditions up the face of the limestone cliff faded into childhood memories along with the blissful nights of sleeping beside her brother on the living-room davenport.

*

Shortly before the girl's twelfth birthday, the driving lessons began. On a Sunday morning she and her brother took off in the Studebaker for Black Road, escorted by Annette Dunham. Things went well, and by the following Sunday the girl was already in comfortable control of the Studebaker. The Sunday before her twelfth birthday she proudly drove up to the dirt plot in front of Brown's Chapel and astonished Cymbaline and Tennyson Butler, youngest children of the current pastor, who always stood around in front of the church until the last minute, hoping as she did that some miracle might spare them the ordeal of the service.

She was eternally grateful to her brother for not exposing her one bad blunder during the course of her lessons. A precipitate move had stalled the Studebaker in the middle of the railroad tracks at the intersection of Ottawa and Center streets. An engine that trailed a single freight car was shuttling back and forth lazily between siding and main track, and it presented to her for one frantic moment all the hazards of Pearl White at the climax of one of her Saturday-afternoon *Perils*. After pressing on the starter until the motor died to a low hum, she realized that she had left the choke out so far that the carburetor was hopelessly flooded. The gas fumes and her own exasperation brought tears to her eyes. As the engineer finally decided upon the main track, she gave up and lifted herself in her seat so that her brother could slide across under her and take the wheel. The motor responded like magic, and the flooded engine sputtered once or twice and then resumed its regular rhythm. The brakeman blew his steam whistle as he leaned out of the window of the locomotive cabin, and one or two pedestrians stopped to look as they waited for the freight car to cross the intersection.

The boy drove the rest of the way home, while the girl

sat recalling his admonition the first time she had driven unaided: "Remember, Kitty, if you ever have an accident he'll never let you drive again. So just don't have one!"

For many years she didn't.

Given proper care and especially proper fuel, the Studebaker might have functioned with reasonable efficiency, considering its age and previous service. But the father exercised the same optimism with regard to fueling motor cars as he did to supplying dry-cleaning tumblers. The gasoline that went into the tank of the Studebaker issued, more likely than not, from the supply tank in the stone tumbler room—and, at times of extreme optimism, even from the tank set aside for settling and skimming off the used gasoline. If it came from the second, there would be no question of avoiding trouble after the first few miles; if it came from the supply tanks, there was always the risk that dust or other foreign matter might have settled in the open pan in which the gasoline was transported from tank to tank. In either case it would be only a matter of hours before the fine wire mesh of the strainer and eventually the feed pipe became obstructed by an accumulation of refuse. In the middle of the Town or on an open country road, the motor would gasp, choke, cough and sputter, and finally come to an asthmatic halt.

The girl had learned all the antidotes—split-second use of the choke, coasting if on an incline, switching the ignition on again to gain a few precious yards, and pumping the gas pedal with the motor shut off in order to force a few drops of liquid into the congested tubes. She also knew how to disconnect the feed pipe and blow it out; but sometimes the blockage had progressed too far, and she would have to phone to the West Side Cleaners for assistance and wait until her father or brother or cousin would arrive, out of sorts and with auxiliary tools and a can of gasoline from a gas station. Desperate pleading on her part and the reasoning of her mother and brother were of no avail. To make matters worse, her father enjoyed the same optimism about rubber as he did about gasoline. Tires worn smooth were recapped over and over, and inner tubes scraped and patched until almost none of the original fabric was visible. It was a great disappointment to Albert Dunham when he learned that neither the tires nor the wheels of touring car and truck were interchangeable; but he compensated for this by stocking up with used tires bought on sale or acquired by a series of shrewd trades, and not once was a new tire bought for either car or for any of their successors.

The girl would sigh as she felt a telltale dragging, forerunner of the thump that would bring her to a stop at the side of a road or, if she were unlucky, a downtown street. The crowning horror would be if there were no spare—if her father had said, "Oh, you won't need that spare tire. I'll get around to fixing it, but those on there are every bit as good as new. I'll bet my bottom dollar you won't need to change a one of them for the next six months."

When confronted by his exasperated daughter or wife, he would exclaim with genuine puzzlement, "Well, I'll be doggoned! I could have *sworn* that tire was good for another six months! Can't understand it. I'm going to take it right back to Duffy's and show it to 'em. Make 'em give me another one."

But of course he never got around to it.

Albert Dunham's consuming preoccupation with buying, selling, bargaining, and trading was not confined to his own enterprises. He thrived on offering business advice to others. His own lack of enough ready cash to engage actively in real estate or other quick-money deals, coupled with his wife's adamant refusal to speculate, aroused in him a chagrin that developed into a bitter resentment toward her, his circumstance in life, and eventually the Town. He did, however, derive a certain compensation from his growing reputation for business judgment.

The arrival of Mayme and Will Humbles, in possession of enough cash to buy a modest house, had offered him an unexpected opportunity to enter the thick-and-fast of the real-estate business. The selection of the locale, the terms, and finally the purchase itself were all left in his hands, with flurries of interest from his sister-in-law. For it seemed that, even as the train had pulled away from the Iowa cornfields and the deserted mines, Will Humbles had begun to draw farther and farther into himself, so that whenever decisions had to be made, he would say wearily, "Whatever Mamie says. Ask Mamie. You-all know I don't know anything about house buying."

The twinkle was gone from his brilliant blue eyes, and while he still wore the wide felt hat, even with his Sunday clothes, his body wasn't straight up any more or proud as if he had just dismounted from the bay gelding. He paid for the three-room house on Hyde Park Avenue, silently moved into it, exchanged his sombrero for a mill cap, took the lunch pail that Mayme Humbles packed for him every morning, and went off to the steel mills to supplement the savings that had been pretty well eaten into by the purchase of the house.

It did not take long for the coke furnaces to break what remained of Will Humbles' spirit. In a short while constant sweating had washed sunburn and windburn from his skin, so that it was waxen white instead of ivory. Before the summer was out the crinkles around his eyes became furrows, and new furrows were added. His leanness turned to extreme thinness, and the girl felt sad and concerned for him as she sat on the front steps of the Hyde Park Avenue cottage and watched the tired, defeated man shuffle down the street toward them, head bent, blue denim shirt streaked with sweat which hadn't dried out on the long ride in a streetcar so crowded that he'd had to stand the whole way. But she felt saddest of all about his thick-soled, ungainly mill-worker shoes—so far removed from the high-heeled cowboy boots of Iowa.

Sometimes her uncle passed the girl and her aunt without a word of greeting and went directly out onto the closed-in back vestibule, where he would pour water from a china pitcher into a china basin and remove his shirt and wash vigorously for a long time, as though to wash away the odor of escaped gas and the blue-white flame of the ovens and the glare of the endlessly churning vats of liquid pig iron. Then he would sit on the back step, smoking his pipe and looking into the evening sky, not seeing the tiny plot of garden or the fence or the neighbors' houses close on each side. He would sit there until his wife summoned him to supper. Afterward he would go into the bedroom, return with his spectacles, and sit on the back steps again or at the dining-room table, if it had already become dark outside, and read the evening paper. There was never any mail for him, nor did he ever write to anyone or ask about the tall sons in the mining town or the old lady who sat under the grape arbor. His wife told him one day that his mother had died, but he went on reading the paper. When he had finished with the news of the day, he would go into the tiny bedroom, undress, get into bed, and move over to the wall, with his back to the open door and eventually to his wife as she lay beside him. He did not intend to be unkind; he just seemed to have nothing to say.

Now and then the two families would exchange visits, at Christmas or Thanksgiving. Then Will Humbles would make feeble attempts to join in the general conversation and once or twice talked for a while about the mining town and the farm and the horses. But he would soon lapse into moody silence and look for a corner apart, where he could be alone with his pipe and his spectacles and the newspaper, even if he had already read it from front page to back.

Withdrawn thus from any social obligations to his present

life, he asked only to be left alone. His wife seemed to feel no loss whatsoever. Her many lodge and church-society activities occupied every spare moment free from household duties, and the proximity to her sister and to her niece and nephew, both of whom were as dear to her as though they had been her own, filled any emotional needs left unsatisfied by the church. Before the end of her first year in the Town, Mayme Humbles had cause to be grateful for her husband's indifference to his immediate surroundings and for his complete delegation of authority to her.

The Studebaker started an epidemic of automobile buying among Annette Dunham's friends. Dr. Williams invested in a new Ford sedan; this was justifiable, because his practice had increased to such a point that it was almost impossible for him to make all his visits on foot and by streetcar. And Agatha Carrington felt that because she supplemented her husband's income she was entitled to certain luxuries: the first week in August she bought a new Nash. It was silver-gray, with solid metal wheels instead of wooden-spoked ones like the Studebaker. She let the girl drive it once or twice, and then the week before school opened, in one of the sudden bursts of frivolity and generosity that endeared her to her friends, she invited the girl and her mother to drive with her to Alton, Illinois, and across the river to St. Louis.

The journey—a confusion of endless highway through prairie and farmland, with now and then a small, summer-lazy Midwest town—delighted the girl. They stopped at a park in one of the towns to rest and eat from Agatha's picnic hamper and enjoy their first glimpse of the Mississippi. Afterward they made a slight detour so as to visit the state tourist attraction called Starved Rock; and the mother explained, from the top of the ravine through which the river flowed, how an Indian maiden had thrown herself into the depths rather than be taken prisoner by her pursuers. Later they crossed more bridges, and then the highway ran for a while beside the now slow-moving, muddy Mississippi, on which the children of Annie and Edward Poindexter had skated when they were young, when the river, free of waste oils and refuse from the factories, had frozen solid every winter.

The three travelers arrived in St. Louis after dark, driving head on into the exotic, exciting sounds and smells of Chouteau Street, which was filled with a kind of Negro laughter that the girl did not remember from the City. At Agatha's suggestion they stopped at a lamp-lighted fish vender's stand, around which casually dressed men and women lounged with collars open, their ebony and mahogany and pale yellow shoulders bare in the hot breeze stirring from the river, looking down into the time-blackened kettles of floating, sizzling catfish chunks, waiting their turn, and all the while fingering a ten-cent piece or jingling a nickel and a dime for a double order.

Everybody on the street watched the strangers in the new Nash, and the good-looking Agatha Carrington fluffed her red-brown hair without knowing it and matched stare for stare and lit a cigarette; but Annette Dunham looked straight ahead and wished that they would hurry up with the order and that if Agatha just *had* to smoke cigarettes, she wouldn't in public, especially not *here*. She took personal offense at the decline of Chouteau Street, which had always had a bad reputation, but which had certainly suffered terribly from the influx of southern Negroes since her own young girlhood. She wished that they would wear more clothes and not stare so impudently, and regretted that she had agreed to Agatha's suggestion that they cross over the river into St. Louis and pass through Chouteau Street and try some of its famous fried fish before ending the journey at Alton.

The girl crossed both arms on the open window of the car and leaned her face as far into the street as she could and thought that she had never before seen in people such abandon and naked joy and fullness of meaning, just in standing and looking and listening and waiting for catfish and in enjoying whatever soft creole humor they were passing back and forth about the three foreigners, who belonged to them in a way though they didn't belong *here*. They could pause here, but they were to be pitied and joked about quietly, and they should take their catfish sandwiches and drive off in their new-looking automobile, which marked them for outsiders by its hard top and conservative color and modest trade mark, as opposed to the automobiles that really sent a thrill up local spines and stirred envy in local hearts—the outlandish, handed-down, open-topped, flashily upholstered, noisy-motored, vivid-colored vehicles in which big-time gamblers and politicians paraded the district on Saturday nights and Sunday afternoons: Chouteau Street's own kind, who had made good and who showed it in a way Chouteau Street understood, with a lot of gold teeth and hair made slick by straightening combs and pulling irons and gleaming with Madame Walker's pomade; and with diamond stickpins and pointed yellow shoes with mirrors in the toes and broad-striped suits and shirts, their women carrying organdy parasols of all colors and wearing many finger rings and necklaces of big glass beads and pastel-shaded silk stockings and dresses cut low over high, cone-shaped bosoms, which their companion would more than likely be fondling shamelessly as they drove at a snail's pace through the heady kaleidoscope of poverty, ready money, moonshine, dice-rolling, poker playing, laughter, razor melees, bawdiness, music, and ecstasy—before going away into their half-life, their sheltered middle-class, tree-shaded, left-over mansions, to continue playing at something they weren't, becoming dimmer and dimmer likenesses of what they should have been and, instead of getting stronger and clearer and more absolute in themselves as people, picking up life-draining habits from the great middle class that they imitated, losing in the process all of the ancient, life-giving ones.

Many of these things Katherine Dunham saw later on other visits. This night she felt deeply stirred by the multiple raw potentialities; and the music that drifted out from every doorway as they drove away toward the bridge followed her and struck so far down into a substance that had never stirred or made itself known before that now, at this moment, began a possession by the blues, a total immersion in the baptismal font of the Race. This music would sometime be her only tie to these people. Deeper than prayer and closer to the meaning of life than anything else—work-roughened, broken-nailed fingers on an untuned piano, a whisky-ruined voice coming out of a mouth filled with remnants of teeth alternating with gold inlays, a head bowed over a steel guitar, or a wet face turned up to the smoky ceiling of a jam-packed, closet-sized room behind a sawdust-floored, spittoon-dotted bar; eyes open or shut, it didn't matter, just so they turned inward, way, way inward, deep into something people are supposed to know about and don't look at, or knew a long time ago and lost touch with. Single road to freedom.

She ate catfish as they left Chouteau Street and crossed the placid, river-smelling Mississippi into the sleeping hills of Alton. She ate eagerly, and the fried fish seemed more savory than anything she had ever tasted or ever would taste again. She felt at peace eating the food of these people they were leaving behind, whose rhythm and feel had entered her body as nothing else had, making her one with them. The piece of catfish assumed the proportions of the first ritualized sacrificial food of the initiate, dedicated through blood for life.

They drove back through a summer melancholy with the oncoming fall, and a few mornings later, after lingering over toothbrushing and hair combing longer than necessary to cover an uncontrollable, gnawing panic, the girl reluctantly dressed, sorrowfully ate a bowl of oatmeal, and set out for her first year in high school, positive that she would lose her way. She felt a great sense of inadequacy and imagined herself to be the only one, among all of those others approaching the dreaded sanctuary like so many purposeful ants, who would be incapable of finding her way to the building and through the mock-Gothic portals to the auditorium.

Eight
The Piano Lessons

*

Katherine Dunham had taken her first piano lessons at the age of eleven. Her father had driven her to the house of a customer who lived on the West Side, a woman of Polish descent named Cusak. After a few visits Mrs. Cusak decided that it would be more expedient for her to come to her pupil, and she would arrive regularly each week in the flat above the cleaning shop, place her wristwatch at the end of the keyboard, open her brief case, extract a staff notebook and sheets of music—and then listen, watch, nod, frown, and write exercises for the girl to copy. Ten minutes before the lesson ended, she would exchange places with the girl, adjust the piano bench, wipe the palms of her hands and tips of her fingers on a lace-bordered handkerchief, and attack the piano in a display of virtuosity that barely concealed her secret desires. At the end of this impromptu concert, she would sigh, pat the girl on the head, give a word or two of encouragement or admonishment, and depart.

At first the lessons were no chore at all. With little practice the girl satisfied her teacher and pleased her watchful father. But when she entered high school, Albert Dunham set a practice schedule so inflexible that every after-school activity not required for credits had to be humbly petitioned for, and even a five-minute delay in her return from school brought on endless questioning and explanation.

She was bitter at having to spend the first hour and a half alone in the flat, where in an emptiness that seemed eerie to her she would fall prey once again to the kind of terror that had haunted her years ago—although the unnamable hobgoblins with which her imagination populated every corner were no longer called "Crandalls," being closer akin to images evoked by Dr. Fu Manchu or Tarzan's apes. Her resentment of the whole ordeal soon turned to an active hatred of the piano and a stubborn resistance to her father's musical ambitions.

To solve the problem of space in the back room, Albert Dunham had fastened two pipes to the ceiling, and on these he hung finished clothing. To lift the clothing into place, he had attached a hook to the end of a long pole, and with this same pole he let his daughter know that he was aware of every wrong note, every overlong pause, every lapse in technique and memory. Sometimes, quaking at an unnatural sound from the old boards of the building, she would risk the next note and turn her head to see if any unearthly creature had actually become manifest; and before she could find her place again, the racket would begin in the kitchen—her father pounding on the ceiling of the shop's back room to remind her of his vigilance. Argus-eyed, he seemed to see through the ceiling and into the front room where she might have taken a few moments' respite, drawn into herself in misery, turned about on the bench to face squarely whatever terrors the room might hold, so that the chill at the nape of her neck and her tense back muscles would relax; but the furious pounding of the pole would send her swiftly back to arpeggios or Mendelssohn's "Spring Song" or "The Wedding of the Winds," for which she had special antagonisms. And she would glance in agony at the clock on top of the piano, which never moved as slowly as when she was on this particular torture rack.

Before evening service at Brown's Chapel had become an

inflexible pattern, Albert Dunham had often devoted Sunday nights to music. Perhaps he was trying to recapture the lamp-lit Glen Ellyn Sundays or times before that when he played for parties in City mansions and dreamed of an orchestra of his own. With his daughter at the piano, his son at the mandolin, and himself at the guitar or mandolin, he seemed to recapture some of the contentment of the early days of his first marriage. The trouble was that his ambitions led him to excessive demands.

He discovered that Dr. Williams had at one time played a violin, and it was not long before the doctor joined the Sunday night musicales. On these occasions the mother and her friend sat on one side, enjoying the music or talking of study-club news or comparing recipes. The brother seemed never to make a mistake, but the girl was forever in trouble. Sometimes, from the corner of her eye, she would see her brother look up quickly from his music stand and know that she was in the wrong place. Her father might be absorbed enough in his own playing for her to scurry to recover herself; but if she was hopelessly lost, she would fall into a cold sweat of apprehension and play more wretchedly than ever. Then her father would stop the others, thread his tortoise-shell pick carefully through the strings of his instrument, and slap her across whichever side of her face happened to be nearest. The notes danced through tears, and she would bite her lips to keep the guests from seeing their uncontrollable quivering. Most of the time she would have to be excused at least once in order to put cold water on her face and blow her nose and dry her eyes and breathe deeply in the kitchen before returning to the piano bench. The doctor made no attempt to conceal his disapproval, and whether for this reason or because of a growing responsibility toward the Brown's Chapel choir, he and his wife were present at fewer and fewer of these evenings, and the quartet once again became a trio.

The girl dreaded these evenings and showed it. Her

brother chafed under them, but with his characteristic self-control doggedly plucked his mandolin—an instrument particularly odious to him because the year before, under a friendly music instructor, he had begun lessons at school on the cello and rehearsed whenever possible with the teacher, who played the viola, and with two classmates who played the violin. His ambition was to own his own instrument, but his savings were still not sufficient; and Albert Dunham, whenever he was approached for the balance, flew into a rage, immediately concluding that the boy felt the mandolin beneath his dignity and had chosen the cello to show up his father's bad taste. So he relentlessly pursued the mandolin practice and the Sunday-evening concerts, as though exacting penance from his son or further proving his own dominance.

Shortly after the New Year, Annette Dunham's mother, Anna Poindexter, moved from her native Alton to the town where her two surviving daughters lived. Mayme Humbles rearranged her cottage to accommodate her mother in the one bedroom and exchanged the couch in the living room for a folding davenport bed, on which she and her husband slept. To take some of the burden from her sister and to occupy the old lady, the girl's mother arranged that she should visit Bluff Street every afternoon. The old lady would stay for the evening meal and then, leaning at times more heavily than seemed necessary on the shoulders of her son-in-law and grandson, descend to the delivery wagon, enter it only after numerous dramatic attempts, and be driven back to Mayme Humbles'. Sometimes her acid humor and biting remarks would rankle with the father, who for the most part tolerated her only because he could see no alternative. Often he would rise from the table at the end of a meal in such a black mood that no one dared ask him to assist in her departure. Then mother and daughter would take one side, brother the other, and, with the old lady clutching her walking stick because she didn't trust their puny strength, they all inched their way down the steps and into the truck.

The grandmother's daily visits were welcome to the girl in spite of the friction that mounted between her parents. The steady creaking of the rocking chair behind her at her piano practice was comforting; and after practice, as she went about her household chores, she would find occasion to pass the rocking chair again and again for further installments of the old lady's account of her courtship in the Illinois backwoods more than a century before. If it were wintertime, a young girl might very well greet her suitor from under blankets, fully dressed. The young man would also climb under the covers, and with a plank between them, the two would exchange trivialities, blushing and holding hands across the barrier, while a vigilant father smoked a pipe beside a log fire and a sharp-eyed mother cross-stitched the very quilt that would some day belong to the girl.

The significance of many of the old lady's confidences escaped the girl: life at that far-off time—revolving around strange and mixed blood relationships, around relatives fleeing the South and stories told Anna Poindexter by *her* grandmother—become a confusion of Choctaw and African mythology and heroic escapades riding sidesaddle on a horse; but it seemed much more real than the present, which daily became more complex and burdensome.

The anecdote Anna Poindexter enjoyed relating more than any other concerned her wedding night: how she was totally ignorant of the fact that the same young man who had courted her fully clothed and on the other side of a wooden plank would expect after marriage to sleep by her side unhampered and unchaperoned, both of them clad in nightshifts! As she reached the climax of her tale, the old lady would lean far forward in the rocking chair, clinging to both armrests as though to rise up in emphasis.

"Ed Poindexter never did see me *once* without my clothes

on! No sir-ee! Not *once* in the whole twenty-six years we were married!" And she would settle back and rock rapidly for a few moments, as though congratulating herself.

"But, Grandma," the girl would say, sometimes sitting at her feet, with books and papers spread before her in case the downstairs door should suddenly slam and footsteps mounting the stairs interrupt these informative sessions, "how on earth did you go to bed for *twenty-six years* and get your nightgown on and off without him ever *seeing* you! And didn't you ever wear a *bathing suit?* And didn't he even see you in your *nightgown?*"

The old lady would settle back in her chair, cackling salaciously at her twenty-six years of ingenuity. "Twenty-six years an' three days, and thirteen children! An' never once, mind you, did Ed Poindexter ever see me *even in a nightshirt!*"

"Well, I don't know," the girl would often answer dubiously. "Mother goes to the bathroom in her nightgown without her bathrobe sometimes if it's hot and the lights are off. And I'm *sure* Papa must see her. I shouldn't think *that* would matter!"

"Not once," the old lady would keep repeating, rocking vigorously. Usually a pinch of snuff would end that particular installment.

Finally the music teacher, puzzled at the plateau from which her pupil advanced not an inch, gave up in disgust, and Albert Dunham was not averse to saving the money spent on the lessons. The after-school practice continued, but as a monotonous repetition of music already learned; each time the girl tried to go a step further and memorize the familiar pieces, the retentive section of her brain closed tightly, and she would sit hour after hour, day after day, listlessly repeating the same notes but unable to go beyond the first page unless the music was before her. Her mind would wander to dancing class, to basketball practice, and to the coming spring track events.

Altercations between her parents because of her grandmother's presence resulted in fewer and fewer visits from the old lady, and by early spring they had ceased altogether, except on special occasions. The mother, never a good loser, took even more umbrage than usual in this instance, and the father's references to his mother-in-law's hearty appetite caused heated arguments long after his victory had been won.

And the girl resumed her after-school practice alone in the flat.

Once each semester a high-school organization grandly entitled the Terpsichorean Club gave a recital under the direction of Miss Phoebe Ann Kirby, head of the physical education department. This year the important event took place in mid-spring. Katherine Dunham, among other extras, was an eager wood nymph, a willing tree, and an obliging scarf bearer. When she wasn't fulfilling one of these functions, she stood at the side of the stage, following, enraptured, the performance of the soloists. One girl in particular enchanted her. She had often seen her practicing at the ballet bar of the smaller gymnasium or pirouetting into the center of the floor on the tips of toes encased in pink satin slippers. On the night of the recital she performed with Phoebe Ann Kirby a *pas de deux,* which was listed on the program as a tarantella. Then she appeared in breathtaking splendor as a Russian princess, wearing a white fur hat, a skirt made of layer upon layer of white satin and tarlatan, a red satin jacket, and, most dazzling of all, white kid boots reaching to just below her bare dimpled knees. There was applause as she leaped into the center of the stage to strike a pose, then further applause and an excited buzzing from the auditorium when she had finished leaping, twirling, and thrusting first one leg and then the other forward from a squatting position with her arms folded. The program listed this *pièce de résistance* as the *hopak.*

Katherine Dunham became obsessed with the determination to learn or at least approximate this particular dance. With difficulty she persuaded her parents to allow her alternate evenings after school to attend special dance classes and, before the semester ended, was permitted to enter the group from which selections for the Terpsichorean Club would be made the following term. She rolled on the floor, ran in circles with other panting, eager-eyed aspirants, and waved her arms in a figure-eight design to the chiming of a gong and the thumping of a tom-tom. She practiced special techniques for sitting, falling, jumping, leaping, and stretching. But in none of this was there a hint of the *hopak.* Once she questioned Miss Kirby about ballet lessons, but was told that these were not a part of the school curriculum. So all she could do was to reconstruct in her mind's eye the vision that had appeared at the recital.

In order to raise money for a new parish house, the elders of Brown's Chapel, aided by such stanch supporters as Annette Dunham and the doctor's wife, decided upon a program of concerts, recitals, lectures, revival meetings, summer picnics, bazaars, fashion shows, contests, and individual pledges. With her mother the girl attended one of the rallies at which these projects were discussed. It was an inspiring occasion. Mrs. McDonald and the Carrington girls and Ethel Donnelley presented plans for a fashion show, with dresses to be solicited from local tradespeople and later auctioned off. Thalia Dishman offered to organize a pit barbecue; Mr. Ivory, a chitterling supper; Mrs. Maddox, a fish fry. Dr. Williams pledged one hundred dollars before the year was out.

The girl sat rapt, envisaging the clothes she would model

at the fashion show, tasting already the smoky barbecue from Thalia Dishman's pit in Manningdale, seeing herself at Bush Park, passing out paper plates bending under the weight of fried chicken, potato salad, candied sweet potatoes, corn pudding, baked ham, and deviled eggs.

At the headiest moment she raised her hand. "I would like to organize a cabaret party," she said.

There was a stunned silence from the few present who had some notion what a cabaret was; from the others there were smiles and nods of indulgent approval. Annette Dunham fell somewhere between the two groups. She had seen cabarets depicted on the screen, and from this her impression was dubious; on the other hand, knowing how limited her daughter's worldly experience was, she could imagine nothing harmful in what she might suggest.

The girl herself could have tracked her idea to its source. . . .

Once or twice a year Albert Dunham would put on his dark blue suit and pick out his best tie and carefully brush his gray felt hat over steam. Then, with the disapproval of his wife pursuing them even after they were seated on the train, he would escort his daughter to the City, where for a few hours he would pay formal visits to old friends, to his sister Lulu, and to the family of his former wife. After the first year the son was not invited to join these expeditions; to the girl they seemed a betrayal of Annette Dunham, and even in her Sunday best she felt awkward and out of her element when visiting her niece and nephew.

There were always gathered at the Weir flat on Sunday afternoons the sons and daughters of people who claimed to be "society." Their fathers were lawyers, doctors, or businessmen influential in politics; their mothers were schoolteachers or, like their counterparts in the society that they worked so hard to emulate, ladies of leisure who spent the day at club meetings and bridge parties or on shopping sprees and beauty treatments, which in their case consisted mostly of skin-bleaching applications aimed at realizing their ambition to "pass."

The sons and daughters of these people, like the Weir children, specialized in a code language of smart sayings, repartee, and a running banter. They looked down their patrician noses at anyone darker than a caramel or with hair that hinted at any attention from the beauty parlors of Madame Walker or her competitor, the Poro hair-straightening system; they talked of the Sunset and Dreamland ballrooms and of Erskine Tate's band at the Vendome; they played a running bass accompaniment on the piano to verses with thinly veiled double meanings. And they tried to outdo each other in first-hand accounts of cabaret parties. And the girl, sitting uncomfortably in a corner, was deeply impressed.

Once she had committed herself to organizing a cabaret party for Brown's Chapel, there was no turning back. Her impression of cabarets was that they were frequented for the dual purposes of nourishment and entertainment; such an event should afford a golden opportunity to fatten the church coffers. Her parents tried to dissuade her from her dream of one thousand dollars, but in other ways, infected in spite of themselves by her enthusiasm, they offered invaluable help. Her father secured the hall under lease to the Brotherhood of Elks and persuaded its treasurer to wait until the performance for the rental fee of ten dollars. His artistic instincts again aroused, he also agreed to take part in the vocal group and sing his favorite solo, "Asleep in the Deep." Her mother, perhaps realizing the girl's disappointment at not having played a larger part in the school recital, offered to help with the costumes.

Most important, of course, was the Russian costume; but to the girl's vexation the skirts were of cotton instead of gleaming satin, the hat was of felt rather than fur, and the boots were white canvas leggings fastened over last year's white summer pumps. But the demands of her first experience as impresario, producer, star, and director were so multiple and complex that she had little time to sorrow over such inadequacies.

Mrs. McDonald, wife of a local chiropodist, had been a star performer in a theatrical company that toured the country following in the pioneering footsteps of Williams and Walker. She joined forces wholeheartedly with the aspiring young producer and delved into her camphor-scented trunks to bring forth her version of the tightly corseted dresses of the Floradora girls, topped off with a mauve-colored velvet hat, rakishly tilted, from whose wide brim flowed a sweeping ostrich plume.

Because of her conversations long ago with the old woman at the top of the cliff, the girl felt quite at home with the former Floradora soubrette's suggestions; the afternoons she had long ago spent at the Monogram Theatre moved out of an almost forgotten dream world into sharp reality; and she drew as generously on this folk material as on the school recital, the Terpsichorean Club rehearsals, and scenes from movies. The score of *Dahomey* and selections from the recent musical, *Shuffle Along,* also emerged from Mrs. McDonald's trunks and were passed into the capable hands of Ethel Fuqua, who was still organist at Brown's Chapel. And partisanship was forgotten, and recruits were called in from the First and Second Baptist churches.

Among her other duties, Katherine Dunham was to act as Mistress of Ceremonies, welcoming one and all to the "Blue Moon Café" in verses written by herself. She was also to introduce each number in verse, to accompany her father's vocal solo on the piano, to sing "Dardanella," and to perform an Oriental dance (to Grieg), which she had reconstructed from a picture of a Turkish maiden on the cover of a pulp magazine and her recollections of Theda Bara as Salome. As if this were not enough, she would lead a chorus in the cakewalk, join the Floradora trio in "Tell Me

Pretty Maiden," and, as a grand climax to the entertainment, appear as the whirling, leaping Russian princess of her dreams.

Neither the producer nor her assistant had reckoned on the time lapses for changing costumes necessitated by this ambitious schedule; but Providence intervened and saved the girl from attempting the impossible. On the day of the performance, excitement and nervous anticipation and overwork kept her in bed with a dangerously high temperature. Her parents insisted that she bypass the dress rehearsal, but she wept so bitterly that they finally gave in. As she stepped onto the floor space allotted for the entertainment and opened her mouth to recite the welcoming verse, not one sound came out. She had completely and totally lost her voice.

So the first fruits of stardom were bitter. Dr. Williams hurried over from his office, peered into her throat, and shook his head, as he had on his first visits to the back room of the shop. But he laughed heartily at her tears. To her it was the end of the world, the collapse of a beautiful dream, and it took some minutes of solicitous attention from the program and refreshment committees to persuade her that the show could still go on, herself with it.

The doctor dug in his satchel for the white powders; Mrs. Williams copied the Mistress of Ceremonies' verses, and Mrs. McDonald offered to read them; "Dardanella" was deleted, leaving only "Anitra's Dance," the cakewalk, and the Russian dance; and the Floradora unit was reduced by one. Otherwise the program would remain as planned.

Voiceless and flushed with fever, the girl helped the refreshment committee to unpack sandwiches and put cases of soda pop into tubs of ice, and the ticket committee to count reports. Later she watched fascinated in the mirror as Mrs. McDonald, perspiring in her unaccustomed corset, arched and extended her somewhat skimpy eyebrows, rouged her cheeks and mouth and eyelids with magenta, patted a pink powder over the whole, and gave her costumes a nervous final examination. An hour before the announced beginning of the performance, the girl was dressed as Anitra, clutching her cotton veils about her to keep from shaking, although the night was unseasonably warm.

When she saw the first guests arrive, look curiously at the decorations, and sit at ringside tables, her heart plunged to her feet and she wanted to run away. Presently she forced herself to stop peering through the black sateen curtain separating the backstage region from the hall, and sat in a corner bathed in perspiration and alternately flushed and chilled, until her mother came to tell her that it was already late and that every seat in the Blue Moon Café was occupied. Unable to function as stage manager because of her voicelessness, she could only sit anticipating her own appearance, feeling more like a prisoner awaiting sentence than the star of the evening. Finally the moment could be put off no longer. The lights were lowered, Mrs. McDonald read the opening verses, Ethel Fuqua played selections from *Shuffle Along,* the vocal group sang "Under the Bamboo Tree" from *Dahomey,* and the trembling Anitra found her way through the backdrop and into the center of the floor, where all the past rehearsing and all her bravado melted away, leaving only cold terror.

She didn't hear the applause on her entrance, scarcely heard the music, forgot her planned routine, blushed painfully in sudden lucid moments when she was aware of crassly amateurish improvisation, ended somehow with the music, and went out through the black curtains, again oblivious to applause and more dead than alive.

The subsequent numbers were never, in retrospect, clear to her. There was an intermission, during which Annette Dunham convinced her husband that the girl could not accompany his solo and persuaded him to accept Ethel Fuqua as substitute. But when she suggested that the cakewalk and the Russian dance be eliminated from the program, she met with stubborn though voiceless opposition.

The Russian dance in fact proved to be the hit of the evening and was repeated by popular demand. The girl, by now seriously ill, leaped and twirled the second time on energy borrowed from the enthusiasm of the audience. She bumped into a ringside table at the end of one dizzy gyration, lost a white legging in another, and, when she found that she couldn't manage the allotted number of knee squats, ended as best she could and fumbled her way through the backdrop, only to be led forth by the transported Mrs. McDonald to share a bouquet of flowers presented to the two leading ladies by the program committee.

She went immediately home and to bed, although the Blue Moon continued with dancing for all in true cabaret style. Some of the elders of the church, who had tolerated the idea of the entertainment, drew the line at public dancing in the name of the Lord and left in a huff; but they were somewhat appeased by the financial report at the committee meeting a week later. The net profit was seventy-six dollars, and, in view of the facts that tickets had cost twenty-five cents and that the capacity of the hall was limited to four hundred persons, the Blue Moon cabaret party was considered an outstanding success. But it also gave rise to a coolness between the more conservative older faction of Brown's Chapel and a progressive younger faction; the chill intensified because of numerous other disagreements within the church body; and the final result was a schism that some years later removed the progressive element once and for all.

Albert Dunham, the son, was never without friends. He was never lonely or fretful like his sister, because loneliness presupposes demands on others, and he made no such demands. He was pleasant, dryly witty, quiet, wise, and modest. He was also never lonely because the world of books was the world in which he believed, and with unerring taste he attached himself to the comet tails of the great, the wise, the tolerant, the thoughtful. He was one of those rare people born into philosophy, and scholarship came to him far more naturally than the usual forms of social intercourse. This was by no means to say that he did not know how to play, to tease, to enjoy the play of others; and during his first and second high-school years, he had shown a real aptitude for athletics, excelling particularly in track and field sports. An excursion into football, however, lasted for only one semester and was replaced by his fervent application to the cello.

His winning personality and intellectual brilliance created acute discomfort among the bigoted element of the Town, which was now suffering in a mild form an inundation of illiterate Negro job seekers from the South such as had precipitated the race riots in the City a few years ealier. What could once have been indulgently overlooked as childhood camaraderie grew, in the boy's last years of high school and his first year at junior college, into steadfast friendships that overrode all artificial class distinctions. The sons and daughters of the "best families" of the Town gravitated into his orbit with unself-conscious ease, so that his nomination for presidency of the senior class, one year before his sister entered high school, surprised only those who refused to take either his intelligence or his popularity seriously. He had won the class election and ended the year in his usual position at the top of the class; but the victory was marred when the scroll of honor students placed each year in the lobby of the school building was defaced by the crude blotting-out of Albert Dunham's name.

The girl had learned about this when she had overheard her brother unsuccessfully trying to dissuade his mother from paying a visit to the principal of the high school. She asked no questions about the outcome, but she knew that

Annette Dunham went out one day with fire in her eyes and returned triumphant. After the girl entered high school herself, she never passed the honor-roll plaque without feeling a tremor of uneasiness, remembering the unkindness toward her brother, whose mild disposition she could never imagine evoking anything but respect.

Then, after the boy entered the Town's junior college, he was one of three students nominated for the presidency of the first-year class there. And the girl sat listening while he told their mother his reasons for having already definitely decided to leave the college the following year and go directly to the University in the City.

At the class nominations a student whom he'd had no reason until now to suspect as unfriendly had asked permission to address the class. In a dissertation the more shocking because it had obviously been prepared, this student had prophesied for his classmates their humiliation in front of other schools if a student of Albert Dunham's racial heritage, no matter how brilliant or how likable, were to be elected two successive years to a class presidency. His having been president of the high-school senior class and valedictorian, too (here some protests from a few not too stunned to answer: scholarship should not be confused with popularity!), was sufficient evidence of the good will of his classmates and the progressive attitude of the school. But, after all, there were limits. Just extend this thing in theory as far as the presidency of the United States! As much as they all liked and respected Albert Dunham, he must not be elected.

It was Mary Barr, daughter of a state senator, who first found her tongue and asked for the floor. She reminded the class of the precepts of democracy and warned them of the dangers of bigotry. In the ensuing heated discussion the boy was forced to confront certain realities of which he had been aware, but somehow only in an abstract or theoretical way, so that they had not seemed to affect him personally. For the first stunned minutes he saw friends turn to enemies and casual acquaintances rise to what amounted to heroism. In the heat of the crisis he offered to withdraw his name, and he remained adamant over the protests of those to whom the issue had passed the personal; so the election continued halfheartedly, with only two of the original three candidates.

An unhappy bystander on this occasion, the girl was soon to encounter some of the same humiliations.

The high school had at this time two music teachers, one presiding over the orchestra, the other over the band. And the band director was the antithesis of the man who had encouraged Albert Dunham, Jr., to study the cello and play in the string quartet. As though charged with a sacred responsibility, he carefully weeded out from among his students all possible non-Aryan elements, his particular anathema being personified in the two Dunham children. Four years ago he had seen to it that the boy was enrolled in his colleague's class. Now he was faced with the problem of Katherine Dunham.

He seemed to feel a particular nostalgia for old American songs, particularly those dwelling upon the scenes of his native South. When she encountered "Old Black Joe," "My Old Kentucky Home," "Swanee River," and others, the girl felt self-conscious because of their evocation of a stereotype that she vaguely felt had something to do with herself—chiefly because of the teacher's satisfaction at her discomfort and the pointed way he had of focusing his attention on her when he conducted such songs.

And then he hit upon a new selection. The wonder was that he had overlooked it for so long. The girl found herself listening to the rest of the class sing about the exploits of a traveler who "jumped on a nigger" in order to cross a river because he mistook the Negro for a horse. Her astonishment at seeing such a word in print turned to consternation as she realized that she, too, was expected to sing the song, which was broken down into two parts: her part was alto, and there was only one other alto. The indignation of the past months suddenly took form, and her distress turned to stubborn anger. The shrill soprano voices of the girls took the lead, and the uncertain voices of the boys followed, wavering from tenor into baritone and bass. The music teacher, beaming with the excitement of victory, pointed his baton at the altos—but only one responded. Katherine Dunham sat tight-lipped while the teacher struck the guiding chord again on the piano, this time impatiently.

"Altos!" he said imperiously, eying the girl as though he had just discovered in her the signs of leprosy. "I don't hear the altos!"

The youthful voices began again:

> "Went to a river and I couldn't get across,
> Sing Polly-wolly Doodle all the day,
> Jumped on a nigger 'cause I thought he was a hoss
> Sing Polly-wolly Doodle all the day!"

This time the second alto, completely unaware of the drama, but intimidated by some undefinable tension in the air, swallowed in the wrong place and emitted a belch. The class broke into titters and giggles which for some reason made the instructor, as he rapped on the edge of the piano and glared through rimless glasses, a ridiculous figure. The finishing bell saved the situation, and the girl filed from the room exchanging with the teacher a stare as venomous as his.

Again Annette Dunham dressed in her Sunday best and visited the principal of the school. This time she was not so readily the victor. While the school board procrastinated, pressured on one side by the bandleader's threat of resignation and on the other by Annette Dunham's undoubted influence in the community and willingness to use that influence to the extreme, the girl sat in the music class and refused to open her mouth for "Polly-wolly Doodle" or any of the other selections. It was as though her decision had given her jaws of steel.

For a while it seemed that the term would end with the two factions in a deadlock. Then one day Annette Dunham again returned victorious from the principal's office. She had taken with her a petition signed by the most prominent citizens of the Town, all of them good customers of the West Side Cleaners and Dyers. Her husband, as incensed as she by the music teacher's effrontery, had secured most of the signatures as he made his rounds of deliveries; in addition, he had lined up a sizable roster of leading civic organizations only too willing to lend support to a cause that might result in vote getting. The combined forces swayed the evasive principal, and by the end of the term it was definitely decided that the offending book would be removed and the bandleader confined to John Philip Sousa, where he was at his best anyway.

Nine
The White Canvas Shoes

*

The summer was the hottest on record. The only relief came at night, when a slight breeze from the river wafted across the canal, bringing with it the familiar sewage odors intensified by the day's heat. The buildings on the west side of Bluff Street suffered most: backed up against the cliff, they received no crosscurrent of air. The father stood at the pressing machine bathed in sweat, his temper shortening with the rise in temperature. Each day the mother seemed more drawn and tired, and the unpleasantness between the parents was so marked that the girl sought any escape from the shop.

Though summer was normally an off season, business flourished at the West Side Cleaners and Dyers. A hired girl named Allegretta helped in the flat on Saturdays, and with her Katherine Dunham was almost entirely in charge of house cleaning and took more and more responsibility for the preparation of meals. Annette Dunham worked in the shop from early morning until late at night, as she reminded her husband when her refusal to let him invest in new machinery and real estate drove him to smoldering wrath and then open abuse.

The girl visited her Aunt Mayme and the doctor's wife as frequently as possible and took again her favorite walk to the locks; she felt too grown up to climb the cliff. Her brother went grimly about his work and studied between times for a special examination that might win him a scholarship to the University. But this was never mentioned.

Fear was familiar to the girl, but most of the time it had been fear of the unknown—the felt and sensed but not seen. This summer she entered into a new consideration of fear—the same kind that she had known once before when the man with his face cut open so that his teeth showed had stopped at the automobile in which she sat waiting on a hot Sunday afternoon in the City. But now this fear was of violence that stemmed from the very roots of her being, from the very core of her own family.

She lay sleepless at night, straining to hear sounds from behind the closed door across the living room, but also afraid to hear them because of what she would learn. On the hottest nights the door would be left open; and still, relentlessly, with no consideration for the boy on the couch in the dining room or the girl in her alcove, her parents would turn against each other, accusing, reproaching, vilifying, disparaging, one vituperation mounting upon another until they ended in stifling sobs from the mother or in the flight of Albert Dunham: half-dressed, he would fling doors open and slam them behind him and finish the night in the delivery truck or stretched out on a table in the back of the shop. Once the girl was certain that she heard blows struck and was afraid to look at her mother in the morning.

The climax of these arguments came on a night when she had fallen into a restless sleep of exhaustion. She awoke with a premonition of more serious trouble than usual and turned and twisted on the narrow bed, trying not to hear the voices and the more ominous sounds from the room facing her. After listening to an unmistakable struggle in which her father seemed to be attempting to eject his wife forcibly from the bedroom, the girl slipped out of bed and went to stand in the center of the living room. The only light was from the dim street lamp, but she could see her mother in her white nightgown, clinging to the frame of the door as her father pushed and dragged, striking her in his fury, cursing in his repeated threats to rid himself of her presence.

The girl heard the cries for help, but was unable to move. She began to think about Mrs. McGuire when her husband had come home drunk on Saturday nights and beaten her; she thought, too, that this must be what it was like to be dead, to have terrible things happening and not be able to move or do anything. Once she tried to reach out to her mother, but even her arm refused to obey her will. Then a light went on, and something changed in her mother. She looked wild with one kind of fear at one minute, then suddenly just as wild but with another kind of fear, this one more real. And the girl heard her brother's name and saw that he had stepped to her side.

"Stop it!" he said, but her mother kept calling her brother's name and saying, "Albert! Don't. Don't. He's your father!" The girl hardly had to turn at all to see her brother, and she looked with curiosity at the gun that he had pointed at his father, who stood with his mouth wide-open, that surprised, young-boy look on his face, which had been black and swollen with rage a second before.

"That isn't my BB gun," the girl thought. "He should be careful with that. It's his twenty-two."

"Stop it," her brother said again, and his voice was so quiet that it hung in the middle of the air between the four of them, not going anywhere, but hanging there like a sign that said just where to go—to turn right or left or stop.

"Put that gun down," her father said.

"I'll put it down all right," her brother said. "Oh, yes. I'll put it down. But if you touch her again, I'll kill you. I mean it." And he didn't put the gun down. He continued to look at his father, who still stood in the doorway of the bedroom.

Forgetting all of a sudden what had gone before and why the boy had come from the dining room in his wrinkled gray-and-blue-striped pajamas, pointing the rifle at his father, his face ash-colored and with dark circles under his eyes because he couldn't possibly sleep enough with so much hate and unrest all around—Annette Dunham tried ineffectually to shield her husband. Her hair had come unbraided during the struggle, and her eyes rolled wildly, and though she really was reacting in the only way she could, it seemed to the girl illogical after the soul-sickening cries for help and the obvious brutality of her mistreatment. After having dragged the boy into it by calling for him, she kept saying over and over in the tone of voice she always used when things happened that could never happen to her, "Albert, Albert, he's your *father!*"

The boy looked at her pityingly, wearily, as though to ask when she would ever understand, how it was that she refused to understand in spite of all their hours of confidences. He turned and went into the dining room, the gun at his side pointing downward, looking spent as though it had been used. The other three stood where they were; then the sister turned numbly to the room where her brother had gone.

"Which is the one?" she thought. "Which is the one with the bent knife, the razor in his hand? Who is doing this? Who is making everything full of fear and hate? Why did she have to holler? Doesn't she know that if she does it again, it will all be *her* fault? It nearly happened just now. It will happen. It's got to happen. It's been happening. Why is it so cold?"

But it shouldn't have been cold, because it was the next morning and she was in her mother's bed, well covered, and Dr. Williams was leaning over the thermometer trying to read it against the light, which was difficult because the green shade was drawn. Her mother stood next to him looking worried about the thermometer reading, but otherwise as though the night before had never been.

The doctor turned to the bed and smiled. "Well, young lady," he said, "where did you pick up that mosquito? Can't say as I expected to run into that around these parts. Malaria, of all things!"

"Why, that's impossible!" her mother said. "It just *couldn't* be malaria! That's only in Florida and Africa!"

"Well," the doctor said, a twinkle behind his thick glasses. "Guess we had to get to Africa *some* way, didn't we?"

Her father came in, and her heart began to pound the way it had the night before. She wanted to look away, but her head felt too heavy. He said something about playing around the canal, but Dr. Williams said No, it didn't have to be that way at all; there was a malaria belt in the Middle West, and no one seemed to be able to account for it or foretell just who would fall victim, but anyway mosquitoes can fly quite a distance, and maybe she didn't go to it, it probably came to her. Then he delved into his black case and took out capsules along with the ever-present white powders and wrote two prescriptions, an unusual procedure for him.

As he left, he told her mother that he thought the "young lady" was a little upset these days. It wouldn't hurt a bit to see that she was kept quiet and without excitement. She would be in bed for at least two weeks and ailing after that. When he repeated his instructions about no excitement, the girl thought she detected some special emphasis. She closed her eyes and turned to the wall, partly because she felt so ashamed that not only Bluff Street, but all of the Town, must by now be aware that the Dunhams were having a terrible time, and that Mr. Dunham beat his wife, and that his son was going to kill him with the rifle that they used to go rabbit hunting with a long time ago.

The malaria was persistent, alternately raging and subsiding for a month. The girl wearied of aching bones and stomach pains and chills and fever, but she was grateful for the comparative peace in the family. She moved again to her small room, and at night when it was too hot to sleep, she would search the heavens for her special Star. But the nights were murky, and most of the time she couldn't find it, and when she did, the Star seemed alien, embarrassed, like a host who wants to tell his guest that his welcome has run out but doesn't know how to say it. She prayed to it in spite of this, forcing herself to stay kneeling on the bed though her head felt dangerously heavy and her back ached and her knees trembled. Mostly she petitioned that everything be set right. And again she asked for strength and courage for herself, somehow sensing that little by little she would be pushed into some position for which she now felt woefully inadequate.

Her brother sat with her as much as he could, bringing her ice-cream cones or bottles of pink soda pop and one day a string of pearls. She recognized it immediately as one of a kind that hung in multiple ropes at the counter she had pored over with Dorothy Jackson. But he told her a long tale about where pearls come from and how these pearls had belonged to a princess in Hawaii. Then he told her such stories about the Hawaiians and what they looked like and what they did that she forgot to ask how he had managed to get the pearls, which by now were wrapped in so much romance that they had become priceless, because by now she believed him, because she wanted to enter into the spirit of things and be as entertained and entranced as he wanted her to be.

She was well again, but the fear stayed inside, settling into her stomach and rising into her chest, so that she felt herself holding her breath and then letting it out in long sighs and still not being able to take in enough air. Her first day up she looked for the rifle, but it was nowhere to be found. Her father's shotgun, which had stood in the corner of the bedroom on the side of the bed where he slept, was missing, too.

Her brother saw her looking under the couch where he slept in the dining room. "He took it," he said, smiling at her confusion. "Never mind. I'm going away pretty soon. I have a scholarship. But not until winter. Don't tell anybody." The bottom fell out of everything, and she sat on the couch and stared at him. "I'll come back," he said, "and then we'll all go away together." She knew what he meant by "all," but the thought of facing days and months and perhaps years without the presence of her brother, with only the terror of her father and what she now recognized to be the constant nagging of her mother, removed all hope of survival.

A spark had gone from her, and those who knew her best thought that it was the result of the malaria and that, as soon as cool weather came, she would recover her old restless energy. But at fourteen she felt old and tired and wasn't even much interested in Allegretta's confidences about how babies were born.

"Mens is terrible," Allegretta lectured, as they washed the white woodwork in the bathroom. "You jus' stay away fum um. Ain' Miz Dunnum tolt you yit?"

"Told me *what,* Allegretta?"

"Tolt you whar babies comes frum! Big girl like you ain't got no bu'ness so unknowin'."

The girl felt ashamed and backward at her ignorance. "They come out of inside," she said, feeling uncomfortable at such intimacy. "I saw a book where the calf was inside its mother. . . ."

"Hee hee!" Tears rolled down Allegretta's brown cheeks whenever she started to laugh. She was not long from Mississippi, and scrawny, and thought that she was eighteen but was not sure. Her hair stayed in tight knots until she prepared to leave on Saturday afternoon; then she undid it and heated an iron comb—which she always carried in her handbag along with a bottle of hot sauce, a can of Poro Hair Pressing Oil, and numerous other indispensable properties—and walked back and forth from the kitchen to the bathroom, where she stood before the mirror and pulled at the kinky knots with the hot iron until they sizzled out into flat, oily strands. At first, separate pieces stood up like the bristles on a hedgehog, but when she had smoothed the unruly ends into place and changed into a clean dress and screwed on pink earrings and put on lipstick and rouge and a little pink powder, she looked quite presentable.

"Ain' stiddyin' no cow!" she said. "Laws, whoever heerd tell talkin' 'bout cows stid of educatin' proper 'bout babies? Babies is *folks,* ain' no *cows.*" She emphatically "busted her suds," as she said of anything to do with washing, and began to fill in the gaps in the girl's neglected education.

"But how do you know when you're going to have a baby?" the girl asked, as they moved into the kitchen.

"*Know!* Lawd, chile, you *knows* all right." Allegretta had covered a good deal of ground during the washing of the bathroom woodwork and was now at what she considered the climax of her discourse. She stopped busting suds and looked at the girl as though to be sure that the impact of her words would receive full consideration.

"Den," she said in a voice husky with awe, "ya pee bags bus!"

"Your *what,* Allegretta?"

"*Pee bags,* girl, ya pee bags busses, 'en den's when ya *knows* hit done be time!" They stood over their bucket of Fels Naphtha soap powder and warm water turning tepid, each lost in her own thoughts. The girl was impressed by all that she had learned, chiefly because of the frankness of her narrator. She didn't want to show her own ignorance by asking more questions, but was unable to figure out a number of things in spite of her informant's meaty colloquialisms and graphic details.

She always intended to ask Allegretta more, as casually

as possible, because she felt that there were some things that by now she should know but that Annette Dunham would never in the world speak of. She didn't get around to it, though, and one day Allegretta didn't come to work. Then her mother told her that if they ever passed her on the street she wasn't to speak to her. The girl was astonished, considering Allegretta one of her best friends, until she overheard a telephone conversation.

"How *could* she?" her mother was saying, in her most "it-couldn't-have-possibly-happened-to-a-Poindexter" tone. "And me trusting her with Katherine and all the time her carrying on like that. I used to see her get all done up on Saturday afternoons." Whoever was on the other end of the line had some choice bits to add. Annette Dunham drew away from the telephone to look at it as though the very words had contaminated it. "Lord have mercy!" she said when she trusted the instrument again. "A *white* man! *Of all things!*" Then she drew upon her stock phrase for the worst that could possibly happen to anyone. "She ought to be run out of town!"

Katherine Dunham was deeply vexed with her mother for her rejection of the hired girl. If Allegretta approached all of life with the same innocent gusto as she had during their Saturday cleaning conferences, what she had done couldn't be so terrible. Allegretta was the only person who talked about such things who didn't make her feel uncomfortable or guilty or as if she were spying on something not quite clean.

She and her mother passed the girl once or twice downtown, and the daughter wondered if all of that under her smock was what they talked about, and what she would do if her pee bags busted while she was walking around window shopping. Her mother stared straight ahead without a sign of recognition, but the girl smiled at Allegretta in spite of what her mother had told her.

And to Annette Dunham's chagrin, she continued to do so on subsequent encounters.

There were many times as the summer drew to a close when the girl would willingly have suffered another attack of malaria if that could have insured against family strife.

Albert Dunham was not appeased by one victory, although to the girl it seemed monumental. He had cajoled and threatened and intimidated his wife all through the summer and finally, on the assurance that the venture was not speculation but a provision for the future, had persuaded her to sign the necessary papers for the purchase of a red brick house which had once occupied a position in the center of a modest estate, but which now encumbered the storage yard of an iron foundry. An elderly Frenchman owned a lot a block away, and by having the house moved to it on immense rollers, the father accomplished one of his lifelong dreams: to buy something considered useless or impractical and make it a profitable investment. It was a ten-room house with an attic and a gabled roof, and to transfer it from the foundry to the vacant lot was regarded as something of a feat. The curious drove to the spot from all parts of the Town to watch, and Albert Dunham absented himself from his business at every possible opportunity, not so much because he was needed to oversee the job as because he basked in the interest and admiration and sometimes the envy that he saw on the faces of spectators who were as driven as he to keep up with the times, but who hadn't been clever enough to think up such a move.

Once in place, the house was remodeled into two apartments. Years would pass before Annette Dunham and her husband occupied the downstairs flat, and by then the two children would have gone their separate ways. But at the time, just the talk of a house, a real place to call home with a room of her own, encouraged the girl. Then she would hear the nightly bickering again, and her enthusiasm would leave her, and she would wonder if people were ever satisfied or if something was wrong with all families. She began to take a great interest in imagining the inner lives of people, in projecting herself into their thinking and feeling, in wondering why they behaved as they did and if the other people around were concealing wounds and hurts and fears and bitterness behind their friendliness and smiles and the nice words that they said to each other. If she isolated her family from the others, she felt lost indeed. On the other hand, if all of life and all relationships were like the Dunhams', then she had been born into an ice age or into a black abyss with only more blackness beyond each door which was opened at so much effort and cost.

Shortly after the girl's recovery from malaria, her mother —as though her daughter's illness had suggested the idea —developed a Saturday-night practice of fainting on the doorstep of the shop, always when her husband was near by, so that he would have to stop whatever he was doing and carry her through the street and up the stairs to the flat. The first time this happened the girl was reading in bed and had just been wondering how late they intended to work. It was after eleven, and her brother was still on the delivery truck.

When her father passed through the living room with the inert figure, puffing and panting and dripping with sweat from the climb up the stairs, her blood stopped circulating and she thought, "Well, it's happened." She started across the room as she had on that other night, wondering why she couldn't move quickly or cry out or do something active or dynamic, as she imagined other people did at times like this. This time she kept walking until she stood in the doorway; she spoke above the pounding in her ears which came from her own heartbeat.

"What's the matter?" she managed to say.

Her father seemed upset, but not like someone who had just committed a murder. She stared at the figure on the bed, looking for blood or other signs of violence, and Annette Dunham began to groan, turning her head from side to side.

"Get some water," her father said.

At the kitchen sink she drank half a glass of water before she remembered what she was there for, and then hurried guiltily back into the bedroom, handing her father the glass from a distance, already condemning him as criminal, already seeing him in jail.

Once in a long while Albert Dunham understood his daughter. "Your mother's fainted," he told her. "Get the smelling salts."

She fumbled in the drawer and found the bottle of lavender smelling salts that her mother sometimes carried to funerals. She couldn't look at her father because she knew he had read her thoughts, and she felt that from now on she would have nowhere to hide. She would have to let him see everything, how she was beginning to hate him, and how she was afraid of him and afraid for her brother even more than for her mother.

The fainting was presently supplemented by attacks of leg cramps, severe and without warning. They would occur in the middle of the night or when there was a guest for dinner or, worse still, in church. A series of low moans might announce their imminence, in which case the girl and her father would leave the dinner table or the church pew, half carrying and half dragging the mother to some sheltered spot. The girl would be the first to rush to the telephone to call the doctor, but he might be away from his office, and father and daughter would then become momentary allies in frantic efforts to calm the suffering woman. The girl went through an apprenticeship in applying hot fomentations and in massage and manipulation, and worked feverishly to straighten the leg that would have been drawn double by suddenly contracted tendons and muscles, strangulating the surrounding nerves, so that Annette Dunham would scream in a voice hardly recognizable as her own.

The girl learned to sleep lightly and to wake at the slightest unaccustomed sound, with her full faculties ready to go at once into action. Hardly were her mother's first cries uttered than she would light the fire under the teakettle, snatch the bottle of Sloan's Liniment and a towel from the bathroom, and take her place at the foot of the bed, where her father would already be at work over the twisted muscles. Her mother was usually so tidy that the girl hated seeing her with her hair in disorder, her eyes wild and rolling, and the corners of her mouth wetter than they should be.

Sometimes in her pain the mother turned accusingly on her two attendants, crying "Do something. Can't somebody *do* something? *Why* don't you help me? *Why* don't you *do* something!"

And all the while they would be pulling, massaging, perspiring, the father dutiful no matter how bitter, the girl numb and driven and guilty because of the revulsion she felt toward such nakedness. She had had no experience with the leveling-down, the stripping of all pretenses, the ultimate groveling of the proudest, which pain achieves so effectively.

Annette Dunham lost no opportunity to blame her condition on overwork and the strain and abuse of her married life. Albert Dunham retorted that her troubles more than likely stemmed from her time of life, to which she rejoined that he should know all about this, having once been married to a woman far more senior to him than she herself was. The ugliness continued and grew until there was another physical struggle, this time while the brother was at a late rehearsal of the string quartet.

Bad became worse and still worse, until one day, having

been told so many times to leave if she didn't like things the way they were, the mother called the girl into the bedroom, where preparations for departure were already apparent, and in the quavering voice she now used so frequently told her that she had been ejected bodily from the shop, that the joint bank account had been closed and a new one opened in the name of Albert M. Dunham alone, that her very life was in danger if she did not turn over to her husband each day whatever payments were made in the shop during his absence or had come in by way of the delivery wagon. When she had objected to expenditures she thought unnecessary, he had told her that her services were no longer needed and that she had tried her best to alienate his children from him. Then he struck her and said things that were the unkindest that could be said to a woman of her age, who had been as much a mother to the children as if she had borne them. The girl wept and clung to her as she never had done before, tired of being brave and stoical and indomitable like her brother, willing to be just for once, a frightened, lonely, sick child, tormented by too much awareness.

Her tears turned to hysteria, and her mother must have been moved, because she agreed to stay, no matter what.

"Take me away with you!" the girl pleaded. "Please, Mother, don't leave me with him. I hate him! I hate him! Please take me away!"

Annette Dunham, because she was a good mother and an upright wife and essentially moral in all of the ways set out by her Puritan forebears, was stabbed and shaken by her daughter's outburst.

"But, Katherine," she said, "he's your *father!* You mustn't say things like that!"

The girl turned hopelessly from her mother, defeated. Surely now it was only a matter of time. She sat in her own room until the sobs had died and tried to stop thinking how near her own panic had been to her mother's nakedness in pain. She set the table and began to prepare for supper. Not a word was spoken during the entire meal.

School started, and each day she turned the corner from the Cass Street bridge the girl had to hold herself back to keep from running the long block to the shop. She felt that one day she would find her mother dead or not there. When she saw her, her head bent over the sewing machine as usual, she felt such relief that she could only stand for the first few minutes and make nonsensical remarks.

That was the first week of school. The Sunday beginning the second week was exceptionally bad.

On Sunday, with rare exceptions, the father prepared the morning meal, and his mood was reflected in his menu: pancakes or corncakes or hoecake bread for average or sullen moods, sour-milk cornbread or baking-powder biscuits when his mood was friendly or elated. And on the friendly days he insisted on waiting on table, jumping up to look into the oven, and returning with a plate of golden butter-filled squares of cornbread or fluffy buttered biscuits.

His son had chosen this Sunday morning to announce his intention of leaving junior college in midterm and accepting the scholarship offered by the University. While the mother and daughter stared at their plates and kept trying to swallow pancakes that didn't taste good any more, the brother sat with his food untouched, presenting his case as reasonably as possible.

He had managed to wrest from his father enough money during the full-time summer work to pay for his cello lessons. Now school had started, and he felt that he could no longer return to the old routine of work before and after school, with only his food and the bare necessities of clothing as grudging compensation. He was perfectly willing to forego lunch and carfare, but not his cello lessons. The tips that he had carefully hoarded as a young boy had diminished to almost nothing, because he was now on more familiar terms with the customers, and they respected him too much to offer tips. Most important of all, he had to save toward the coming winter. The scholarship, valuable as it was, would pay only tuition, leaving him with no means of support unless he could find work that would not interfere with his studies. Until now he had outwardly lived the life set out for him, all of the time a different person inside. Now he wanted to prepare for life as he saw it and felt that it should be; and without his saying so, the others at the table knew that he meant a life very different from the one he had so far led.

All of this seemed reasonable enough to the two holding their breaths over the already cold pancakes. But to the former German tailors' apprentice who, as he learned their trade, had listened to the saga of their Black Forest childhood—how they had been tied to the bedpost and thrashed for disobedience or gone without food or locked in a closet for days until chastened—it represented the final abnegation of "blood" and "descent" and "inheritance." It meant also the final break with his first-born, the last of the line, who should have dutifully learned more about solvents and tumblers and repairs and trading and business, in order to carry forward the Name and consequently the Race.

The father said to his son, "Eat your breakfast."

And the son said, "I'm not hungry." The father repeated, this time rising from his chair at the head of the table, "Don't talk back to me! I said eat your breakfast!"

"I don't want any breakfast," the boy repeated. "I was talking to you about what I intend to do, what I have to have, that's all."

The chair at the head of the table fell over backward as Albert Dunham reached across and struck his son. The girl sat with her mouth full of pancakes that refused to go down and stared into her plate, wanting badly to run from the table and out of the house and keep running.

Annette Dunham said, "Oh, Al, don't hit him! He was only *asking!*"

And the father, nostrils wide and voice thick, picked up the chair and said, "When I tell you to do something, you do it."

The son turned pale where he held his lips tightly together, but his cheek was dark red where his father's open hand had struck it. He ate the pancakes, and the only sound in the room was the scraping and clattering made by the man at the head of the table, who had expected further resistance or something else, but not just this.

When his plate was clean, the son excused himself from the table and went through the kitchen and into the bathroom. He closed the door, but it was easy, in the dead stillness not even disturbed now by Albert Dunham's knife and fork, to hear the sounds of retching. When the boy passed through the room again, he looked at his father triumphantly, even hesitating slightly as though to ask, *"Well, anything else?"*—and then went out of the room and down the stairs.

It was ill advised of the mother to pursue the subject further that day. The stormy discussion was carried from bedroom to kitchen to living room to dining room, until when time came for Brown's Chapel Christian Endeavor the girl was eager, instead of reluctant, to go, and even asked her mother if she might stay through for the evening service. But the two church services were only an interlude, and again in the flat above the shop the bitterness between husband and wife continued into the night.

The son returned home after everyone had gone to bed and began his habitual reading in the dining room. A moment later the father streaked through the living room and down the front stairs like a madman. Then the house was in total blackness, all electric current cut off from the main switch. The father found his way back to the bedroom by flashlight, gloating aloud over the victory. There was no sound from the dining room, but when the girl turned the corner at the Jefferson Street bridge the following day after school, she felt the emptiness and didn't bother to run the rest of the way home. The sewing machine was silent, her father sullenly worked over a skirt on her mother's pressing board, and upstairs the dishes were still in the sink from breakfast and the suitcases were gone from the bedroom closet.

She stood in the middle of the living room and wondered why everything seemed so empty, because her mother was almost always in the shop at this time anyway. Then she began mechanically to put things in order, noticing that the bed was still unmade and so guessing that she had left in the early morning.

Her brother came in while she was washing the dishes. "She must have left early," he said.

The girl agreed.

"Did she tell you anything yesterday?"

The girl shook her head.

"Did she leave you a letter?"

"No, did she leave you one?"

"No."

"Where do you suppose she went?"

"I don't know. She'll come back or let us know."

"Are you going away if she's still away by winter?"

"I have to. Don't worry. She'll come back before then. She said before that she was going, and didn't."

"I don't want to stay here alone. Suppose she never comes back!" The girl was crying, and he was drying the dishes without thinking about it or having to be asked to. Then he began to wash the dishes because she couldn't see what she was doing and just kept mopping helplessly at one plate that had some streaks of hardened egg left on it.

"Don't wash the dishes," she said. "It makes your fingers soft for the cello. You always said that."

"That doesn't matter. . . . Say, Kitty, wouldn't you like

to go to the University, too? After junior college here?"

"Yes," she said, a little dubiously. "But it costs a lot, and I'd never get a scholarship."

"Never mind," he said, wringing out the dishcloth and handing it back to her. "By that time I'll be able to help you. Just keep going and don't pay any attention to him. You've got to think about getting away, that's all. Why, you could even go to Africa after you finish at the University!"

He smiled at her; now she had a secret to live by and for, and the flat didn't seem so empty, and instead of being cold and suffocated and without any hope at all, she felt strong and ready for anything. He was standing in the door, already too long away from the West Side Cleaners' truck.

"Don't give up Kitty," he said. "Don't ever give up. You'll make it all right!" And by the way he said it she somehow felt that he meant she would make it whether he did or not, though he was so superior to her in every way that she could see no doubt anywhere as far as he was concerned—except for a smile that sometimes seemed to be hinting at a sweet and sad and wise farewell, as though actually making the farewell just wasn't worth the effort.

After a few days a letter arrived from Delavan. The girl had avoided her father as much as possible and had said nothing about her mother. Once she had to ask for lunch money, and her father told her then that it was time for her to begin learning how to work in the shop, how to remove the spots from dresses and answer the telephone and keep books and press knife pleats and lengthen or shorten pants cuffs and skirt hems.

The letter was from Annette Dunham and it said, "Dear Katherine, I couldn't stand it any longer. I was sorry not to tell you but I had to take the morning train to Delavan. I won't come back until your father can treat me decently.

Be a good girl and take care of the house. Your Aunt Alice is very sick. It is a good thing that I came when I did. Tell Albert not to cause any trouble. It doesn't do any good to argue with your father. After all, he is your father. With love, Your mother."

The girl sat at the desk with the open account book before her, and read and reread the letter for some sign that life might again be resumed as it had been before, even with its troubles, but with her mother there. She tried to find the comfort and love and affection that she knew must be hidden somewhere between the lines, and felt that her own incapacity kept her from discovering them.

Her brother read the letter with no expression and said, "She'll be back. You just watch and see. She won't stay away." But he didn't seem too happy about the letter. The same day the father received a letter, and whatever was in it only added to his habitual sullenness.

The volume of business continued to increase; by the second week of his wife's absence the father, even after hiring a replacement and conscripting his daughter's help, found the efficiency of the shop deteriorating. The girl was beginning to feel the strain of added duties; she refrained with difficulty from showing her discontent at having to forego the late-afternoon dancing classes, and she had to beg a letter from the dean of girls to convince her father that two evenings a week were required in out-of-doors sports to fulfill the requirements of the curriculum. These he allowed her, with the understanding that she still put in a certain amount of daily time in the shop if she expected her school expenses.

Toward the end of the first month of the semester, she took stock of her clothes and found that, although she could manage well enough with dresses by lengthening skirts and switching combinations, her shoes presented a real problem. Last year's shoes were impossibly small; her good patent-leather slippers, saved especially for funerals and club meetings and church suppers, were hopelessly outgrown; and the shoes that she had used steadily during the last part of the summer were worn through on the soles, so that the shoemaker just looked at them and shook his head; besides, she would have had to stay home from school while they were in the shop, because she had absolutely nothing else to put on, not even bedroom slippers. So she put pieces of cardboard in the shoes every morning and wrote and asked her mother what to do. Her mother wrote back immediately that she should ask her father for the money to buy shoes, especially since she now worked in the shop and took care of the flat and cooked most of the meals. She would have sent the money, she said, but things were going very badly with Aunt Alice and Uncle Ed. She would explain later.

All at once the shoes went to pieces. First the cardboard fell out while the girl was walking along the corridor between classes, because the holes had grown much larger as she went to and from school. Then it began to rain every day, and the sodden cardboard would have disintegrated by the time she reached the school steps. She started carrying extra pieces and would go into the girls' washroom to make a replacement before the first class, flushing the bits down the toilet so that no one would suspect her dilemma. Then there was the embarrassment of taking her shoes off for gym class and having to hide them quickly away in the locker and spirit them as quickly out again when she dressed. And of course her stockings were abused because of the holes in the shoes and had to be darned nightly.

One day as she walked home in the rain, the squish of water between her toes and the roughness of the pavement where the cardboard had given way, roused her from apathy to anger. She hated her father for subjecting her to such discomfort and indignity, and her mother for having left her in such a position.

"She should have stayed!" she thought over and over,

and then she said to herself, "He's got to. He's got to get me a pair of shoes. I'll stay home from school, and they'll put him in jail." Her anger gave her the courage to burst into the shop and rip both shoes off in front of Mr. Crusoe and the new sewing woman.

"I've got to have some shoes," she said. "Mother said to get them. She promised them before she went away. I can't go to school this way!"

"I have nothing to do with what your mother promises," her father answered, not looking at her or at the shoes, but going on with his pressing.

Her anger became hysteria. "I've got to have shoes!" she cried. "I won't work here any more if I can't have shoes!"

Mr. Crusoe put on his hat and went out the back door, as he often did when a crisis was in the air. He was a mild man by nature and disapproved of his employer's violent behavior. He was, however, well paid and knew that he would risk his job by taking a stand; and he had a family of his own to think about.

"You ran her away," the girl cried. "I want her back! You make her come back or I'll go away, too!"

The pressing iron stopped in midair, then slammed down onto its stand. She should have been afraid then and flinched or drawn back. But resentment had piled up and been held back until she had no control whatever; she was swept along in her assault on injustice. Her father may not have intended to strike her, but she didn't wait to find out. She darted to one side and found the electric iron from the ladies' pressing board in her hand. Then she was calm.

"You touch me," she said, "just touch me. And I'll kill you. Maybe Albert didn't do it, but I will. I'll kill you, I tell you!"

And she almost hoped that he would make the move, so that it would all be over with. There was only the sound of the gas in the pressing iron and her own heart pounding out its triumph over fear. Her father reached for his battered felt hat and turned to the back door and went out. She realized that she was in her stocking feet and picked up the soaking shoes, from which wet gray wads of cardboard fell. As she passed the sewing woman, she could hardly walk straight because her head felt light and her throat felt as though someone with steel fingers had just squeezed it in both hands. She walked into the rain and up the stairway to the flat. She saw that her father had peeled potatoes and left two T-bone steaks on a platter to be cooked for dinner; he had also washed the breakfast dishes. She made his bed, set the table, and gathered enough courage to return to the shop for her evening duties.

Her father was alone at the pressing table. It seemed early for the others to have left, and she felt uneasy, wishing that her brother would happen in. Her father pressed for a while in silence, and she began marking bits of tape with the names of the owners of the last lot of clothing that had been put into the bin under Mr. Crusoe's pressing table. After a while her father spoke, and the quality of his voice disturbed her, because she couldn't believe it meant defeat, and she knew nothing about what might be buried far beneath the virulence that had effaced the father she remembered from Glen Ellyn or even from picnics and Bush Park and rabbit hunts and ice-cream freezing in years after that. She saw only one side of it; that her nights were fitful and her heartbeat unruly and her mother gone and her brother resented and beaten and herself unwanted and beaten, too, if she didn't behave exactly as she was supposed to; and her feet were wet and her shoes worn out, and even so she was not allowed to stay and learn more and play more after school like other girls of her age, but must spend the evening hours in a tight confinement filled with odors of gasoline and steam and pressed wool, or in the flat above, cleaning, cleaning, fighting a losing battle against the dust wheel.

"I wrote your mother today," he said, "asking her to

come back. I had already written her. I told your brother about it, but you didn't give me a chance."

The girl stood quietly at the basket of dirty, half-sorted clothes. She could hardly believe what she was hearing, but the warm flow in her veins and the glad thump of her heart were real.

"I'm glad," she said, after a moment of trying to keep the sound of tears out of her voice. "I'm glad you asked her." At that moment she didn't hate her father. She loved everyone, even people she didn't know.

"About the shoes," her father said. "Business is good, but there are a lot of payments to be met on the new house. Making it into two apartments takes more money than your mother realizes. That's why we have so much trouble."

The girl felt suddenly deflated. She would rather not hear anything at all like criticism of her mother or justification for her father's behavior. She would just like to think about her mother's return and perhaps about a family like other people's—and above all, she admitted to herself with a fleeting feeling of guilt, a new pair of shoes.

"How much would a new pair of shoes cost?" her father asked.

From long experience with her mother's efforts to extract money from her husband, the girl quoted an outside figure, the sound of which surprised even herself.

Her father looked up in astonishment. "Why, I could put another window in the attic for that!" he said. "You'd better wait till your mother gets here!"

The girl's heart dropped to the floor. "Oh, I *can't!*" she cried. "Can't you see what my shoes are like? And I'm so ashamed. Everybody looks at me now. They can see the cardboard."

"They can be half-soled," her father said.

"But they *can't!* The man won't do it! And, besides, what would I wear while he did it?"

"I saw some shoes of your mother's in the closet," her

father said. "They should be just about right for you, and the soles are good and strong. I'll get them."

The girl wondered what shoes they could be. She went on wetting the strips of tape on a damp sponge and marking names with an indelible pencil. Then she sewed the names into the cloths and after that went through the pockets and seams for forgotten articles.

Her father returned with a pair of shoes. They had medium heels, higher than those girls of her age wore. They were narrow, as all of Annette Dunham's shoes were, and certainly long enough for the girl. The soles were strong, and they were tie pumps. But they were of white canvas. Shoes that the mother wore only on the hottest days of the summer, and then most of the time at picnics. The girl concentrated on a green stain on the toe of one of them and wondered what picnic it was a souvenir of. She felt sick with apprehension as she took off the wet shoes and tried on the white ones. Then she sighed with relief.

"They won't go on," she said. "See, just half my foot gets in."

Her father seemed pleased with himself. "Take your stockings off," he said, "and dry your feet and put a little powder on. Then they'll fit. They're good and strong and will do fine until your mother gets back."

Her brother entered in time to witness the triumph of the shoes. She stood stockingless, her instep and ankles covered with the powder used to whiten freshly cleaned kid gloves. Her feet had slid in with the greatest of ease, while she tried to make them expand and prayed that they would stick halfway. It was the end of October, and cold and rainy nearly every day, and in the Midwest the traditional day for taking off straw hats and white shoes was Labor Day. She would surely be the laughing stock of the whole school. What good had it done to make the hockey team and get ninety-nine in Latin and be asked into the Girls' Athletic

Association? She bit her lips to keep tears back and refused to look at her brother.

He paid no attention to the shoes. "Did he tell you?" he asked, his voice light and gayer than she had heard it for a long time. "Did he tell you that Mother's coming back?"

She felt ungrateful to be near to tears about the shoes when her prayers had been answered and soon everything would be all right again. "Yes," she said, and managed to smile at her father.

"Now you'd better go and fix the steak," her father said. "Put the potatoes on, and I'll be up in a few minutes to mash them. Those are fine steaks. Henry Simon did all right this time!" And, as she went out the front door: "Don't cook mine too long. Nobody ought to eat steaks like you and your brother eat them. All of the taste is cooked away."

Dinner was almost friendly, and every time she remembered the white shoes, which were warm and comfortable until she realized that they were way out of season and for a grown woman, she thought instead of her mother's return, and the shoes didn't seem so bad.

But when she wore them the next day and the rain had soaked through to turn them a dirty gray, she wanted to turn and run away or take them off and go barefoot. She even wished for her old shoes, but her father had thrown them out, feeling actually pleased with himself for his brilliant solution of the problem.

All that she had feared became fact. She was looked at, and her shoes were pointed out, and she could hear snickers that in her misery were amplified to raucous laughter. When she was worn out with blushing and trying to look as though nothing were wrong and it was the most natural thing in the world to wear her mother's white shoes to school in late October, they developed a new way of embarrassing her. They now squeaked when they were dry, so that if the day was not rainy, she soaked them in water before leaving home, hoping to be spared at least a part of her suffering. To make matters worse her mother had written that Aunt Alice's condition was so grave that she was not expected to live, and that Ed Poindexter was taking it badly, and that she would have to stay until the crisis was over one way or another.

Two weeks passed in waiting, and one night as her brother helped her with the dishes, she burst again into anger.

"I don't think she's coming," she said. "I think he's lying anyway. I don't think he even asked her. I don't think she'd stay just because Aunt Alice is sick. I bet he didn't even ask her. He just wanted to make me stop asking for shoes and put these on me for good!"

"No," her brother said. "Don't forget he needs her every bit as much as we do. I think this has taught him a lesson. Nobody can do as much as she does, and, besides, he doesn't have to pay her." The logic of this quieted the girl, and she resigned herself again to the white shoes.

A telephone call from Delavan announced the death of Alice Poindexter and the imminent return of Annette Dunham. She would not arrive alone, however. Ed Poindexter had lost all interest in his beauty salon during his wife's illness, and her death had deprived him of any wish to resume his profession, and the doctor had said that he shouldn't be left by himself.

The Sunday before their arrival the girl spent the day at Mayme Humbles' house. The Oldsmobile had not been out of the tin shed during the recent crisis, but this morning she was allowed to drive it to church by herself, then to go with her Aunt Mayme to the cottage on Hyde Park Avenue.

The first light snow of the season settled on the windshield and powdered the grass plot in front of the house. Inside, Will Humbles had lit a fire in the kitchen coal stove, and he sat by this methodically reading the morning papers, while old Annie Poindexter sat at the front window, her "courting" quilt over her knees, peering at passers-by, wondering out loud about the happenings that she heard talk of but always felt left out of, and rocking when she hoped for attention.

It was a pleasant day, and even Will Humbles went out of his way to make conversation, reminiscing about coal mines and cattle ranches and real Indians. But he looked tired and thin, and the blue veins in the depressions of his temples kept up a steady throbbing.

Her grandmother seemed as astute as ever, but her flesh was shriveled and her hand trembled as she tried to cut pieces from her favorite part of the chicken, the back, so that her daughter said, "Mama, just use your fingers."

And Will Humbles, bent well into his plate, cackled for a long time as though he had hit on something extremely funny and original, and said, "Fingers's made before forks."

The girl wondered why people seemed the same for so long, then all of a sudden different: much older or thinner or fatter or more worried or peculiar acting.

When she talked about the excitement of her Uncle Ed's arrival, her Aunt Mayme looked worried and shook her head.

"Nett says he's a sick man, Kitten. Now don't you go making plans to cause any more trouble with Al Dunham!"

"Can't stand to be told," Annie Poindexter said. "That's what's the matter. Him and me never *could* get along. But I told him a piece of my mind, I did!" The old lady still couldn't manage her chicken, and her daughter had to lean across and arrange it for her in smaller pieces and wipe some gravy and dumpling from her chin. It was her trembling that caused the untidiness, because she had always been neat as a pin.

The girl thought, "They don't know Uncle Ed like *I* do. We'll go for long drives on Sunday afternoon, even if it *is* winter, and he'll be well and maybe start a beauty parlor here."

Sitting later in the intimacy of the kitchen, while her Aunt Mayme washed the dinner dishes, she went into fancy flights of wild escapades in a brand-new roadster, saw herself in a white uniform mixing creams and lotions in a beauty salon on the main street of the Town, and imagined her family at peace: her father and Uncle Ed would be buying and selling real estate in all kinds of clever deals, so that there would be no more cleaning shop, no more dust wheel, and no more arguments. And they would live in the new red brick house.

It was unheard-of to stay home from school except for illness, so Katherine Dunham didn't bother to try to wheedle her father into letting her go to the train to meet her mother. Instead she awoke early in a state of nervous excitement and swept and dusted the flat thoroughly before leaving for school. She braided her hair with special care and considered putting blackening on the white canvas shoes, but thought that perhaps her mother wouldn't like it and brushed them vigorously instead. Her classes dragged through the day, and each hour bell seemed to hold off with studied deliberation. At four o'clock she raced from the school and ran home, not even trying to protect her books from the rain.

Her mother was at the sewing machine as though she had never left it. Uncle Ed sat beside her, looking at a newspaper. He was wearing glasses, and the bushy mane that had given him the air of a distinguished foreign potentate was tinged with gray. And as she leaned over to kiss her mother, she noticed that he was holding the paper upside down.

Her mother hugged her tightly, and all at once she felt traitorous because of her fears and distrust and doubts of the past weeks. The display of affection was unlike her mother and embarrassing. She said, "Katherine, Katherine, I'm so glad you're all right!"

Then, pushing her away to see her better, she said, "My, how you've grown!" The girl looked at her feet, and Annette Dunham gasped. "What on *earth* are you doing with those old white summer shoes of mine! Have you lost your *mind,* a rainy day like this?"

The girl had rehearsed over and over the story that she would tell, the tearful unburdening. But now that the moment had come, she felt that it would be some betrayal of her father, who had so reformed that it didn't seem fair to bring up those things that were all forgotten and over with now. She said nothing and continued to stare at her feet, and her mother said, "Go upstairs and get the umbrella. We're going right now and get you some shoes."

Everything gladdened at once, and then she remembered that she hadn't spoken to her uncle. Ed Poindexter had dropped the paper and was looking at his niece with the benign, untroubled recognition of a child who has come across a lost toy that everyone but himself has considered irretrievable. He had trouble forming words, and his effort was painful.

"Hello, Kitty," he finally stammered. "This is Uncle Ed." He repeated the first two words of the last sentence a number of times, and though he was smiling, he sounded as if any minute he would cry. She nodded to him, smiling, too, but her own smile felt unnatural. She wondered why she thought of the house in Glen Ellyn, of Grandma Buckner and the dolls, of a boy with Uncle Ed's smile leaning over a baby crib and talking a language that wasn't like the language the others spoke.

She heard her mother speaking and knew that she had missed some part of a conversation. "Why, of course, Ed. She knows you! Katherine, why are you standing there like that? Tell your Uncle Ed of course you remember him and then go upstairs and get the umbrella before your father gets back. We'll have to take Uncle Ed with us. He can't be left alone, and I have to wait until Albert gets back to take him to Aunt Mayme's. Mama will want to see him. Maybe when he sees Mama . . ." She didn't finish the sentence, but swallowed hard and bit off a long piece of thread that she drew from the bobbin of the machine.

Ed Poindexter was docile as a child, but he could not be left alone any more than a baby. He had other infantile ways, having some of the time to be reminded where the bathroom was or comforted when someone spoke harshly to him and his feelings were hurt and he cried. All afternoon he would sit smiling and vacant beside his sister, asking now and then for a glass of water or sucking happily at candies.

The blow was a bitter one to the girl. She was not allowed to drive the Oldsmobile alone with her uncle, and it became her duty to walk with him back to the house on Hyde Park Avenue when she returned from school. At first it seemed like some terrible jest, and she felt certain that she would wake up and find it all untrue, and that the man who loped beside her, whimpering about the cold, his hands in woolen gloves dangling outside his pockets, would change while they waited at a crossing and become the dashing man she had loved in Delavan. He would dry his nose with a spotless white handkerchief, instead of running his tongue out to catch the dripping from his nostrils, and stand upright, instead of shuffling half-bent, and smile a real smile, instead of that painful empty grimace, and say, "Well, Katherine. I certainly had everybody scared, didn't I? But *you* knew all along that I was just playing!"

But it didn't happen, and once when he didn't understand something that she had said to him and she spoke sharply and he burst into tears, she felt so upset that she had to hide her own tears—tears of shame and vexation with herself and with him and with the way things happened to the Dunham family.

Once when the sisters had risked letting Ed Poindexter walk alone from Bluff Street to Hyde Park Avenue, he was lost for hours. It was a Saturday evening, and neither father nor son could be spared from work. The two sisters consulted frantically by telephone, debating the consequences of appealing to the police. The girl offered to search for her uncle, and in the Oldsmobile, shivering because the temperature was below freezing, she slowly combed one street after another in the neighborhood between Hyde Park Avenue and Bluff Street. She abandoned this and turned the automobile to the other side of town. Nearly at Brown's Chapel she came upon the dejected figure of her uncle. She recognized from a block away the bent, shuffling, aimless form in an overcoat that was beginning to show signs of wear. With her feeling of relief came a pity that made her ashamed of the times when she wished he hadn't come or that he would sit somewhere else besides right in the front window of the shop.

Her uncle had turned blue with the cold, and tears streamed from his eyes and ran over the woolen scarf that Mayme Humbles had wrapped neatly at his throat before he left on his first trip alone. He climbed into the automobile and accepted the handkerchief the girl took from his pocket in fingers too numb to function.

"I t-t-t-tried," he sobbed, over and over again. "I tried but I couldn't find the way. Every time I asked, somebody said something different!"

The girl realized that he had made a tremendous effort to fit into things and lessen the burden to his sisters; and that all the times before, as he sat smiling vacantly, somewhere in the dim recesses of his shut-off self there must have been a recognition of things as they were and a will to emerge.

Sometimes she admitted to herself that she was afraid of

him, in a way that she couldn't control. She hated the fear, because he seemed so helpless and childlike. But at times, like the time when her father had decided to trust him with turning the hand crank of the tumbler but had carefully warned him not to enter the room with matches, she had seen a look on her uncle's face that made her uneasy, with the same prickling at the back of her neck that she had felt when she passed the halltree where the "Crandalls" lurked. Later, when her father returned unexpectedly and found Ed Poindexter dropping the kitchen matches, unlighted, one by one into a pool of gasoline which formed as it dripped from the full tumbler, she wasn't at all surprised and wondered why her father had taken such a risk, why he had put the idea into Uncle Ed's mind in the first place.

She hid her fear and showed more gentleness and understanding than the others, who acted some of the time as though he didn't exist. Gathering together the dim memories of her babyhood, she learned, as it were, to join in her uncle's own game. She would seat him where she could see him well enough so that he could not take her by surprise, even in fun, and play the piano, which he enjoyed immensely. She tried to interest him in beauty concoctions, but the subject made him gloomy and restless, as though the painfulness of trying to put pieces together was too much for him. The times when she felt closest to him were when they sat looking at each other, she not letting her eyes fall before his, even though it was not easy, and smiling back at him even though there was nothing at all funny unless it were the wordless conversations that they carried on.

The most difficult thing of all to support was the weekly morning service at Brown's Chapel. Annette Poindexter had always spoken highly of the Poindexters of Alton, but her brother Ed had been her greatest pride and joy; and it was especially hard for the entire family, with the exception of Mayme Humbles, to decide to take him with them to church. The sisters arrived early on the first Sunday and held their heads high, pushing their brother forward if he lagged behind. The girl blushed and writhed inwardly, seeing the stares of astonishment and the heads nodding in recollection of Annette Dunham's proud boasts, hearing the sudden outbreak of whispers. Worse than anything else was when Reverend Dyett said, in his precise, clipped British West Indian, wiping his hands on his immaculate handkerchief as he always did at the finish of his sermon, a little nervous because this was his first diocese and not an easy one, "Let us turn to page . . . and sing . . ." Everyone stood, and after a rustling of pages Ethel Fuqua struck the chord, and the choir took the lead. But leaping ahead of them and over them and writhing through their well-modulated singing came a tortured dissonance from the throat of Ed Poindexter. Transported into some kind of obscene yet holy worship, none the less valid because it belonged to him alone, he threw back his head and, still holding the hymnal as though it were guiding him, raised his cacophonous paean to the Almighty.

He was not set free until the following spring. At the burial his niece offered as honest a prayer as she could for his well-being, standing by the first of the family grave plots—this one a little removed from the willow trees that would eventually shelter Katherine Dunham's father and her brother and her second mother.

Ten
The Cello Lessons

*

One of the paradoxes in Annette Dunham's nature was her occasional willingness to switch from an apparently fixed and unswerving attitude to its exact opposite. Her agreement to accept Helen Weir into the household on Bluff Street came as a complete surprise to friends and family and most of all to her husband, who, although he doggedly continued to make periodic overtures to the Weir family, had not foreseen this particular victory. Once over her first mistrust of everything associated with her husband's and children's past life, Annette Dunham had by degrees made grudging adjustments, to the extent of inviting Lulu Dunham for an occasional Sunday dinner or closing her eyes to those infrequent trips to the City when the father took his daughter to call on her half sister Fanny June Weir and her family. She herself made no overtures and discouraged any on their part.

So Katherine Dunham was astonished, too, when her mother announced that Fanny Weir, concerned over her daughter's many social distractions and their bad effect on her studies, had asked that Helen be installed in the Dunham household so that she could attend the local junior college. The girl was delighted: there would be Helen's companionship, and perhaps her presence would relieve the darkening atmosphere of the Bluff Street household.

Helen Weir arrived in midwinter to begin her first term. Her fair skin and light brown hair caused an initial flurry of curiosity, but no one could deny the unmistakable resemblance to her younger, darker uncle and aunt. Her racy, sophisticated wit made her immediately popular with her classmates, so that there was no need for her to excel in either scholarship or athletics. She straddled comfortably the barrier between the two races, needled her aunt and uncle about the effort put into their scholarly and athletic achievements, and silenced by ready and cutting repartee any impertinent questions about her lineage or about the fact that her aunt and uncle were her juniors. Katherine Dunham and her niece shared the single bed of the cubicle; it was not comfortable, but at least a sleeping companion made the room seem less cold. At school—though the two seldom met, lunch hour for the college being set apart from that for the high school—the girl was aware of curious stares and felt a return of the old discomfort that had made the childhood move to her half sister's flat disagreeable. But the presence of an outsider softened her father's ill temper and drove lurking terrors from the upstairs flat.

During this period the director of the string quartet began to urge his pupils to further individual achievement. By one means or another, often with the surreptitious aid of his mother, the brother had managed to continue his weekly cello lessons. His main problem was to find time for practice. Whatever moments he tried to insert between his delivery rounds were quickly claimed by his father, who, seizing the wooden pole with which he had formerly telegraphed commentary on his daughter's piano practice, pounded furiously on the ceiling of the shop at the first notes of the Bach exercise that the boy had chosen as his special assignment. Sometimes the music would continue uninterrupted. Then both downstairs doors would slam in furious succession, and the father would leap the hall steps two and three at a time to confront his son, by this time carefully packing his instrument away in its canvas cover. On such occasions the combined physical and emotional stress would seem to strangle the man, so that, unable to articulate, he could only gasp through flaring nostrils and point to the open door and stairs leading downward. More than once his arm was raised to strike his son as he walked past, but the direct glance and tightset features must have flashed a warning; muttering, he would turn and bolt down the steps ahead of the boy, to be prepared to thrust at him any duty, real or concocted, as justification of his act.

Whatever restraining effect Helen Weir's presence may have had on the father soon wore off, and by the middle of the school term, the flat and the shop again became the scene of violent quarrels between husband and wife. For the first time allusions to the Glen Ellyn family passed freely back and forth. Much that the girl had told her new mother during the first year of confidences now became useful to Annette Dunham, and she reminded her husband of the years of negligence when the two children were called into court as witnesses against their own father. In short, Helen's presence seemed to serve as a catalyst for whatever bitterness had not yet found expression in earlier quarrels.

At times church came as a welcome relief. This winter there was a series of revival meetings of the kind more usual in the summer months, but especially instituted by Reverend Dyett as a fund-raising device. Reverend Scott, the famous revivalist chosen to head the series, was a florid, freckled man of a coloring known as "meriney." He was young for his position, but the "call" had come to him early, and as a child of seven he had toured from tent to storefront, whipping exalted congregations into frenzies of religious ecstasy with his treble-voiced declamations about death and resurrection in the Valley of Dry Bones. As a man of thirty he still had a childlike, almost puckish air, accentuated by a broad and unlined brow under crisp, red-dish-gold, tight-cropped curls, large sparkling brown eyes, a golden-red mustache, and a full red mouth.

Although Annette Dunham was in principle opposed to public demonstrations of emotional catharsis, she would certainly not have missed the social opportunity of welcoming the renowned spiritual leader to her own church. At the initial service the entire congregation was immediately captivated. The men admired Reverend Scott's well-tailored, carefully matched clothing; the women strained forward to catch the full beam of his smile and to stare hypnotized at the sparkle of clear polish on his manicured fingernails. As he walked from the rear of the church down the aisle to the carpeted, flower-decked platform, followed by a band of brushed deacons and starched deaconesses, an odor of expensive cologne trailed in his wake.

At first sight Katherine Dunham, along with Helen Weir and almost every other female present, fell madly in love with Reverend Scott. The silence was nervous, expectant; a moment later it was broken by a sigh of admiration and a burst of applause led by Reverend Dyett. The girl felt that she had never seen such warm, humorous eyes and wondered how such a man could have brought himself to a life of denial and service and privation such as she imagined the ministry exacted. He smiled as he reached the altar and turned to his audience, and she was sure that there had never before been a smile like his or teeth so white, the whiteness marked by fine dividing bands of gold, so that each seemed a well-set pearl.

His first words dropped like a bomb on the expectant congregation.

"Brothers and sisters, I am a sinner."

He spoke softly in a low, deep voice which sent a shiver down the rows of pews. He leaned forward intimately, his smile dissolving under some inner fire as he spoke. The deacons and deaconesses sat stiffly in the front row; visiting pastors sat self-consciously in the high-backed chairs on the altar platform.

"Brothers and sisters, my sins are the following." He began a deliberate enumeration, from the thievery of a cake from his mother's pantry at the age of five, through high-school and college peccadillos which had the ladies blushing into their handkerchiefs and the men trying to suppress smiles, right up to visitations of temptation as recent as the present stage of his career. His voice had been humble, a little abashed, but open, asking their forgiveness. One or two women were moist-eyed. And then suddenly he slammed his freckled fist on the Bible, lying opened on the stand before him, and cried out in a voice of thunder.

"And *who,*" he shouted, "*who* among you has not sinned in the sight of the Lord? Even the little babies! Even the old ones who can't get up and around any more to commit abominations, but just sit and *think* about it! There you are, a-looking at me. There you sit, hypocrites every one of you, wallowing in your own sin and happy to see a fellow brother down on his knees before you. Down in the dust!

"But let me tell you, a-sisters and a-brothers!" (The transformation was complete: at one moment the cultured, pleasantly controlled young visiting minister; the next, a raging, accusing fury, working into the sing-song rhythm that marked communication with the Spirit, lapsing into folk idiom, rocking on the balls of his feet, gripping the lectern so hard that the knuckles of his hands turned white under their freckles.) "You don't a-*fooooooo-ul* a-tha Lord! You *cain't* a-fool a-tha Lord-Jesus-praise-His-holy name. I *was* a sinner, but I'm *a-saved,* bless-His-holy-name-by-the blood-of-the-Lamb, SAVED!" He glared into the petrified congregation as though searching one who dared refute him. He continued, sing-song, eyes closed, rocking, a poetic chant as though all to himself. He was entering onto the territory of the wailing blues singer, voice lifting on the last syllable. Someone began a hand clapping, someone else cut across it with a counter rhythm; then foot stomping began in the same pattern.

"Oh I thought that I mus' die,
An' I ast de Lord's forgiveness,
For a-tellin Him a lie!"

The stanzas broke form.

"But, brothers and sisters, I REPENTED and I was SAVED. Washed clean in the blood of the Lamb. SAVED, I'm a-tellin' you. SAVED a-by the blood of the Lamb!"

The air crackled. Mrs. Meadows jumped from her seat like a marionette on a string and shouted, "Hallelujah!" The temperature seemed to rise by twenty degrees. Coats were shed amidst "Amens," and Reverend Scott wiped his brow with a spotless handkerchief as he began to pace the short span of the altar platform with heavy measured steps. Then, just as suddenly as his poetic trance had arisen, it subsided.

"Brothers and sisters," he whispered, "I will ask your pastor to bless this congregation."

Reverend Dyett's short, if crisp, blessing seemed too long. Then Reverend Scott, still controlled, his original groomed self, read the text whose exposition had given him his greatest triumphs.

"From Ezekiel, 37th chapter—first and second verses. *'The hand of the LORD was upon me, and carried me out in the Spirit of the LORD, and set me down in the midst of the valley which was full of bones. And caused me to pass by them round about: and behold, there were very many in the open valley; and, lo, they were very dry.'* "

"Yes, Lord!" the congregation answered.

"Amen!"

"Praise be His holy name!"

Reverend Scott closed the Bible and paced the length of the platform. He stopped at one end and pointed a long finger toward the back row of pews.

"And so what did I *do* to wash away those sins? Those sins I was a-telling you about. Those sins against the Lord. A-those abominations to His HOLY name?"

The girl watched entranced as the evangelist seemed to grow and swell. His brown eyes became glassy, water rose on his forehead, his breath came in short gasps, and his voice shifted a quarter-octave in register. Between gasps he sucked his breath inward, making a hissing sound as it passed through his gold-bordered teeth. The revival meeting was under way.

"Well I'll tell you what I did."

(Breathless silence for ten seconds, as though they didn't know; then a great sigh of relief, even sobs, tears, gasps, as—stopping dead in his tracks—he triumphantly bared his innermost being as though it were a scientific revelation or a military secret.)

"I went-down-into-the Valley of *Dry-y-y* Bones!" He tromped and trudged the stage, lowering into the dread valley, losing physical strength, falling to his knees with no respect for his sharply creased tan tweed suit, battling demons and doubts and temptations, gnawing his anguish as he clung to the pulpit and called on the Holy Ghost, water streaming from face and eyes and body as he relived his monstrous trials. His red-brown eyes flashed like twin searchlights and fastened on one after another of the rocking, moaning, quivering crowd. He draped over the pulpit and pointed at one, then another, in rapid fire.

"And you, sinner! And you, adulteress! And *you,* coveter of thy neighbor's wife! And *you,* spreader of evil tales!"

The girl tried to follow his accusations without turning her head and was astonished at the accuracy with which his targets hit home. The accused hung their heads or jerked convulsively, falling back onto neighbors or leaping up into the aisles at the sledge-hammer blows of the evangelist's attacks. No one paid much attention to them, as by now the room, with its windows nailed tight against the subzero weather, had become stifling. Through the thick, swirling atmosphere the sword of the avenging angel struck left and right, guided by the transported Reverend Scott.

Annette Dunham intensely disliked displays of this sort, and in this opinion she and Reverend Dyett were in complete accord. The preacher sat at one side of the high-backed chair reserved for the officiating evangelist, drying alternately, with a spotless white handkerchief, the palms of his hands and his high, bemused forehead. Annette Dunham sat staring stonily into the empty chair behind the evangelist. The fiery sword seemed deflected as it passed before her, the Spirit wavering an instant under her grim displeasure, then beating a retreat to more receptive ground. But Mayme Humbles, in her starched white deaconess' robe and cap, stood up in the front pew and said, "Praise the Lord!" in a loud and determined voice. Agatha Carrington dried her eyes on a dainty lace handkerchief and said, "Mama! Mama!" A few regular chapel members moaned and wept a little and stood up to shout or make a turn or two in the aisles, arms waving, eyes closed at the fervor of the message. But it was the guests from the Baptist churches and the newly formed Church of God in Christ who caused most of the commotion.

" '*And he said unto me, Son of man, can these bones live? And I answered, O Lord God, thou knowest!*' " Reverend Scott cried out sepulchrally, at the base of the altar.

"I said, sisters and a-brothers, can these dry-y-y bones a-live again? I see nothin' but bo-o-ones all aroun'!"

"A-a-a-umph!" answered the members of the Church of God in Christ, who were given to a form of vocal expression known as "trooping."

"Seen the finger bone"—holding high his index finger.

"Praise be His name!"

"Seen the leg bone"—lifting high his well-formed leg

with such a movement that the tweed trousers rose about the straining calf.

"Seen *all* a-them a-back bones. A-them a-hip bones. A-them a-thigh bones. A-them a-*other* bones. A-dry, without no *flesh*. A-dry, without no *skin*. A-dry, without no *blood*. Jus' *bones!*"

The trooping rose to a concerted gasping intake which sounded like a children's classroom smitten by whooping cough. At each anatomical exposure Reverend Scott whipped higher the flame of participation in the ladies and identification in the men. Those removed from this personal association were either hypnotized by the unfolding of the solo dance-drama or had given themselves over to the message behind the words.

At one moment the evangelist was on the floor, writhing in the throes of his combined torment and ecstasy, frothing at the mouth, veins in head and throat as tight as cable cords. But when Brown's Chapel seemed at the exploding point, he was suddenly on his feet, emerging calm and collected from behind a fresh white handkerchief. He spoke now almost in a whisper, reading from the big Bible, which had somehow not been dislodged during the drama, soothing the heaving, perspiring, weeping congregation, spiritually and physically and emotionally exhausted.

"*So I prophesied as I was commanded: and as I prophesied there was a noise. And behold, a shaking, and the bones came together, bone to his bone.* Oh, brothers and sisters, are *you* going to come together tonight, bone to bone, to be breathed upon and made to walk upright again?" His voice was tender, pleading. It was the cue for the choir to sing "Dry Bones." As the verses led from one bone to the other, joining one skeletal fragment to its partner, the pews emptied and enemies shook hands, friends embraced in tears, and all who could reach the revivalist—who hid his triumph behind a well-rehearsed boyish display of modesty—grasped his extended hands, pumped them up and down, even kissed them.

Among the few who remained seated during this processional were Annette Dunham and her daughter, but Helen Weir rose and joined the line of handshakers.

The younger girl had been aware of Helen Weir's unusual interest in Reverend Scott. She had seldom seen her niece in eclipse for so long a period, willing to be absorbed, drawn into, possessed by someone else, some power outside that left her without volition for banter or facetiousness. Her curiosity turned to consternation when, at the "call" from the pulpit for repentant sinners to go forward and kneel at the mourners' bench, Helen Weir arose, grabbed her by the arm, and piloted her to the front pew from which the officers of the church had risen to make way for the overflow of penitents. Her heart rose to her mouth as she felt the electric presence of the evangelist, who leaned across the pulpit, directed his burning gaze, pointed to one and then another of the sinners, and commanded them to kneel at the step below his feet. Some didn't wait, but threw themselves weeping and moaning onto the elevation, draped in white linen sheets for their reception. Panic seized the girl when she felt the finger point directly at her. Helen Weir had already stood up.

"Come on, Kitten," she said, addressing her aunt, but staring enraptured at the man. The girl felt her cheeks flush with embarrassment and beads of perspiration form on her upper lip and forehead. In anguish she turned to her Aunt Mayme, who stood to one side in her white frock, but to her dismay Mayme Humbles smiled and nodded in encouragement. Even Mrs. Williams, two rows back, leaned toward her as though to join the phalanx of "Shepherds" and "Shepherdesses" who would lead this unredeemed prize into the fold.

It had always been assumed by the congregation that

both Dunham children would one day officially "join" the church. (Their unbaptized state was, of course, not suspected.) This seemed as opportune a time as any, the rich interflow of spiritual communion making all feel an almost inebriated sense of brotherhood. The girl felt herself the victim of some horrible trickery. The surrounding sympathetic faces became coercive; the penetrating gaze of the preacher stripped her of her clothing and made her feel wretched and impure; her niece seemed a hypocrite, the wallowing sinners ridiculous, the whole scene unreal and dangerous. She wanted to cry, but fought against it by biting her lips and breathing deeply. She thought of her brother and how he would look at her with compassion, even disdain, if she allowed herself to take part in such a naked mass demonstration. She craned her neck toward her mother, and what she saw there gave her courage to rise on trembling legs and force her way through the crowded aisles, past surprised and shocked and disappointed glances, to the seat that she had just vacated. All of this had taken not more than sixty seconds, but to her it was an eternity. As she walked, she felt the hot gaze of the evangelist following her and was afraid to look up after that, for fear of whatever perturbation he might transmit to her because of his thwarted effort to save a choice soul.

Annette Dunham would not have stood in the way of her daughter's conversion, but she would not have approved of its taking place in just these circumstances or at the feet of a man as agilely exhibitionistic or as liberal in the exposition of subjects usually not brought before church congregations as Reverend Scott. She therefore turned to the girl with an almost imperceptible nod of approval and later explained her support of the child as parental liberalism, recognition of the free choice that all should have in regard to such individual properties as "soul" and "religion." But, true to the paradox of her nature, this respect for free will did not extend to her daughter's physical presence in church. She continued to exact from both her daughter and Helen Weir the full measure of Sunday attendance; and more than once Helen lamented her "conversion" as a moment of weakness, which she later attributed to the hypnotic quality of Reverend Scott's brown eyes. As a confessed and baptized Christian, a full-fledged member of Brown's Chapel African Methodist Episcopal Church, Helen Weir was honor bound to attend all services for the length of her stay in the Town.

When Helen Weir first became a member of the household, it had been difficult to decide how she should address her somewhat intricately conjugated relatives. In actual fact Albert Dunham, Sr., was her grandfather by marriage, but to have proceeded on this basis, especially in view of his being younger than her own mother, would have seemed ridiculous. In the end, "Big Albert" was agreed upon for the father, "Little Albert" or just "Albert" for her half uncle, and "Kitten" for her half aunt. After much deliberation Annette Dunham accepted "Madre" as preferable to "Aunt Nett," which she reserved for all second-generation relations of the Poindexter family. The use of the Spanish word gave a certain air of worldliness to an already complicated relationship and served to confound the inquisitive who would have questioned "aunt" or "grandmother."

Helen Weir's chief concern in life was enjoyment. Her most admirable quality, as far as the girl could see, was a genuine interest in people and a conscientious effort not to cause trouble. Her nature was essentially generous, and her family life had been on the whole a carefree round of parties and club meetings, sorority dances and dates. In the Bluff Street household she tried hard at first to ignore the unpleasantness at mealtimes, the black moods of the father, and the constant threat of physical violence, withheld now from the boy but periodically meted out to his sister in a backhanded slap or by the belt strap.

During Helen Weir's second month in the Town, Katherine Dunham became aware that a new mood was developing in her father. She realized that some business crisis was affecting their lives and that, although the shop was operating on a heavier schedule than ever and the dust wheel was churning through its ponderous rounds from early morning until late at night, although extra help had been taken on, there was a falseness in the apparent prosperity: there never seemed to be enough money. The girl was not familiar with the word "inflation," but she knew that her mother sent her to Simon's grocery store less and less often for porterhouse steak and that bitter words far into the night behind the closed doors of the bedroom were most of the time about money: how there wasn't enough for food and proper clothing or a family car, because the cost of living had outdistanced even the doubled and tripled income.

Once she was startled to hear the sounds of scuffling in the bedroom and then to see the door jerked open and a handful of coins flung onto the floor and a silver dollar rolling in crazy circles. The light was on because her niece was sitting at the living-room table with her open books.

"All right! You want money," her father said in the thick panting voice that marked a real crisis. "Take it! You accuse me of stealing it—take it and get out!"

That night her mother had a return of her old attack of contracting leg muscles, the first Helen Weir had witnessed. The ordeal left her shaken; but her initiation into the Dunham household was not yet complete.

A Saturday evening came when on one flimsy pretext or another Albert Dunham refused his son the allowance that would permit his cello lesson for the coming week. Sunday was made miserable by the boy's aloof resentment, the mother's arguments in his support, and the demoniacal outbursts of the father, who seemed goaded beyond measure by some inner passion quite unrelated to the immediate dispute. Helen Weir was not her usual cheerful self, but had fallen into the deepest kind of depression. While she and the younger girl were washing the dishes from the Sunday meal, the father stormed in and out of the kitchen, rattling pans, gathering scraps from the plates and morsels from his supply of partly spoiled butcher's leavings and setting them to stew for the dog Rex, slamming the door between hall and dining room with such force that the flimsy walls trembled. The boy practiced steadily at his cello in one corner of the living room. The mother sat darning stockings; her trembling fingers as she threaded the needle betrayed her pent-up emotions, and from time to time she wiped moisture from the spectacles she had recently acquired. When the dog food bubbled over and trickled onto the floor, Helen Weir threw down her dishcloth in disgust.

"He makes me sick!" she ground out, with such vehemence that her aunt stopped, hands in suds, and stared at her. "Imagine not giving Little Albert money for his cello lessons and offering me a box of chocolates for Valentine's Day!"

"He *what?*" The girl was astounded.

"Yes, he *did!*" Helen went on heatedly. "And he didn't even give Madre a *card* for her birthday." She snatched a saucepan and began vigorously polishing it, forgetting that she had just set it aside. "And he keeps hinting around and asking me to go to California with him! Just wait till I tell Madre! I bet he'll sing another tune. Or I'll tell Pop. Only I just didn't want any more trouble. There's enough already."

The hall door opened and slammed. Albert Dunham came in, turned the fire from under his bubbling kettle, and went out again. His daughter still stood with her mouth open.

"It isn't true," she said, half whispering, fighting to keep her voice steady. "I don't believe it. He *wouldn't.* He doesn't have any money. You saw what he threw on the floor the other night. It's because everything costs more and there just isn't enough money, but even if he has enough for the cello lessons, he wouldn't give it to you. He wouldn't ask you to go away with him. How *could* he? You're a *relative!* He——"

She stopped, because Helen was looking at her with something of the same pity and disgust she had seen on her brother's face when he found her too stupid or unknowing for words.

"How can you be so *dumb,* Kitten!" Helen put the pan away and went on drying the rest of the dishes. The girl knew that she had been protecting her father, justifying his impossible behavior, betraying her mother and her brother. But she felt that her denial might change things, turn things back to where they had been a few minutes ago, before the pot boiled over.

"He wouldn't do that," she repeated stubbornly, and the steaming pot began to double and triple and lose focus through the tears in her eyes. She let the tears brim over and fall into the tepid dishwater. The only important thing was to make what trembled on the brink of crashing down upon her take some other turn and be true for someone else's life, if it must be true at all. She felt the nearness of total disaster, the victory of the lurking shadows and unnamable terrors of childhood if this new thing were to be so.

"I just don't believe it," she repeated.

Her father came for the dog food and left.

When he had gone, Helen said, "All right, you don't believe me. He writes me notes all the time and tries to get me to talk to him alone. I always tear them up, but you just watch and see. There'll be another one."

The girl felt the truth in her niece's statements, but hung her head over the dishpan without speaking and continued uncommunicative for the rest of the evening and for several days following.

The cello lesson was on Friday, and, hearing her mother and brother in conversation, the girl knew that there had been no solution, no way to filch or borrow or earn the money to pay for it. An apprehensive gloom had settled on everybody in the household except the father, who strained the gasoline in his tumblers and hauled carpets in and out of the dust wheel and planted the pressing iron with its spouting gas flame on the wet pressing cloth with a grim singleness of purpose that presaged more trouble than tantrums or arguments. The girl kept well out of his way, and, as though she blamed her niece for what was going on, she stayed far over to her side of the narrow bed at night. She missed the warmth of the body that she had grown accustomed to and, because of the cold and her gnawing fear, slept hardly at all. She dragged home from school on the day scheduled for the cello lesson to find the fire dead in the base-burner and the ashes unemptied. This indicated that her brother was in rebellion and her mother and father in open feud. Without removing her coat or overshoes, she emptied the stove of its ashes, rebuilt the fire, washed the stacked-up dishes, and began to prepare supper. In the shop her father grunted in response to her greeting. Her mother sat at the sewing machine constantly adjusting her glasses, which, moistened by tears, slipped from her nose more frequently than usual.

The Cardwell brothers, Roy and Meredith, had been onetime playmates of the brother and sister during their earliest days in the Town. Meredith, the older, now in his second year at the junior college, was a good football player; his brother was a dogged scholar. Both young men had supported themselves through all their school years and for this were accorded a certain respect by Albert Dunham. During this winter of increased business he had hired the older brother to alternate evenings between the dust wheel and the pressing machine, and Meredith Cardwell had immediately become infatuated with Helen Weir.

On the evening of the cello lesson the girl went about her chores so immersed in her own misery and her indefinable apprehensions that she was not aware of an additional disquiet until Meredith Cardwell, making a special trip to the kitchen, pointed out that Helen had not returned from college and had sent no word of explanation; and he hinted darkly that she had not seemed at all herself lately. The girl turned from him to hide her flushed face and followed him back to the shop, where she telephoned first her Aunt Mayme and then Mrs. Williams. But her niece wasn't at either place; so she braced herself and advanced on her mother, who sat stonily at the sewing machine.

"What could have happened to Helen?" she asked. "She's never late like this!"

Annette Dunham stopped stitching on a gray skirt. In her surprise she forgot her role of silent martyrdom.

"Why, isn't she with you? She was home early—your father was on his way from Mrs. Fitzpatrick's as she was leaving school and brought her home in the truck. She came in and went right out again, and I thought she went upstairs. Where in the world could she be?"

The daughter could only shake her head, but none of her fears were dislodged. Leaving the shop, she met her brother.

"I can't find Helen," she said, genuinely worried now. "She came home from school and left right away. Where do you think she went?"

"Probably dead," her brother said, shortly. "She'd be better off."

The girl stared at him. Then she turned and ran up the stairs, past the door to the flat and into the back room, where the dust wheel sat in one of its rare periods of repose. A single bare electric bulb lighted the bleak, icy hall.

She went as far back as the small stone tumbler room before pulling the string of the dim light, which scarcely penetrated into the yawning mouth of the wheel. It swung back and forth in a feeble effort to dispel the shadows. Somehow the dust wheel had been from the beginning associated with trouble; she peered into the cavern beneath, but could distinguish no limp form, no mutilated body. She hardly knew what to look for, but was glad that she had not made her discovery there.

She went through the flat again, stopping to set the dining-room table and put more coal on the living-room fire. Her brother was at his cello practice, fingering over and over again the same exercise. She wanted to ask him to stop because it was sure to cause trouble, but her initiative faltered as she saw the grim set of his mouth; she continued her search, which had begun to take on a desperation she was unable to control. This time she turned the corner at the bottom of the stairway and buried her face in her coat collar against the blast of cold wind that blew down from the cliff. The hall window threw a square of light on the muddy snow in the side yard, and a light from the entrance to the tumbler room cut across the far end of the yard. Between the two were the skeletons of the most recently discarded delivery trucks.

The girl climbed from one to the other in a fruitless search. She moved farther toward the cliff, staying well out of the range of the dog, whom she saw framed for a moment in the opening leading to the cellar rooms. He snorted once or twice, and turned from the cold to drag his clanking chain farther into the cave. Then, as she walked a few steps farther, she saw the outline of Helen Weir's body, crumpled in the snow just out of range of the dog. She stood petrified, then bent over and began to tug at her niece's shoulder, trying to pull her into a sitting position; but the anxiety of the search had taken all of her strength. Turning, she stumbled back over the icy path of the side yard, bumping her shins against an old wagon shaft in her flight for assistance.

At the top of the stairway she heard her mother's voice and her own name. Bursting into the dining room, she saw Annette Dunham wildly waving both arms and dashing frantically between kitchen and living-room doors. Then the dining-room table heaved onto two legs, dishes and silverware crashed to the floor, and the girl grasped the oil lamp that slid in her direction across the white tablecloth. Holding the lamp high, she saw her father and brother on the floor, locked in the kind of lethal embrace that she knew only from motion pictures. Her mother sounded much as she did when racked by her morbid night attacks.

"Help! Katherine! Albert, he's your *father*—oh, Al, *don't, don't, he's your son!*"

The girl felt a rush of blind loathing for her mother. Sickened by the shocking sight of the two bodies rolling, panting, struggling for an advantage on the floor, she stood for a moment unable to move; then she put the lamp out of reach on the floor and began yanking on her father's jacket. It was already torn in the seam around the arm; now the sleeve ripped from the coat. She went suddenly blind, and her sickness turned to fury. She grabbed the flying coattail and didn't notice that father and son were suddenly both standing, gasping, glaring at one another with hatred and that Meredith Cardwell stood between them, his muscular body blocking their efforts at further attack. Her father shoved her roughly aside and snatched the dangling sleeve from her hands. He brushed past his son, panting.

"Get out of my house," he said. "Tonight. And don't ever let me catch you in it again."

"Al, Al, you don't know what you're saying," her mother cried, still aimlessly wandering from door to door, stopping to pick up wreckage from the upset table, waving knives and forks in front of her as though trying to find a focus. The father stormed down the stairway.

"I'll kill him," her brother said, his voice shaking; the old calmness was quite gone. "I said I would if he ever touched me again!" Then savagely to his mother: "He's no father of mine. And *don't ever say it again!*" He was trembling and seemed terribly thin and for the first time helpless. The girl wanted to bury her face against his shoulder and cry, but instead she turned to Meredith Cardwell.

"Downstairs," she said. "In back. By Rex. Helen." Then she sat on the couch and felt all of her joints turn to water.

Her brother went by with a cardboard box tied with string and an armload of books, and her mother clung to him saying, "Albert! Albert! Not tonight. He didn't mean it! Where will you go tonight? You haven't had your supper!"

For the first time he didn't seem to know she was there, or his sister, but went straight out and down the steps as though he had lost all faculty for speech with his last words.

The girl stood up when Meredith Cardwell came into the room, carrying her niece, who had begun to regain consciousness and was shivering spasmodically. Their entrance must have seemed like some unreal anticlimax to Annette Dunham. She still stood with knives and forks in each hand, but her arms had ceased their arabesques and hung limply at her sides.

"She went out because she was so upset, I guess. And passed out," the girl said listlessly, tired now and so drained by the past few hours that she only wanted to be in her room alone.

"Passed *out?* Is she *sick?* Oh, Katherine—when I already have more than I can bear!" Her mother placed the silverware on the table and started helping her daughter to undress Helen.

"Meredith, put some water on to heat and phone Dr. Williams. All of this trouble, with Albert put out of the house. I just can't bear any more. And with Uncle Ed just buried, too. Katherine, go phone your Aunt Mayme—no, that would just make more trouble with your father because she's my sister. Oh, why did they have to fight over a cello lesson!" Her fingers trembled and her glasses were wet, so that she didn't notice the crumpled piece of paper that fell from Helen Weir's fingers, still numb with cold. The girl picked it up and put it into her own coat pocket. She knew immediately what it was, and she wanted to tear it up without reading it or hand it back to the writer.

Meredith Cardwell returned, bringing extra blankets from the couch in the living room, and fixed the fire and lit the gas in the oven in the kitchen without being told, and put water in the hot water bottle, and stood to one side looking worried, while the girl and her mother wrapped their patient in warm blankets and massaged her fingers. Dr. Williams' comforting step on the hall stairs saved an awkward situation, because Helen Weir was beginning to gasp and try to sit up and wanted to say something, and Annette Dunham was asking her what on earth was the matter with her, why had she been so upset that she went outside without a coat, while the girl was hoping and praying that she would keep her mouth shut or stay unconscious until she could regain composure.

Dr. Williams said, "Well, now. Just look what we have here!" Then he listened through his stethoscope and felt her wrist and took her blood pressure, and after he'd heard the story of how she had been found, he took out a needle and syringe and a tiny vial of clear liquid.

"Well, well. Might've been worse. Young girls do have their problems—nothing serious—just watch out for a cold. Keep her good and warm." He looked significantly at Meredith Cardwell, who had lurked partly out of sight just inside the kitchen door, and burst into a good-natured guffaw.

"Take her to a football game, young fellow," he said, a twinkle in his eye. Then he buttoned his overcoat and buckled his overshoes and said goodbye and left.

Meredith Cardwell followed him down the stairs, then returned. "Mr. Dunham isn't there. Mr. Crusoe wants to go. I'll close the shop." He said his farewells and left.

Helen Weir was already asleep. The mother started to speak, as though to ask for some explanation, but seemed to think better of it and turned away, dazed again as the climactic event of the evening recurred to her. The girl went to her room, on the pretext of removing her coat before she put the kitchen in order for the night, and took out the crumpled piece of paper. It bore her father's distinctive slanting handwriting, and her face burned as she read, not without some pangs of conscience, the proof of her niece's accusations: insistence that she accept a small gift, coy reprimand for her rejection of his advances, and clearly, concisely, the offer of the clandestine alliance. The lure: magic, golden California, flight from the Middle West. The justification: his need, his desire, the rectification of the loss he had suffered in his first wife's death.

The food stayed in the kitchen untouched; the father remained in the shop below until far into the night; Annette Dunham cried herself to sleep; Helen Weir, lulled by the doctor's sedative, slept soundly on the dining-room couch, wrapped in blankets and hot-water bottles.

And Katherine Dunham, drawn into a knot in the middle of her bed, stared dry-eyed at the square of sky outside the window. As though tired of endless petitions, the Star had gone out of sight. This night she marked as a turning point in her life, a matriculation from the faltering, fumbling, accidental knowledges of childhood; from naïveté and wonderment and straining to decipher in the dark, and asking favors of stars, and hoping for a house warm in winter with concealed sources of heating, and yearning for tender love, and looking forward to never feeling shame or fear—a matriculation from juvenile optimism. She felt that she understood her brother better now and the way he looked at her pityingly, because she was so gullible as to hope for something better, to hope at all, to kick and struggle and try—to run from one sprung leak in the structure of their combined four lives to another, trying to stop the flood with her eager, inept fingers. She thought of her mother with contempt for not having done something about things before now, of her brother with anger and humiliation at some betrayal not quite defined, and of her father with cold hatred.

Helen Weir went to board with the Williamses. Annette Dunham had announced her intention of leaving her husband if he made no effort at reconciliation with his son. The boy had written from the City; he had entered the University with high recommendation from the Town college, but was without means for the barest sustenance. He had applied for work in one of the University dining rooms in exchange for his meals; meanwhile his situation was critical. Albert Dunham not only maintained his unyielding position toward his son, but forbade either mother or daughter to make any overtures of assistance, and to insure respect for his authority he cut off both of their allowances. From somewhere the mother produced small sums, and the daughter forfeited every other day's lunch. But mere exchange of correspondence with the son would throw the father into fits of rage, more volcanic than ever as the fortress of his visionary life crumbled. Meredith Cardwell, victim of some of these moods, found other employment.

When the girl felt that her mother might waver in her decision to leave, taking her along, she braved possible further disaster and showed her the worn, crumpled note that Helen had dropped. Annette Dunham glanced at it cursorily and looked for some time into space. Then, turning her face and compressing her lips, she tore it into small bits, threw the pieces into the coal pail behind the stove, and continued brushing her hair, partitioning it into sections to be rolled into knots and tied down for the night.

The following day, seated in the cold living room, surrounded by suitcases and other signs of exodus, Annette Dunham waited for her daughter's return from school. Her face was swollen; her eyes were red behind their magnifying lenses.

"Your father struck me when I asked for money to send Albert for food," she said, her voice unsteady. "His own son. He broke my glasses." The girl noticed that one side of the spectacles was without its gold frame, but was fastened to her mother's hair by a string and hairpin. Pity for her mother and gratitude that at last some forward step would be taken melted the hard core that was by now a familiar part of her being. She touched her mother gently on the shoulder.

"Don't cry, Mother," she said. "Don't cry. We'll go somewhere and have a house, and Albert can come back. I'll work hard and help. Maybe we can go to the City."

The mother drew back to stare aghast at her daughter, as she so often did, as though she couldn't possibly be in her right senses.

"Move away from *here?*" she exclaimed. "With Mama and Mayme here and Ed buried here and your father here?"

Plans for escape died in the girl as suddenly as they had been born. She was again the victim of her own naïveté. Perhaps she herself was not involved in her mother's plans. Perhaps she would be left as before, to a fall and winter of white canvas leftover shoes. Not Mrs. Williams, not her Aunt Mayme, not anyone would take her in, in defiance of Annette Dunham's disapproval or Albert Dunham's strictures. She sank back into her feeling of impotence and waited to be told what to do, whether to go or stay, to prepare to leave or to remove her wraps and make the fire and fix her father's dinner.

"You're going with me," her mother said. "Pack your clothes in the case on your bed. It's started, but I just didn't have the strength to finish. We're going to Rebecca Brown's. I've rented her house, and she'll move into the attic. I certainly hope I never have to see her. I wish there was another way for her to go in and out excepting down that ladder in the bathroom."

For a moment the mother forgot her immediate problems in anticipation of future ones. It had been a bitter defeat to seek a favor from her first benefactress in the Town, to retract in the feud that she herself had initiated. But the locale was respectable and the house familiar. They went in the truck, driven by a boy who had been recruited just that day. The father worked steadily at his pressing machine and did not look up at their departure, though the girl entered to help Mr. Crusoe load the sewing machine. There were no farewells.

A cold March wind was blowing, but the streets were miraculously clear of snow and there was a faraway smell of spring in the air. The girl passed familiar landmarks of her childhood with a quickening pulse and imagined, as they rounded the corner past the stone steps leading from the park bordering the creek, that she smelled tiny new dandelion flowers and freshly baked bread. Rebecca Brown was not at home, but the key was in the mailbox and the lights were on and the small cottage was warm and cheerful. Avoiding conversation, they set about installing themselves in their new home.

The fluctuating economy just before the Great Collapse threw the Town into the same uncertainty as it did the nation. Individual lives followed the strange current of things, feeling at one moment drunken exhilaration, at the next the bewildered uncertainty of the blind at some completely unfamiliar sound or smell. For Katherine Dunham an unexpected blossoming of popularity at the school followed the disruption of her family life. She was elected president of the Girls' Athletic Association almost before she realized that she had been nominated. And as though embarrassed at previous miserliness, Destiny bestowed a double bounty in the form of membership in the Terpsichorean Club. Then, with an overwhelming burst of generosity, it accorded her center position on her class basketball team, and a few weeks later on the school team.

Then the pendulum swept downward. Her father, stubbornly refusing reconciliation with either wife or son, had been unable to find or afford adequate assistance in the shop. For a short while he supplemented his wife's earnings at her private sewing trade in the cottage with small donations toward food and clothing for the girl. At the height of her newly found freedom—when she could enjoy the evenings set aside for the important extracurricular activities, with only the stipulation that home duties be discharged later—Albert Dunham decided to withdraw his contribution unless his daughter paid for it by working after school in the shop.

There was no way out, as ends in the cottage on Elm Street could not be made to meet without added income. Fortunately the basketball season was over, but no manner of manipulation squeezed enough time out of the rushing moments of the late afternoon to attend meetings, follow the routine of the beloved Terpsichoreans, and train for the coming track season. The promise the girl had shown in track events, particularly in high-jumping, she clung to stubbornly; but before the spring track meet she was forced to withdraw because of excruciating flashes of pain in her knees and shinbones. Weeping in her frustration, she told her mother, who agreed to a consultation with Dr. Williams. He diagnosed the trouble as "growing pains" and prescribed white powders and less activity.

There was no one to intervene on her behalf with her father, and midspring found her dispiritedly following the old path across the Jefferson Street bridge to Bluff Street. Her first sight of the front office of the shop disturbed her. The plate-glass window was streaked by spring rains, the letters spelling WEST SIDE CLEANERS AND DYERS were faded, and their gold edging had started to peel. The shop door stood open, and the cloying smell of gasoline reached her before she entered. Inside there was complete chaos. Unsorted clothing covered the desk, the chairs, the sewing machine that had replaced her mother's, and the floor. The hanging racks were crowded with undelivered clothing. Cousin Howard Owings, again recruited for work, was loading the delivery truck with carelessly wrapped suits and packages. Thalia Dishman's sister stood at a pressing board, and the father, battered gray felt hat pulled down on his head, struggled through the back doorway with an armload of reeking woolens. The girl sorted and marked the clothing, dusted and scrubbed the front office, and then, no longer able to avoid the inevitable, went out into the spring evening and up the familiar stairway to the flat above.

Here the dissolution was even worse. There had evidently been no fire for some time. Dust coated the living-room furniture and windowpanes; the cot in the dining room, where her cousin evidently slept, was an unmade nest of soiled quilts; mice scattered from the kitchen sink and stove, where they had been foraging in moldering food remnants and their own droppings. She realized sharply and for the first time the enormous effort that her mother had put into organizing their lives, into making something more than just passable out of nothing. She, too, had made her contribution to the endless battle against the invasion of weather, time, rodents, the base-burner, the dust wheel, working instinctively beside her mother, not recognizing the drive as one for self-preservation as much as for order. Now she stepped gingerly into the kitchen, the soles of her feet tingling as she avoided grease spots and rat leavings on the once spotless linoleum. She balked at scouring the scum-coated pot in which the dog's meals were cooked, but lighted the gas stove, heated a small washtub of water, and began cleaning the kitchen.

That night her protests to her mother were so vehement that she was, after the first few days of divided duty, required to do service in the shop only.

The most popular girls of her class were sewing gold wool letters on navy blue sweaters—the school colors—and a boy named William Booker, who like Meredith Cardwell was a good football player, became friendly with Katherine Dunham. The Bookers had only recently arrived in the Town, but because they appeared on several occasions at Brown's Chapel, the girl felt that she could consider them among her acquaintances. With some misgivings she allowed William Booker to escort her from school as far as the bridge, and, after halfhearted protests, sewed his gold letters on her sweater. She avoided telling her mother that they were for a boy's athletic achievement, not for hers.

Albert Dunham, however, with what seemed to his daughter a sixth sense, but was really only deduction based on observation and astuteness, gauged the moment of her departure from school and stationed his delivery truck in some conspicuous spot, so that she would be forced to say farewell to William Booker and relinquish his company for her father's. If he was delayed by his work, she might almost reach the bridge; but it seemed to have become a compulsion with him to forestall any companionship of his daughter's that might lead to escape from his authority. It was he who discovered the provenance of the embossed letters and he who forced her to return them.

After this she avoided personal contact with her father as much as possible, discharging her duties and waiting impatiently to be driven home. The school term ended; Helen Weir returned to Chicago; Annette Dunham worked at building a business following of her own and was increasingly depended upon by her husband for the execution of alterations to clothing, which he delivered and called for at her home. There was little money and no talk of reconciliation between the parents. The unrest of presentiment flooded the entire country. Late in the summer there was a flurry of excitement over a brief visit from the brother, who shocked both mother and sister by his thinness and aloofness—by an estrangement from them that they could not fathom but assumed had to do with the City, the University, and a way of life remote from their own.

Eleven
The Creek

*

In spring the creek running alongside the wooded park that separated Rowena Avenue and Elmwood Avenue stayed continuously swollen—in early spring because of melting snow, in late spring because of heavy rains. Now it was late spring, and the creek was at its most turbulent. Both snows and rains had been unusually heavy that year, and the muddy water rushed down its path carrying dead tree branches, pieces of shingle torn off in lightning storms, lumps of limestone marl, and even boulders. This rubble would butt against the time-worn retaining walls with such force as to crumble sections of the concrete or congest to form dams that forced the overflow onto the paths, byways, wagon roads, fields, and woodlands that followed the creek from the source of the Illinois River to a tributary of the Desplaines River just beyond the town.

One evening in late spring, full of stormy resentment against her father, the young girl left the Rowena Street tramway and descended the stone steps leading from the street down into the park. It had become his practice to make her wait night after night in the shop until he could drive her home himself in the truck, partly to forestall the innocent conversations she might have with the youth who was the current delivery boy, partly to have occasion for his own increasing demonstrations of intimacy, which bewildered, terrified, and sickened her.

The strain of her confusions and of her coming final examinations was beginning to tell on her, but she was left with one bright hope—that of escape. She wanted to apply herself more earnestly to her studies and to devote consecutive hours, rather than stolen ones, to classes in eurythmics and interpretive dancing. And especially in the spring it became harder than ever to force herself to turn off Desplaines Street and into Bluff Street and go to her father's shop. The odor of gasoline, the confusion of bits of paper with scrawled orders and numbers left for her to enter in the ledger, the pile of fume-filled woolens and silks and satins to be sorted, gave her a feeling of utmost despondency. The sewing woman hired after the split in the Dunham household came early and left early, so that the girl scarcely ever saw her, and only Mr. Crusoe was left working in the shop: he would shut off the steam-pressing machine shortly after her arrival and depart, leaving the more expert hand finishing for her father. Then, outside or upstairs in the carpet room behind the disordered flat where her father lived alone now, there might still be Old Man Ferguson, mumbling, bending over the hand-cranked auxiliary tubs, skimming the murky sediment from almost clear gasoline and sorting it into tin drums, to gratify that endless, hopeless, pathetically optimistic belief of her father's that waste could be done away with, that if one treated dirty gasoline with care, it would become virgin again. So tubs and pails and kegs sat in the tumbler room upstairs and out in back, and her father and Old Man Ferguson drained and skimmed and mixed and strained, losing more in the transfer and in clogged and choked pipes and pistons, and eventually in dissatisfied customers, than if they had thrown the used fluid out.

But, fired by an almost naïve confidence in his inventive and rational capacities, Albert Dunham continued in his own way, dreaming of becoming affluent enough to transport his daughter to a warm climate (California became more prominent in conversation as the winters of the Town grew colder) and there establish her permanently, in a bungalow that he would design himself, as a sort of hostess and loving daughter and willing mistress combined. It is doubtful that he understood the full significance of his desires. He must have felt only the drabness, the treadmill inescapability of his life as it seemed cut out for him; and as she grew in likeness to the woman who had first meant love, security, social prestige, and hope in life to him, his frustrations became focused upon his daughter.

On this particular spring night, her work finished, Katherine Dunham had refused to wait longer for her father. Keyed to hypersensitivity, she had begun seeing in every gesture or overture, whether from her father or the delivery boy or even a friendly customer, a possible aggression. Her uneasiness became especially acute now, as the warm spring sun dropped out of sight, and the delivery boy said a good-bye that seemed too intimate, and children stopped playing, and Bluff Street quietened into the hush that meant dinner hour. She went once or twice to the door and looked toward Western Avenue, from which the delivery truck should turn into Bluff Street if her father was on his regular route. The palms of her hands were moist and cold, and she wiped them across the canvas-covered ironing board. She picked up Mrs. McFarland's black pleated skirt with its Paris label and put it down again. Then on impulse she hurried to the rear of the shop and slid the bolt of the back door, felt her way between the pressing machines and out of the front office, and stepped into the strangely deserted street.

Books in hand, she ran the length of Bluff Street. Passing the bottling factory, she glanced aside into the cheerful kitchen-dining room of the Byfields: Helen sat at the table with the books, and her mother stirred something at the gasplate by the sink. Crossing Jefferson Street with a quick look left and right for cars, she almost collided with Art Simon on his new bicycle. They "Hi-ed" at each other, and she went on to the car stop on the far side of the street by the bridge and leaned against the lamppost in front of Adler's fish market, trying not to show that she was out of breath.

Her old feeling of fearlessness, of being able to run or fight her way out of any harm as a boy would do, came back to her. This was a feeling rarely experienced since the shame of her first blood flow and since the alternate tension and hopelessness that had come over her with a full understanding of her father's attentions: the wanting her to sit close to him in the truck or kiss him goodbye, or the touch and fondling that made everything about her in life seem smudgy and unclean and waiting. (For what? She still didn't know. It was something implied, its very vagueness making it worse, shattering any hope for the love or affection she saw other fathers show their children—comradeship, games together, playful chiding, a check now and then to go shopping with for anything you wanted. The terrible *unknown,* the unclean thing smirked at, was in some way associated *unnaturally* with her own father. Had she done something wrong? Did the closed upstairs room and the gray sweater of her childhood have anything to do with this?)

The Jefferson Street car came, and at Chicago Street she transferred to the smaller, more rural Rowena Avenue streetcar.

The spring evening remained balmy despite the increasing dusk, and she leaned her head wearily against the iron window bars, giving way to the seductive promise of warm weather; smelling the rain over and the rain to come; almost hearing the pushing of buds on trees that leaned toward the open windows; feeling the swell and thrust of small things in the earth under the quiet touch of approaching night. As the streetcar neared the park, she roused herself to decide which path to follow home—the one through the park or the one down the tree-darkened lane past the fretful chained police dog. She chose the former, though she had agreed with her mother not to take this route, even at early dusk. Now the street lights were coming on one by one, pale against the rich red and purple glow of the sky. She stood, swaying in the nearly empty streetcar as she adjusted her middy blouse, and pulled the cord overhead. She waved to the conductor and walked across the bridge, pausing to look down into the littered muddy water, and then descended the wide stone steps to the park.

She felt excited and sure of herself and utterly, independently brave as she stepped from the third step onto the creek wall and started her walk. The narrow path was muddy and full of pockets of water, so she walked along the top of the wall, as she and her brother had done when the whole family had lived so long ago in Rebecca Brown's cottage, or as she did sometimes even now on mornings when she walked all the way to school. There was a certain amount of danger attached to her daring because at this time of year the cement might give way, leaving the rubble interior of the wall to crumble into the water that lapped and swirled against it.

She saw a weak spot ahead, chose a reasonably dry spot in the path, and jumped down. Carefully watching her steps, she had kept her head lowered; and it was only as her feet touched ground that she became aware of a quite different and more immediate danger.

Just ahead of her there was a man, blond, not too young, unshaven, unwashed—the kind of tramp that her mother always hurried her past when they walked home late at night, or scornfully turned away from the back door when one begged food or yard work at the Elmwood Avenue house. There was another kind of tramp—old, ill, used hard by time and circumstance, bleary of eye and shaky of hand

—to whom her mother would willingly allot a small amount of yard clearing now and then as payment for a cup of coffee or some left-over scraps of food. But this man was the shunned kind, and curiosity about him distracted the greater part of her fear; she stood in the path, frankly examining the man, holding her ground, with the crumbling wall and rising water on one side, the dark woods on the other. In the gray cast from the sky and a pale flicker from a hanging lamp on the bridge, she could see pale eyes close set on either side of a high, thin-bridged, narrow nose. A small line of mustache detached itself from the unkempt stubble, but it in no way concealed the pathetic weakness of a mouth that kept working, saying things, mouthing things, exposing stained, cracked teeth and a tongue that continuously licked back saliva between muttered words, whose meaning passed completely over her head.

Her first flash of reaction was that he was ill or hungry and that he would take food or the means to procure it in any way that he could. They were *thieves* then, these shifty-eyed others, and for that reason to be feared. She felt safe in having nothing—only two books, a transfer stub, and the three cents left from the ten she had given the Jefferson Street conductor. And he wouldn't want the books, so he could have the rest. Her relief must have made her smile, because the man relaxed a little from a tense watchfulness and moved a step closer. She felt suddenly chilled and retreated a step. Here it was again, that feeling of unknown danger, coupled with revulsion and a kind of fear that gripped all of her hollow parts and made her want to pray out loud for some relief, some passer-by, even a child or a dog.

She noticed the agitation of one hand which had remained in his pocket and of the other which reached toward her as she drew back, ready to grip her, to stop her flight, to do—what? She called on memories of her brother. What would he have done? He would have smiled and told her in so many words not to panic, not to quake—above all, never to show what was going on inside. *Don't cry out, don't give in to fear, don't give the gods the cheap satisfaction of seeing you weaken.* She had been trying to live by that through the bewildering labyrinth of this past year. And so now it was not hard, in spite of deep disquiet, to stare with what she believed to be regal command at this abject person.

"Please," she said politely, trying to step to one side and eying the crumbling line of embankment to her left.

The man moved into a vantage point that crowded her against the wall. He stood at an angle, prepared to block her escape either forward along the path or sideways into the already dark woods. And backward? Up the stone steps and across the wooden bridge? Suppose he grabbed her in the second that she turned to run on the slippery path, in the concealment of the hollowed-out bowl of woods? Who would know, who would see what might have happened, and what would it be? Murder? But why? For three pennies and a used transfer stub?

Her hand moved to the pocket of the middy blouse to extract the proof of her insolvency. But she stopped because the man was saying words directed at her; and garbled as they were, panted, incoherent, she learned that he wanted her to look, to look at him and at what he was going to do. And whatever he was going to do required an accomplice—not an active one, but a spectator. She pieced together words for which Jimmy McGuire had had his mouth washed out with soap, but this man was using them not in anger, not at a playmate who had worsted him in a fistfight.

"Son of a bitch," he said. His words became clearer, steadier, surer as she stood rooted in combined fear and fascination. Here was a person in great and deep and mysterious infinite pain, and still there was no mistaking the mounting need, the concupiscence behind those small burning eyes as they fixed far into hers.

"Son of a bitch." He was beginning to pant now, and, unable either to understand fully or fully reject the meaning in his eyes and voice, she dropped her own eyes and found that while talking he had unfastened his loose-fitting, soiled trousers and inserted one hand into the opening.

She wanted to look away, because what was happening was too intimate, too naked for her to be watching. She knew that by participating even this far she had taken a step from which there was no recall. She would never be able to look again with innocence at men of this kind or even at her school friends or at her brother or her father. Inactively active by being there, by not raising her eyes or closing them, she lost the crystal-clear virginity that had until now carried her, untouched, past a knowledge too long held off. Not a part of the act, she nevertheless knew that she was sharing herself with, losing herself to this tramp, not only because she was afraid, but because in a moment she would know what had a moment before been unknown and would breathe easier for having been given some answer to her own dark questioning.

Then distaste arose within her, and she wanted to escape, to save herself any further knowledge of intimacy. She looked behind her, measuring the distance; she looked at the tramp. He read her movement, but then all along he had been reading her thoughts—aware, in spite of preoccupation with self, of her fascination, of her acceptance of his tutelage, of the chain of revelations that were leaving her no longer young. The slit beneath the mustache widened, and the tongue and lips worked faster, accelerating the single monotonous theme. "Son of a bitch. Son of a bitch. Son of a bitch." His breathing became a continuous groan, and, unable to carry the weight of his excitement, he backed up to the tree and leaned against it, rolling his head from side to side against the rough bark, his body striking the trunk convulsively, so that the branches rattled an accompaniment to his ritual.

"Jesus Christ," he said, adding to his vocabulary. "Jesus Christ. Son of a bitch." The obscenities became a single long cry whining up into the tree and descending into a low, helpless, grief-filled moan.

She closed her eyes and leaned trembling against the wall. Then she looked at the man and, loathing him and herself, too, she began to run. Water and mud splashed over her ankles, and her eyes stung with tears of anger and shame. At the other end of the park she stumbled on the top step and fell on knees and palms into the road above. She picked up the Virgil and the Greek mythology and wiped them off with her sleeve. She drew her arm across her eyes and held her trembling body to a slow walk, under the street light, past the Stevens' house, around to the back door of Rebecca Brown's, and into the warm safe glow of her mother's kitchen.

In the dining room Annette Dunham was bent over the sewing machine. She looked up as her daughter entered.

"Katherine, you're late. And you shouldn't have left before your father got back. He phoned twice already and is pretty much annoyed that you would go away and leave the shop like that. Why"—drawing the thread out long, breaking it between her teeth—"just look at you! What on *earth* happened to your dress? And your *shoes!*"

"It's muddy, Mother, I——"

"Did you come by the park, Katherine?"—stopping dead, garment half withdrawn from the machine pedal.

"Yes, Mother, I did"—trying to get as far as the bathroom.

"But, Katherine! Haven't I told you never to——"

"Yes, Mother. I'm sorry. It was such a nice evening, and I wanted to see the creek. It's right up to the top and running over in places. I fell on the steps and skinned my knee a little"— Looking down: maybe she could get away now.

Her mother released her, turning again to the sewing machine, inserting a different part of the dress.

"You shouldn't have left without your father," she said.

(*Carefully guarded, so well protected from anything unclean or suggestive. Why, a boy couldn't even have a dance with her at the Christmas charity ball without first asking Mr. Dunham! And then not always getting his consent, because Mr. Dunham loved to dance with his graceful, growing daughter and over and over he would say that he was sorry but she already had this dance with her father, and she would look down and blush with embarrassment at the embarrassment of the boy. And what would she think now when her mother would say to some visitor in the next room:*

"Oh, that's all right. You just speak right out. Going to have a baby! *You don't say! With that* horrible *old man!"*

Hushed voice from the visitor again, then Annette Dunham again, sure of herself and her faultless upbringing and her upright, sturdy pioneer forebears:

"Oh, no, Katherine wouldn't even know what we're talking about. Why, she doesn't know a thing about such things! And never asks questions. Just as innocent as she was at six!")

She passed her mother and went into the bathroom; she clung to the water cabinet above the toilet seat and hung her head down over the bowl, but was able to render only clear mucus and saliva. She gagged once or twice, and Annette Dunham, pausing between seams, heard the sound.

"Are you all right, Katherine?" She called anxiously, all mother, all concern, all curious.

"Yes, Mother. I'll be right there." She bathed her face in cold water and closed her eyes for a moment. Then she went into the dining room.

"We have veal with green peppers and noodles for dinner," her mother said. "The noodles have been in so long they might be too soft. Just light the fire again and set the table. I have to finish this alteration—Mrs. Hardy will be coming first thing in the morning. She's going to Springfield for her daughter's wedding. My! How time flies! You don't remember her, do you, Katherine?"

No answer needed because the sewing machine whirred on, and Annette Dunham, foot busy on pedal, didn't look up.

"They tell me her husband's one of the richest men in Springfield. Don't see how they managed it. She's a nice girl, but certainly not *pretty*. But he's a widower. Over fifty, Bessie says. Money or no money, I don't see it!"

At the table set in the combination dining and sewing room, mother and daughter sat facing each other while Annette Dunham said grace. Short and to the point.

"Dear Lord, we thank thee for what we are about to receive. Amen."

Before, on Bluff Street, grace had been chiefly a special acknowledgment for Sunday dinner. Now in her self-imposed widowhood the mother seemed to feel that this courtesy not only added a certain dignity to her martyrdom, but emphasized the decorum she was instilling in her daughter. The steaming platter remained in front of the girl.

"No, thank you, Mother. I'm not hungry. I—I just can't eat. And I have a lot of work to do tonight." Head down, she toyed with a piece of bread. Her mother did not like food to be refused or rejected; and growing girls should eat; and food was expensive and shouldn't be wasted.

"Are you sick, Katherine?" In spite of pique, the anxiety was real. "Is it your . . . No, it's not time for that. You'd better eat something anyway. Noodles aren't good the second day."

The daughter shook her head, and the mother decided to say no more. She enjoyed her meal, musing over the strange ways that beset girls during adolescence and particularly wondering at this girl who became daily more enigmatic, more closed, more a stranger.

After dinner there was again the hum of the sewing machine in the dining room and the sound of order being established in the kitchen. That night the daughter sat late over her Virgil. Heavy with exhaustion, she still knew that she would not sleep. Whether she kept her eyes open, fixed on words, or held them tightly closed, the quick, treacherous camera of her mind had developed its print, and before her she saw her last glimpse of the tramp—stolen as she recovered from her fall and picked up her books. He was hardly distinguishable in the darkness and distance, but what she had seen was vivid: one hand still gripping closely, as when she had fled; the other straining at the branch above so that it bent low, its dry ends over the creek wall; Promethean, the white face moving from side to side—chained to the tree, but with enough leeway to keep moving, just so far, left and right, talking, talking.

Through summer and fall and the following winter the West Side Cleaners lost more and more customers and had fewer dresses to alter, and need was growing acute everywhere. Letters from Katherine Dunham's brother thanked her for the stamps or the twenty-five cent piece or the mangled cigar that she had filched from pockets of incoming suits and sent to him, but thanked her in a way that revealed how important these small tokens were, so that she felt deeply uneasy for his well-being.

One evening after school she had looked for a long time at the drawer where petty cash was kept, waiting for her father to leave the front part of the shop. Each time he had gone out, though, he had returned immediately, as if he had sensed some uneasiness in the air. During one interval, her heart pounding, she had at last managed to extract from the drawer its only one-dollar bill; but her sense of guilt had been so great that at the first opportunity she returned it. She went on trying, however, to be first to go through the soiled clothes as they came in from the delivery wagon, turning pockets inside out, feeling in seams, securing nickels and dimes and pennies to exchange for a larger coin for mailing.

Her brother had received his first fellowship by now, but the two years since he had left home had begun to take their toll, and he wrote of ill health and chest examinations and a possible stay in a state sanatorium: not a great deal of information, but enough so that her heart beat fast with anxiety and her mother's brow furrowed when she read the pages, and she repeated over and over, "He ought to come home. No sense in carrying a thing too far. Not eating enough and working all night to be able to study all day!" And sometimes Annette Dunham's voice quavered, and emotions she seldom displayed rose to the surface: bewilderment at the turn that her marriage had taken, and a conflict in loyalties. The father's rage had been wrong, but then the boy should not have struck his father, should not have left home: he should have continued in the business and not gone on with this nonsense of philosophy, no matter how brilliant he was or how many scholarships he won. Her worry for him always ended intermingled with indignation. But suppose that he *was* ill, that it *was* that dreaded illness that often attacks young people, especially if they don't eat enough. But surely not *her* son. Surely not *Albert!* She would read a page again, trying to see it differently, trying to push off the gnawing fear between each line.

"It may only be for a year. Don't worry. They aren't sure yet."

Once her mother had spoken to her father, on one of those rare occasions when he had stayed to dinner.

"Al, I'm worried about Albert. He wrote Katherine a letter about a chest examination. Do you think it could mean . . . ? Don't you think you could send some money?" (She herself did whenever she could, always secretly in fear that her husband would find out and fly into one of his black jealous rages. But there would not be much left after she had paid the rent and coal and light and a part of the food, because Albert Dunham, accepting the separation from his wife as final and voluntary, contributed less and less to the upkeep of the house on Elmwood Avenue; and as business became worse, he lapsed frequently even in this respect.) "Or ask him to come back? You know, after all, he *is* your son!"

But his son's rebellion was still a sore subject with the father. He pushed his chair back from the table and prepared to leave.

"He is no son of mine," he said, "and if he thinks he's big enough to strike his father, he is certainly big enough to make his own way. And furthermore, Nett, I've told you not to bring that subject up again."

Angry, headstrong, still too young, Albert Dunham flung himself out of the cottage and down the snowy steps to the delivery truck. Mother and daughter sat close in misery, staring at unfinished food, thinking each in her own way, each with her consuming love, of the son, the brother, who might be at that very moment without warm clothing, without shelter, without food. What the scholarship would pay they could not know, but imagined that it would be not much more than enough for the University tuition, perhaps not even enough for the precious and necessary books, for which he would gladly go without food.

At her father's denial of paternity a brief wild hope had arisen in the girl. Suppose it were so? Suppose they had belonged first only to that dim and distant mother of the past and now to Annette alone? But her mirror had belied this a thousand times during the past three years, when she had turned to it looking for some trace of that dead mother, some definite feature to wash out the stamp of *Dunham.* There they were unmistakably—her father's eyes and mouth and nose, her father's round face. *Aren't you Albert Dunham's little girl? She certainly does resemble her father, doesn't she! Just look at that smile! Just like her father!*

And her brother, too, despite the high-bridged aristocratic nose of Fanny June Guillaume, was unmistakably the son of his father.

Wild hope, born to die quickly in the light of reason: she looked into her plate and ate without tasting the food.

Business worries increasingly beset Albert Dunham in these months. New establishments were springing up left and right, but all other things being equal, they would not have worried him. They came and they went, and few remained, and some even called him in for consultation. What did worry him was the increasing difficulty of finding and keeping responsible help that he could afford to pay, and the rising cost and declining quality of gasoline. The competing plants seemed untroubled by the introduction of lead, ruinous to fine silks and ultimately to machinery. But despite all the straining and skimming that he and Old Man Ferguson did, there never seemed to be enough clear gasoline.

With things as they were now, the big tank of solvent was seldom full, often empty. To do justice to a fragile or fine or special garment, he sometimes had to drive to the filling station at the corner of Raynor and Western avenues with a gallon or a two-gallon can and have it filled for this job alone. Bitterly, as he drove through the winter night on deliveries after hours, he thought of his dreams, his thwarted ambitions, the storms a few years back when he had tried to persuade Annette Dunham to invest in more up-to-date machinery, or to sell out to new companies—then anxious to acquire the clientele of the West Side Cleaners and Dyers—and move the entire family to California. But to the mother further investment in a business already established had seemed a useless luxury, and the idea of such a move had been unthinkable.

So Albert Dunham, Sr., turned his dreams inward. "Asleep in the Deep," "The Wedding of the Winds," "Melody in F," "Dear One," "The World Is Waiting for the Sunrise" had not left the piano-bench drawer since the family separation. In the freezing, dust-covered living room above the shop, the fire was never lighted, and one by one the strings of the guitar strained and snapped in the bitter cold. Sometimes at night as he lay awake in the room where once he and his second wife had slept, he could hear the tension rising under ghostly fingers, the taut wires giving, the squeak of ivory pegs, and then the twang as the fractured ends snapped back and struck the polished satinwood body which had once been his pride and joy; that had, during the best days of Bluff Street and family life, still been a tie to the past, to a life too remote even to dream of any more. . . .

The famous *salons* and musical soirees at the Potter Palmer mansion on Lake Shore Drive: carriages and gaiety and polished floors and shimmering candelabra advanced and receded before his eyes as he lay sleepless in the black room above the shop. In an alcove where four mahogany-colored musicians were tuning their instruments, he, Albert Dunham—young, not long from Memphis, full of a kind of rural charm and wonderment, brimming with hope and ambition—fingered lovingly the strings of his guitar, the polished surface of which reflected candlelight, cut glass, sparkling jewelry, white shoulders, fire glow, and then his own dark face as he leaned closely over it.

His pride was all the greater because he had bought the guitar by the true sweat of his brow: by cuttings and fittings and careful pressings of seams under a twenty-pound hand iron heated on a gas jet in the back of a German tailor shop on the fifteenth floor of the Fair Building in the heart of the fifth largest city in the whole world. At the end of a long day he gratefully inhaled the clear lake air; shoulders aching from hours over the basting needle took new life in this glittering fairyland, where often the musicians were the last to leave, in the hours just before dawn. Albert Dunham was anxious to stay in the midst of such beauty and refinement, but eager, too, to finish, to be away without even touching the table in the servants' dining room, because already he had wooed the glamorous divorcée, and already she had accepted him. . . .

Perhaps as he lay in the arctic isolation of the room above the shop, he would move on to other, later scenes with this same guitar—to Sunday nights in Glen Ellyn before the illness had lined the pale sad face with pain, before the door of the upstairs room stayed shut: lamplight on a gilded harp, a small boy watching the tuning of the instrument, and a smaller child, a daughter, perhaps in his arms as he carefully turned the ivory pegs of the instrument on his knee and plucked the strings, ear bent close, shifting the child in order to lean over and tune to a note on the piano. He could not know then about the glass-topped coffin or the gray sweater or the canal or the creek or the boy who would turn from his father and take the love of his sister with him; nor could he know that the girl would one day grow in likeness to her mother, even though she had inherited none of her actual features, but only their inner meaning. He could not know how disturbing the resemblance would be when the child had grown into a young girl and the young girl had reached the threshold of womanhood. . . . At night, when he could hear the busy working of the mice and the creaking of the giant wheel groaning even in rest under its own weight in the dust-thick back room, and the reverberant yield of a broken guitar string—then, unable to sleep, he would take stock of the frenetic pattern of his life, of the velocity with which change after change in the wrong direction was taking place, and—lonely, rebellious, hungry of soul, and bewildered of spirit—he would conjure up the ideal existence in a California known only from newspaper travel advertisements or the bragging description of an occasional customer or a rare motion-picture travelogue. When finally he fell asleep to dream, it would be of this: that there, in his own house, with her, he would recapture his lost love and lost youth.

Two years earlier, on a bright Saturday morning in spring, a girl hired to clean the Bluff Street flat above the shop had splintered the pane of one of the front windows and, in her hurry to finish her half-day on schedule, placed the fragmented glass on top of her scrub bucket in front of the window. Katherine Dunham, eager to be off to a track meet, had pulled herself inside the frame from where she had been polishing the outside of the window, swung down from the sill, and felt stocking and skin sever in one stroke and seen warm blood ooze from the wide-open, laid-back flesh, before she realized what had happened. Cloth in hand, she stood looking at the incision and watching with curiosity the increased flow of blood, while the servant girl ran for her mother.

Annette Dunham abandoned her sewing machine, called a taxi, and hurried her daughter to Dr. Williams, who shook his head gravely, applied antiseptics, and sewed the wound together. She must be careful, he warned, to move as little as possible, to come to him for redressing at least twice weekly, to abstain from all unnecessary movement until he should declare her fit.

At that time physical activity was particularly important to the girl, and though she nodded docilely, she avoided a direct promise. The wound healed slowly because of stolen moments of exercise, and as soon as the stitches were out, there was no holding her back. One day when she was at basketball practice the scar reopened, and the flesh exposed beneath was not clean; the treatment had to be started over. But, despite all Dr. Williams' resources, the wound continued to suppurate, and one morning while dressing the girl noticed, inches above the wound on the soft skin behind her knee, a small round blister, sensitive to the touch and filled with the same yellowish matter that oozed constantly through the gauze bandage below.

Without question Annette Dunham threw aside loyalty to Dr. Williams and his wife and made an appointment with a German specialist newly established in the Town. With him the girl proved to be a more co-operative patient than she had been with Dr. Williams: she was subdued by discussions at dinner about the exorbitant charge for each visit to the specialist and by his reluctance to take the case at all in such an advanced condition. And in the end he saved her leg.

At first the wound seemed to have healed level with the rest of the skin surface; but even now, two years later, the surrounding area would grow numb in cold weather and the lesion itself would form a tight mound, not painful but disagreeable enough to prompt a new consultation with the specialist. His advice was daily massage, and for a time the girl would herself engage in this treatment while waiting by the stove in the back room of the shop; but the watching eyes of her father soon discouraged her, and she returned to her open books and her brooding impatience.

One night Albert Dunham began the courtship of his daughter, as he had so many times before, naïvely and almost childishly.

"I don't see why anyone would want to stay in a town like this and in this kind of weather when they could be in a place like California."

No response: just a tightening of throat and stomach muscles and that sick feeling which couldn't be controlled and which she prayed would soon pass if she kept her head buried in her books.

"If your mother had lived, I bet we would have been out of here and settled in someplace like Los Angeles or Hollywood a long time ago."

The girl knew that these were only romantic names to

him, and, although she might have been able to support this wool-gathering in anyone else, in her father she found it absurd, and the references to her dead mother seemed indecorous. Feelings of loyalty toward Annette Dunham made her turn from her father at every allusion to Fanny June Dunham, though at heart she hungered to know more of this by now mythical creature whom, according to her father, she daily grew to resemble more closely and who, according to his reminiscences, must have been possessed of infinite beauty and all the graces combined.

When these overtures evoked no response, the father turned the gas out in the steam iron and began the adjustments of stove, pressing apparatus, and back door that normally announced departure. This night, however, as she closed her book and started to rise from the chair before the stove, he emerged from the front office with the desk chair and placed it near hers and as directly in front as possible. Caught off guard, she must have shown her alarm, because his gaze fell and the rehearsed lines were indistinct and unsure.

"The doctor said that your leg should be massaged." He reached for her ankle and extended her leg across his knee. To keep from touching the stove she had to shift her chair so that she was facing him. "I notice that you haven't been doing it lately," he went on, gaining confidence from her helplessness. "You'd better let me do it every night."

The suggestion had become an order; there seemed to be no retreat without admission of panic. She felt blood drain from her entire body, and she clamped her tongue between her teeth to keep them from chattering. Then, as he reached out to unroll the top of the woolen stocking held in place by elastic below the knee, anger and shame replaced fright and she felt a rush of blood that brought her back into equilibrium. Ignoring his touch, she exchanged her Virgil for a French grammar and began poring over declensions of verbs.

From the corners of her eyes she watched her father's hands. She had forgotten how they felt to the three-year-old child; touched by them now, she felt vague stirrings of memory. As they made persistent, regular strokes, working above the numb spot and to her knee, she pictured them as she had known them since: lifting the pressing iron, tuning the guitar, pointed in anger at her or her brother or her mother; an open palm drawn back to strike again an already smarting cheek; competent hands on reins guiding Lady Fern over the asphalt of Black Road. These same hands now stroked the flesh above her knee which led to the tender exposure of inner thigh, seeking farther: hands of a lover in first caress.

She had seen mounting desire before, had witnessed its culmination. Instinctively she began to connect the tramp with this man who was her father. The cold room became stifling; her hunger was now distant. Distant, too, the snowbound cottage, the sewing machine, her mother. Only the lute strings of the sirens and a swimming sea, with the hum of the winter wind in the chimney of the dying stove, and the waning of sounds in the pressing machine as steam turned to water and murmured comfortably, settling into the pipes for the night.

As she swung dizzily on the edge of an abyss, an image saved her. The image of the rabbit at the end of a Sunday hunting trip years before. A rabbit hanging limp and blood-spattered. Slate sky, white snow, a child waiting for a man and a boy to return across ice-bound fields with the kill. A child shrinking from flannel underwear moist with urine, wiping a nose raw from dripping on the back of a woolen mitten . . . stinging eyes holding back tears of defeat . . . helplessness in the bitter cold . . . long ride home. Then the kitchen, and her father's hand forcing its way into the rabbit's enlarged anal opening, emerging with viscera bulging between blood-shiny fingers; again and again, the same hand that lifted the twenty-pound iron, the same efficient fingers caressing guitar strings, the same fingers massaging, intruding, insinuating toward secret places still scarcely known to her.

Nausea drew her violently from the brink of some terror that she defied to take form. Blindly, with deep breaths, she fought her way back to safety, nearly succumbed, nearly drowned finding air again. But life rose triumphant over death wish; over a drawing-back to womb and even farther, to the swirling engulfing plasmodium before conception. Her relaxed muscles contracted into resistance, and from somewhere her own voice sounded—from across the room or an outer door or an outer space.

"That isn't where it hurts," she said calmly, and surprised herself with this control which seemed to have come from beyond herself. "I don't need that any more anyway. If I do, I can do it myself." She added, without bothering to notice the reaction of the man before her, his progressive motion arrested, "I'm hungry. I don't like to wait so long before going home after school. If I'm going to have to wait so long, I would rather walk."

She used her new-found freedom from guilt like an avenging weapon. Now she could hate with reason and not blindly. She could give all of the justifications to her mother and to him if he demanded them—but, most importantly, to herself. She did not know where intimacy would have ended, but by putting together knowledges and glimpses gathered since that spring evening when the tramp had revealed himself to her, she knew it would have been in a place where father and daughter could never meet again in daily life with other people—in some dank, dark, forbidden fen, desolate, stark, lost, never to be returned from. The protective, instinctive mechanism of revulsion gave strength to her limbs and sureness to her conviction.

She talked with malice, pleased to watch the man before her pass from transport to realization to shame. Spitefully, feeling power, she said as she stood up to replace the stocking, rolling it carefully over the elastic, "And about California. If you have that much money, I need a pair of shoes. And Albert needs food. And mother needs money to pay the rent." She said the words carefully, someone else speaking for her. "And I don't want you to touch me again, ever. Not touch me or kiss me or ever get near me, and if you will give me the money, I will go home by myself every night. I don't want anything from you. Anything at all. Because now I know that I hate you!"

Years later, when she understood more about the complex nature of men, when she had been host to loneliness, she would have taken back the words and left only the action. On this night, however, she fastened well the protective mantle of aversion into which she had been retreating farther and farther since childhood; and for many years, until greater wisdom and tolerance and understanding allowed the slow unfolding into mature love, this was all that Albert Dunham was to know of his daughter. As she spoke she saw the beginning of his disintegration, and she knew that she had for the first time consciously exercised the law of self-preservation; to save herself, it couldn't have been otherwise. He would have to place his illusions—his dreams of recapture of things lost, his blind belief in a giving back of something to substitute for things taken away—somewhere else. But the things and places had narrowed down to the Town, and the Town was not generous enough to provide compensation.

Having now accomplished the total estrangement of both his children, Albert Dunham drove his daughter silently through the night, refused his wife's invitation to dinner, and, avoiding the eyes of both mother and daughter, returned to the truck, to the drive through frozen deserted streets, to the room above the West Side Cleaners where he would lie in the darkness and lock into his innermost being his dreams of love and warmth and escape.

Left alone with her mother, the girl lost touch with the

Voice, the Thing, the Prompting Angel that had been with her a few minutes before: she felt on her own again, uncertain, miserable, bewildered. What proof had she? What act to point out that could not be construed, if one needed to avoid truth, as fatherly attention and affection? How could she expect her mother to listen with sympathy to the most damning of accusations? Would not she be the one finally blamed? But she knew the truth and reassured herself by reliving situation after situation until no doubt was left.

She decided to speak to her mother after they were in bed, where the shame in her own face and the distress in her mother's would be hidden by darkness. But she waited too long, and when she did summon enough courage to speak, it was with many hesitations, frequent repetitions, a voice sometimes almost inaudible. She began with the seemingly innocent familiarities that might have been mistaken for paternal solicitude—his insistence on her proximity in the delivery wagon, her endless waiting at night after everyone else had gone home, the nightly offers of the house in California.

At one point Annette Dunham rose up on her elbow and stared through the dark at her daughter. Her voice expressed the astonishment that her face must have shown. "*Why Katherine!* Of *course* your father should bring you home at night! Why, what *are* you trying to say? Are you trying to find something *wrong* with that?"

The stress on the word "wrong" completely discouraged the girl and made her feel suddenly the offender, unspeakably cheap and unclean; made her feel almost in league with the object of her attack. How foolish she had been to hope for some glimmer of understanding, some motherly denouncement of the outrage. She lay in the darkness, scarcely breathing for fear of being called upon for further explanations, and she knew now that there was nothing to say and never would be.

Receiving no reply, Annette Dunham concluded that the matter was dismissed; she turned her back on her daughter and slept.

The subject was never again brought up, and out of it all, the mother was the only survivor not in some way defeated, not in some way loser of a dream.

The girl moved on toward young womanhood; the household remained split; the brother was hospitalized while his mother and sister stayed helpless and grieving. What Albert Dunham felt about his son at this time he kept well within himself, but bitterness was there, and blackness, because both showed plainly on the face that not so long before had been still open, still seeking. Business did not improve, and the nation moved steadily toward the last days before the landslide into deep depression.

The mother stayed bent for more hours over her sewing machine, with less to show for her work at the end of the month. In his fanatical search for some magic solvent that would render clean gasoline from soiled, the father spent restless nights in the tumbler room, alone now because Old Man Ferguson had died and he could not afford a replacement, and Mr. Crusoe had gone to seek more profitable employment in the steel mills. The daughter continued to work at the shop after school, but the battle against stains and rips and tears in increasingly poor material was a losing one; and the pockets of incoming garments yielded few stamps and coins to be secreted for mailing to the hospital outside the City.

At the end of the term, when photographs were taken for the class annual, the girl looked at hers and knew that she was as old then as she would ever be in her life. She would know more, much more, but she could never later be older in the true sense. The sadness in her eyes frightened her, and she begged the mother to let her have new pictures taken, because the secrets captured by the lens belonged to her. But there was no money, and the picture printed in the school annual was a permanent witness not only to her own suffering, but to all of the hidden things in families that one shouldn't tell or be let known: her mother living in one house and her father in another; cardboard neatly folded into shoe soles, but not very useful in rain or snow; her father and brother tossing, locked together on the dining-room floor, with murderous intent; her secret knowledge of the experience shared with the tramp, long ago but still there; and now, for her brother, the sanatorium, because he had gone without food while he studied and lived in winter where there was no heat except a kerosene stove, and because—not being the kind to turn outward, bearing his privations—he had turned inward, and somewhere something had given way.

Twelve
The Quarry

*

The soft limestone base on which the Town was built yielded the material for most of its public buildings and for a number of the business buildings, too, and for the more imposing residences. At any point on the outskirts of the Town could be seen evidences of the excavations, many of them abandoned because of the poor yield or quality of the stone or because the network of wells beneath made further quarrying impractical. As though the scaffoldings, runways, towers, chutes, and tackles were of no intrinsic value once the decision to suspend activity was reached, they were left in place, brooding like fossilized monsters over the deserted cavities beneath.

The quarry that Katherine Dunham explored one spring afternoon during her senior year in high school, when for one reason or another classes had finished early, was the largest and most dramatic in the Town's vicinity. The streetcar conductor, who knew her well, applied his brakes and turned to her expectantly as they reached the park. But on an impulse she decided to investigate the territory beyond her accustomed stop. By now she was aware of the fascination that the deserted and decayed and skeletal held for her—of a nostalgia for past splendor reflected in present ruins. So when the streetcar continued on and passed the deserted excavation, she had at once been drawn by the lonely outlines of the towers and scaffoldings against the sky, by the rays of the afternoon sun slanting across great slabs of cut stone fallen into grotesque angles, and by the desolation of the whole area. But what had seemed irresistible and made her press the button to halt the streetcar was the body of still water that the ruins surrounded, even seemed to rise out of.

She crossed the dusty road and followed a path leading through a rank growth of weeds which stopped abruptly at the brink of a sloping cliff. Down this she skidded and slid, feeling completely possessed by the walls that rose above her as she descended and by the expanse of utterly motionless black water below, cradled in the base of the quarry like some mysterious volcanic lake. At the bottom of the decline the giant limestone slabs circled the water in a series of disorderly shelves; she climbed and hopped from one shelf to the other, feeling the glow of heat where the sun struck, but an eerie chill where the path lay in the shadow of the cliff.

Across the water wooden skeletons jutted starkly into the sky, with here and there a hanging plank or dangling chain. A row of overturned miniature iron boxcars rested beside a narrow-gauge track which led from a gravel pit to the edge of the water and then plunged suddenly out of sight. The girl had stopped to examine this phenomenon when a movement on the shadowed surface of the block on which she would have stepped next caused her to start and then freeze in terror. The thick, mud-colored body of a water moccasin slid over the edge of the rock and into the water. Several seconds passed before the girl dared move. She breathed without sound, trying to stop even the pounding of her heart, holding herself suspended; then slowly she allowed all her muscles to relax.

Farther on she leaned gingerly over the edge of the slab and saw in the water only reflections—her own face, the sky overhead, and a wooden tower on the other shore. The sun suddenly withdrew, and rocks and water were thrown into chill shadow; the sense of danger was intensified, and she turned and scrambled up the gravel incline, through the weeds, and back to the road. There was no streetcar in sight: she walked most of the way home, and it was quite dark when she reached the white cottage on Elmwood Avenue.

Her seventeenth birthday was long past, the first days of Indian summer had come, and Katherine Dunham had started attending the junior college before she returned to the abandoned quarry. During the interval she had heard stories about the place that had whetted her curiosity. On one day it had been a thriving enterprise, on the next ruined and abandoned, all because of a capricious stroke of nature combined with man's ignorance and avarice. A rich layer of limestone paving the floor of the quarry concealed a cavity porous with countless quiescent springs. An injudiciously placed explosive had released the imprisoned water, which rose with incredible rapidity, sucking down the toy railroad engine with its tracks, several boxcars of gravel, numerous slabs of limestone piled around the edges for further cutting, and (legend added) a wooden tower with all of its pulleys and chains and a score of panic-stricken workmen. There had also been stories of schoolboys who dared each other to dive from the gravel shafts into the obsidian depths, never to rise again. Now and then a daring fisherman would venture out in a rowboat, tempted by stories of catfish and perch fattened on the occasional sacrificial flesh; but after one boat had overturned, its oars hopelessly entangled in hidden cables and its occupants swiftly and silently drawn under the surface, the fishing excursions ceased. All of these stories, fact or fabrication, fascinated the girl, and she was anxious to explore the quarry again.

Indian summer had aroused in her a feeling of daring

and luxury. College gave her freedom to skip classes here and there, to adjust schedules to her after-school work, and —greatest license of all—to enlist the aid of one or two understanding professors in obtaining more time for herself from duties at her father's shop. And her father had been somewhat awed by her entry into the college; although he had resented his son's drive for learning, he took some pride in his daughter's. So, aside from the infrequent stolen evenings, she was allowed one Saturday afternoon a month for the social activities of the school. But she attended only a few football games because she had to attend them alone. These were days of serious courtship for all her former companions: every girl she had ever known, it seemed, now had a beau to take her to football games right through to the end of the season, and to basketball games after that, and then, when the winter skating season was over, to track meets in the spring. But she, forlorn in her solitary state and not daring to risk a clandestine escort, began spending her free Saturday afternoons in the public library, reading books reserved for adults—D'Annunzio, Huysmans, De Quincey, D. H. Lawrence, and James Branch Cabell. And on one heady, balmy, enchanted afternoon of false summer she rode out to explore the quarry again.

The sun was warm, and golden light scintillated from the rock slabs, made the gaunt skeleton shafts glow, played on the clear surface of the water. As before, the girl was entirely alone. She walked halfway around the quarry, examining carefully each rock before clambering up on it, not exactly anticipating the appearance of the water moccasin, but nevertheless wary. She stretched out on a warm stone and stared at a cloud bank suspended in the sky, and the stories about the quarry seemed suddenly slanderous, though she knew some of them to be true. She had never learned to swim, but when she turned on her stomach and looked out across the wind-dimpled water, she longed to feel it on her face, thighs, armpits. But the afternoon stretched ahead, and she was in no hurry. For a while she turned the pages of her guide to English literature; then, propping herself against the rock behind, she began reading D'Annunzio's *La Fiamma.* But after a little while she closed the book and began thinking about her own life, about herself, as she did much of the time now.

She thought first of Albert Dunham and wondered if the repugnance she felt toward her father was usual among young women. Her experience with other children and their parents was limited, but from her reading she would have said No. She decided that much of the abnormality of her own situation, if it was abnormal, could be traced to the death of her first mother, who was more than ever in her consciousness these days. She was well aware of Annette Dunham's loyalty and devotion, but as she drew back into her buried self, searching paths of memory in an effort to find the answers to her confusion, she felt sure the change in her father had begun that day in the parlor of the Glen Ellyn house when the two lines of family faced each other across the glass-topped coffin. Then another stream of memory entered, seeking its way toward truth, and reminded her that long before that day her life had seemed troubled, overcast, full of presentiments of all that had happened thus far and of much more to happen in a great, mysterious unfolding. Only somehow she herself—and at this she marveled—felt in some innermost, unexplored, primary retreat a bond with a kind of knowledge apart from and beyond the darkness, the bewilderment, the terrors that had shadowed most of her life until now.

Sometimes she lay in bed at night, as she lay on the stone now, and felt that she was listening, far beyond sound, to the circulation of her own blood. The knowledge without enlightenment which carried her always onward and acted as a silent dictate to her life moved with this circulation. She would hold her breath and shut out all other sounds, waiting, hoping; but the secret assurance would continue its steady circuit of her body, suffusing every nerve and fiber and yet not making itself known. This was something quite different from the Star, which was outside and pierced its rays of hope into her as she grew from childhood; this was something inward and walked as her quiet companion, guiding her—so that now, as later in life, some great crisis would be met and grappled with and over before the conscious self that was called by her own name was aware of what had happened. She felt at times like a driver who, having skirted some precipitous cliff in darkness, halts his vehicle, sleeps until dawn, and then looks back in surprise at his achievement.

Her father had continued to reminisce about his first wife, still missing no opportunity to point out resemblances between Fanny June Dunham and her daughter. Although she would pretend to be deaf to these recollections, secretly she longed to hear them, to find a path in the maze of spider-web filaments, blurred films, and fragmentary designs which constituted her earliest memories.

She thought about Annette Dunham and wondered what constituted fulfillment for her and if she had ever felt deep emotions of love and tenderness or allowed herself to show them—to give out to people, instead of insisting that they pay homage to her. She had seldom seen Annette Dunham weep for others—only for her own offended person or wounded pride.

She turned her thoughts to her brother and wondered if his growing-up meant a change in the old, protective relationship toward her; if he no longer felt himself a part of the mother and sister, left behind, who continued to grieve for him and to serve him faithfully by letter writing. He was out of the sanatorium now, with scars instead of lesions on his lungs. But he seemed in his letters, as he had on his last visit, suddenly much older, much removed, as though a generation separated them in thought. His scholarship had been held in suspension during his illness;

now, once again, he had been forced to seek work between classes in order to survive, and he was sharing an unheated flat with a boy named Nicholas Matsoukas. He conveyed to his sister his excitement at enrolling in the courses of the octogenarian father of American philosophy, Alfred North Whitehead, who rode to his classes on a bicycle, white beard flowing in the wind. Otherwise, he communicated little about his personal life, his deeper delving into his chosen field, or his theses, which were already beginning to attract the attention of his teachers and command the respect of his fellow students in philosophy.

The girl longed to follow in her brother's footsteps, though well aware that on his scale she was no scholar. She wondered about herself, and what would happen to her in life, and if she would ever be able to escape from the West Side Cleaners and Dyers, the dust wheel, the smallness of the small Town, the loneliness, the unfulfillment. She poured her longing to do and to be into the red-brown oak leaves and the jagged wooden towers, the opalescent Indian-summer haze and unclouded sky. She turned on her stomach and faced the water, below whose surface the corners of the blocks had a delicate coating of green. There was no bottom: where the blocks became invisible, the water turned to ink. A few yards farther on, the rusted tracks curved off over the edge. As she sat up to continue her tour of the quarry's secrets, the quickened beating of her heart made her aware of the importance of this moment, which, without knowing it, she had been so long anticipating. She walked slowly, as though in suspended animation, to the rail bed that had been the death trap of the workmen and of how many unremembered others.

The rusted rails glowed warm in the sun, and the miniature boxcar that rested at the edge of the water was hot to her touch. She pushed it, but it remained rooted and motionless. Then she brought herself to the edge of the water and followed the twisted descent of the rails until they disappeared in a tangle of cables passing under and over and around blocks which formed angular, precipitous shelves beneath the water. At first she peered gingerly, afraid of what she might see. Then she became so fascinated with the labyrinthine network, so engrossed in the lazy passage of a single fish, that she did not notice the thickest of the rusted cables detach itself and lash out in a whiplike movement in pursuit of the fish—which, electrified, plunged out of sight into the inky depths. She fell back in fright and disgust and leaned trembling against the rusted boxcar. A shadow touched it, then grew across it from a cloud bank over the sun. The iron planks no longer felt warm to her touch, and all innocence seemed to have washed out of the air with the darkening of the sun. She stepped, quivering, from one track to the other and to the rock on the far side of the car. The sun filtered through the cloud bank. Turning back, she saw the snake emerge from the water, white-mouthed, sated, gliding majestically and insolently across the tracks to rest in loose, ready coils on the shelf she had just vacated.

The winter introduced only a few variations on the restricted pattern of her life. Reconciliation between her mother and father seemed far more likely to the girl than reconciliation between her father and herself. Young womanhood and the introspection and reflection now habitual with her gave form to earlier scattered feelings and reflexes. She regarded her father's extravagant displays of temper as a weakness degenerated into wanton destructiveness, and his refusals of her needs and her brother's as deliberate cruelty. Her mother, with her facility for turning all things finally in her own direction, might take pity on him and invite him more and more often to evening meals or accept meekly his tardiness in payment for her untiring services at the sewing machine; but the girl remained coldly aloof.

But she found one contact with her father impossible to avoid. The Annual Charity Ball given by the Mary E. Gaston Study Club always filled her with excitement over her new or made-over party dress, the colored streamers festooning the Oddfellows' Hall, the ten-piece orchestra with Ethel Fuqua at the piano, Claude Wilson playing violin, and the Dougherty boys on various brass and reed and percussion instruments. She looked forward, too, to the indescribable thrill when one young man or another would place himself determinedly before her father, pass his rigid censorship, and lead her off over the crowded ballroom to the strains of the Charleston or the newest foxtrot or two-step.

Waltzes were by strict order reserved for her father, as was her first dance of the evening. Sometimes the Dougherty boy who led the orchestra seemed to avoid her father's eye deliberately, and there might be selection after selection through which she had to wait while her father stiffly ignored the perspiring young men who would leave the floor after each dance and head hopefully in her direction. She would look pleadingly at the musicians, trying to catch the eye of one friendly enough to pass on to the leader word that Mr. Dunham was waiting to dance with his daughter. But as often as not the delay would be intentional: Albert Dunham's jealous guardianship of his daughter had severely strained his relations with most of the young men present.

Then the moment to dance with her father would come, and she was invariably torn by a conflict beyond her own powers of reason. She wanted to get the first dance over with, and she hated it because it meant the closest possible proximity to her father, and yet she found herself palpitating with all the anticipation of a bride at the first strains of the Wedding March when the floor cleared and only the mature and adept took over in a gay or stately waltz. She would adjust herself to her father, at first shrinking, then giving herself wholeheartedly to the sweep and dip and cadence which reached a fullness unattained in the chopping, bobbing frenetics of the current dances. She admitted with reluctance that as a waltzing partner her father was superior: the irregularities of the floor melted under his expert guidance, the self-consciousness about her height that she felt with anyone else dissolved, and she glided, whirled, dipped, and sashayed to the local musicians' imitations of Paul Whiteman and Wayne King and Guy Lombardo in the latest waltzes of Irving Berlin or perhaps an old favorite like "The Blue Danube," arranged for in advance by her father. For the brief duration of the waltz she forgot all her antagonisms and all her physical revulsion; by the time the dance ended and her father, out of breath and reaching for his handkerchief to dry under the edges of his starched white collar, had led her to the row of seats where wives and younger children sat watching the dance floor, her feelings toward him were almost kindly, almost daughterly.

This warming of sentiment, this momentary relaxation of her usual rigid reserves, surprised her when she became aware of it. Once back in line beside her mother, however, she immediately resumed her feelings of distaste at proximity to her father, of chagrin that every young man wanting to dance with her had to win Albert Dunham's approval and could be accepted or rejected by him on the most capricious of whims. William Booker, the young football star, was of course among those consistently rejected.

Annette Dunham did not dance herself, but enjoyed vicariously the pleasure her husband derived from it and seemed to understand her daughter's love of physical activity, her need for physical expression. And by the time the girl was attending junior college, she reluctantly admitted that the Annual Charity Ball at Christmas, the annual picnic at Bush Park during summer, and club and church and athletic-association meetings could hardly be considered a sufficiently well-rounded social life for her daughter. (Even if a proper escort for school functions could have been found, he would surely not have passed Albert Dunham's censorship.)

Then there was the constant reminder, in letters from the girl's brother, that the Town held little or nothing for the future of anybody with ambition or talent. Part of his concern must have been genuinely for her welfare; another part must have been an urge to consolidate his own victory, so bitterly won.

Influenced by all of these factors, though scarcely daring to hope, Katherine Dunham in her second and last year at the Town's college became aware of subtle changes in the current of her life that might lead to an escape into almost undreamed-of freedom. Her brother, now a full fellowship student in his senior University year and enjoying his first period of relative financial security, frequently visited his mother and sister on weekends; and often he brought with him one or another of his school friends, some of them serious and scholarly, some of them pleasantly frivolous. He and a young man named Barefield Gordon started early one Saturday morning on a novel-writing marathon, with Sunday night as a deadline: they had laid a bet with an admirer of F. Scott Fitzgerald that far too much was made out of the simple writing of a book, that twenty-four hours for two writers, or forty-eight for one, were quite enough time. The light stayed on all night in Rebecca Brown's cottage, and they won the bet, but the novel was never published.

Another friend of her brother's, Isaac Clark, taught the girl new variations of the fading Charleston, and the Mooch and Slow Drag which had supplanted it. Her brother was a bystander at such sessions and turned to his books while the irrepressible Ike Clark would sit beside the girl at the piano, which had been transferred long since from the flat on Bluff Street, and teach her the "Dirty Dozens," a blues with a dozen verses and a rolling bass in the left hand, or the verses to a long saga of *double-entendre* called "Shake That Thing." If her mother showed too much interest in these unfamiliar compositions, the girl would leaf through the sheet music on the piano and play "Always" or "Stardust" or "The World Is Waiting for the Sunrise," which she would sing because it was in a key reasonably near her own range.

She felt herself very near some port of exit and knew that her brother was again guiding her destiny, as he had when they were small children. But she sensed that, despite her brother, despite chance, much depended upon her behavior—upon her continued tie with that inward guide which she was still unable to identify.

Invitations came that winter for parties in the City. They were sent by Helen or Fanny Weir or by friends of theirs, and because such invitations had never come before, the brother's influence was evident. Annette Dunham—guided by her own sense of justice, faced again with the inevitable, and fortified by the judgment of her son—stayed late at her sewing machine, preparing the wardrobe necessary for her daughter's debut into the society of the "elite" represented by the Weir family. To the mother, skirts seemed too short and the girl's legs too long for decency, but she conceded to fashion, delved into her trunks again, and remodeled—conservatively, of course—her party dresses of two decades before. For her part the girl studied harder, making every effort to live up to the scholastic standards set by her brother, and worked doggedly in the hours after school at the West Side Cleaners and Dyers. And one Saturday morning she took her first trip to the City by herself.

The train passed close to the high school and skirted the track field and tennis courts, before leaving the comfortable limestone houses of the East Side and leveling down to woods and open fields. A mile beyond the high school the street leading to the cemetery crossed the tracks. The wooden gates descended with a steady clanging of the warning gong, as the engine steamed by, and lifted in the wake of the coaches, as they had so many times while she sat praying that the Oldsmobile or Studebaker would behave properly, that gas or tires or battery would hold out for the climb to the hill at the top of the gravel cemetery road and back across town to Bluff Street. Snow dusted the leafless trees and dry underbrush of the forest where in childhood springtimes she had gathered lady's-slippers and May apples and bitter young dandelion greens.

Later the train plowed past open fields and farmhouses and ample barns, and she was reminded of the Sunday rabbit-hunting trips, of the slate skies and bitter cold and her father or brother crunching over the icy fields, with the limp blood-spattered prey, to where she waited in the merciless cold, gripping her BB gun while tears ran down her cheeks and into the sagging roses on each side of the gray knitted cap. She looked away from these bleak pastoral scenes and began to examine the other passengers; then she opened a magazine.

Eventually the feel of the great flat ugly sprawling City insinuated itself into the coach, and a stir of preparation began among the passengers: a stretching and yawning, a folding of papers and magazines, a fastening of galoshes, and, finally, as they drew into the tunnels beneath towering skyscrapers, a concerted struggling into overcoats, scarves, gloves, hats.

Now Katherine Dunham felt the same excitement, bordering on panic, that she had always felt on her first approach to a new school. Borne out into the vast marble disinfectant-smelling arcades of the La Salle Street Station, she drew back into herself, quaking with a presentiment of some confusion in schedule, some mishap in connection, until she saw her brother signaling to attract her attention.

Then she felt ashamed of her inexperience and tried to cover self-consciousness with a wooden smile and the formalities of greetings.

The streets beneath the station seemed unchanged. Police mounted on giant seal-brown horses clattered over the pavement; others stood at crossings, blowing the two-toned whistles unique to the City; buildings reaching higher than the station kept the streets in semishadow; and on elevated tracks crowds shoved and hustled in and out of sliding doors controlled by impatient conductors. The sound and sight of so many people made her feel an isolation, yet an urgency to join the movement of going somewhere. And all other sounds and sights and smells seemed to be permeated by the nostalgic odor of The Fair's cafeteria, with its piles of wooden trays and white crockery and its mounds of golden fried fish. She thought of the small child tagging down the corridors behind Lulu Dunham and felt guilty about having called on her aunt so infrequently.

These trips to the City were repeated, but much as the girl longed for and looked forward to the sorority and fraternity and "elite" society dances that she was allowed to attend during her last years in the Town, they were without question a trial and tribulation. It would be hard to determine which was more painful: the gaudy sorority and fraternity balls that she attended in the barnlike South Side Dance Hall, or the small house parties given in the ballrooms of the once splendid mansions of the City rich or in apartments remodeled from the lower floors of the same dwellings and often still maintaining drawing rooms and *salons* of various degrees of elegance. In either instance she was painfully aware of being an extra person, without an escort of her own, following along in the wake of the gay sophisticates paying court to her niece, Helen Weir. Once her brother accompanied them, but left early in boredom. Once each, Barefield Gordon and Isaac Clark escorted her, but with little effort to conceal their motive as a return for hospitality shown on Sundays at Annette Dunham's cottage or as a favor to her brother.

Whether at the mass balls graced by the music of Erskine Tate or Duke Ellington or Earl Hines, or at the more snobbish and intimate house parties, the girl always felt herself a stranger, out of her element—awkward, unglamorous, inept. The texture of her hair was not the most fashionable in this particular society, and the color of her skin barely passed the rigid censorship that operated far less liberally for young women than for their partners; and though she could not doubt her mother's conservative good taste, her party dresses always seemed inappropriate. She was tall for her age and had passed from an absorption in athletics to an awakening interest in scholastic pursuits without ever having acquired the brittle accomplishments needed for competition with the young people of this age and class.

The result was that most of her time at the crowded sorority and fraternity dances would be spent in anxiously twisting the strings of her unsigned dance program in damp fingers, while she stood in the least conspicuous corner of the ballroom, searching the crowd for a single familiar, friendly face. Or she leaned into the mirror in the ladies' room, making over and over the same reparations of her discreet makeup; and when other girls suffering for one reason or another from unpopularity would begin to notice or, she imagined, comment among themselves on the frequency with which she adjusted her hair or scrutinized her face in her compact, she would enter the swinging doors to the inner recess and stand counting minutes, crowded against one of the overused toilets, until some debutante, radiant with her evening's success, would knock impatiently, and she would be forced to give up her retreat, trying to look unconcerned as she again edged her way to a place at the mirror over the washbasin, or went again into the ballroom.

Sometimes, in her extreme self-consciousness at the paucity of entries in her dance program, she would hurriedly scribble a fictitious, illegible name. Once or twice she paid dearly for this deception: the very dance filled in her own handwriting would be miraculously requested, and she would be forced to disappear again into the haven of the washroom to escape detection of her fraud. There were times, however, when the satin richness of Johnny Hodges spotlighted in solo alto saxophone variations from "Stardust" or "Mood Indigo" or "Sophisticated Lady" would make her forget her aloneness, and she would wander off into a world of her own, choreographing beyond and through the gliding figures. And she thought of her father during the long waltz medleys, in which the graces of the four inseparables—"Charmaine," "Marie," "Diane," and "Jeannine"—were crooned, hummed, harmonized, and modulated into falsetto. Then the familiar strains of "Good Night Sweetheart" or "Three O'Clock in the Morning" would release her, and she would make her way to the cloakroom, between bedraggled couples interlocked in noisy farewells, to wait for the convoy she had scarcely seen since her arrival.

The parties given at private residences were just as painful, but in a different way. All her accustomed sets of values she felt to be an encumbrance. She was not brilliant at the piano, knew almost none of the latest slang, felt acutely embarrassed at the familiarities that seemed to determine popularity, and shared no common daily experiences with the young men and women who, though of her age, lived in a giddy, unfeeling, extrovert world of their own. Once, grateful to have been rescued from her isolation, she could think of nothing to talk about with the young man who had so honored her. After a soporific Slow Drag, during which she struggled to keep what she felt to be a respectable distance between herself and her not-too-attractive partner, she said, as he led her to her seat against the wall, "Do you play basketball?" A moment later she could have bitten the end of her tongue. The young man stopped in his tracks, looking at her as though scarcely believing his ears. Then he hurried away to repeat her question to first one, then another of his colleagues, and soon she was the target of a continuous stream of jests about basketball playing. She couldn't imagine what had led her to choose this of all things to talk about at a party where "Round the Clock Blues" was the favorite piano and vocal selection of the evening and where, as one floor lamp after another was extinguished, pocket flasks added zest to a punchbowl already so fortified that she dared not touch it.

A girl named Billie Lawson was frequently a companion wallflower on these trying occasions. Katherine Dunham found a certain comfort in the fact that Billie Lawson was extremely good-looking and came from a family securely established socially and financially; but she, too, was tall for her age, conservatively dressed, shy of manner, and obviously thus far sheltered from the ritual initiations of the era.

Distressing in themselves, these periodic forays into the City did not serve, either, to free the girl from her father's constant, jealous, nagging interference. At eighteen she had never been kissed by a boy except in the game called "Post Office," and she was still forbidden to go out unchaperoned with a young man. Her rebellion began to take final form. She saw with increasing clarity that unless she made a final break with her father, which would in effect be with the Town, she would find herself before long entirely subjected to his will and facing the prospect of full-time work at the shop or perhaps an eventual teaching job, if enough pressure was brought to bear on the local school board. Neither of these prospects was in the least attractive to her. Her brother had suspended his visits, and the dream of escape faded with the passing of winter. As the hopelessness of her situation clouded her days and troubled her nights, she was increasingly obsessed by the quarry, and morning after morning she would awake exhausted from a recurrent dream which was to follow her through much of her adult life.

The body of water took on diverse forms. At times it would be the quarry itself, but most of the time it was a stream, sometimes clear as the quarry water, but just as full of an undefined danger. At other times it was a stagnant, sluggish stream, on which she drifted Ophelialike in her own shallow sarcophagus. A presence, wraithlike and calm, but always unseen, gave her assurance on these nocturnal passages, which never ended before her waking. As she remembered the loneliness of the forest through which the stream made its way and the utter, primordial solitude which shrouded the reclining figure, she identified the comforting presence with her dead mother. Haunted though she was by her desolate nocturnal voyage, she would feel similarly protected during the day, and with this feeling came a growing confidence in her capacity to fulfill whatever destiny lay ahead.

During this period she had retreated so far within herself that a letter from her brother, enclosing a form in which to apply for a Civil Service examination that might lead to a post as junior librarian in the City's public library, went almost unnoticed. She filled it out mechanically and mailed it to her brother. The details of the questionnaire, however, brought her physical self to her attention.

She was then eighteen years old and would turn nineteen shortly after graduation from her second year in junior college. She had reached her full growth of five feet six and three-quarter inches, weighed one hundred and twenty-three pounds, and had dark brown eyes and dark brown hair, with a streak of auburn buried in the middle. Her skin was a light brown, so tinged with green that in strong light

—as, for instance, in the spotlights focused on her in her later stage career—she might appear startlingly pale. Her bosom was smaller than she would have chosen, and her hips were fuller. She had no high opinion of her legs until the first impresario of her full-fledged professional career decided to insure them with Lloyds of London, and even then she regarded them as useful objects, but not especially remarkable. She did appreciate an extraordinarily high arch in her feet, and she enjoyed imitating with her hands and arms the fluid movements of Oriental dancers as depicted in photographs. She found her features exceedingly plain and, because she had no hope of equaling her brother's scholastic brilliance, foresaw no exceptional future for herself. The most that she could hope to do was find freedom from the parental vise that so rigidly confined her conscious life and had infiltrated into her unconscious.

The Great Depression had struck its first blow, and she wanted desperately to earn enough to offer some security to her mother, who was aging rapidly in her struggle to make ends meet and to survive the failure of her marriage.

The application for the examination was accepted. The girl had given her half sister's residence as her address and slightly falsified her date of birth to fit the age requirement. But now she found herself in the awkward position of—should she pass the examination—being scheduled to graduate from the college two weeks after the starting date of her employment. She had no idea whatever about the nature of the examination, and had it not been for a final crisis with her father, she might have allowed her trepidations to discourage her from attempting it.

The young football player, William Booker, had repeatedly asked her to accompany him to an out-of-season basketball game that would determine the state championship. Much as she would have liked to accept the invitation, she kept refusing on one pretext or another; but she finally admitted that her father was the obstacle. Without her suggesting it, William Booker went directly to Albert Dunham with his request, and when it was refused, he demanded to know why. Albert Dunham dismissed the young man brusquely, jammed on his battered felt hat, and tore through the streets in the delivery wagon to Elmwood Avenue. Over the years the girl managed to forget the bitter words that followed, but the shock of her father's unjust accusations, the vision of his face distorted with fury, and her mother's ineffectual attempts at mediation converged on her with an electrifying effect. She heard herself answer as she never had before, and felt a bursting of bonds, a dropping away of shackles, which immunized her to the blow on her face that followed her remarks. She remembered later that, as she had repeated her taunts, nimbly keeping out of her father's reach, she had said to herself, and perhaps aloud, over and over, exultantly, "It's the last time. This is the last time. The last time that he will ever touch me. The very last time!"

Her mother stood aghast, feebly teetering from one side to the other, just as she had during the final battle between father and son, repeating the old incantation, "Katherine, he's your *father!* How *could* you say such a thing! He's your *father.*"

And when the girl turned on her, a blaze of injury, making the same denial of paternity that the boy had so long ago, mother and father both fell silent, as though hearing a death knell or seeing a picture through a window that had always been curtained before. Something happened in her father, and the girl knew later that it was a breaking, an inner crumbling, and that—no matter how many false starts there might be hereafter at recharging the person who had raged and browbeaten and fought and struggled, unable to channel dreams into reality—this night in May marked the end of Albert Dunham as he had been until now. For one split second, while they hung suspended like actors waiting for a cue with breath held in and time and the two clocks stopped progressing, everything stood out clear-white and sharp. Her father saw the future in its bitter truth, picked up his hat, and went out without a word. The girl saw it, too, and turned to the closet to lift her one suitcase from its shelf. But her mother went right on as though the clear-white moment had never happened, as though a page of the future hadn't been held there right before her eyes.

"Katherine, tell your father you didn't mean it! Al, Al, don't leave this way! You shouldn't have struck her! After all, she's nearly nineteen!"

Hamilton Park Branch Library was located in an upper middle-class suburban district of the City where Jews were unwelcome, foreigners of less than two-generation citizenship scarce, and Negroes unknown except as part-time hired help. As for the McLaughlin sisters, they were in the highest echelon of the City's librarians. They were small, neatly formed, soft-spoken Irish spinsters, separated in age by seven or eight years, but so much alike in looks, dress, and manner that patrons of the branch where Bernardine might be stationed would at some other branch immediately recognize Blanche as her kin. Bernardine, the elder of the two, governed not only the tastes and behavior of her sister, but was believed by most of the librarians junior to her to wield an influence over the political structure of the library system comparable to that wielded by her countrymen in the City's politics in general.

When Katherine Dunham descended from the streetcar that had taken her, after a series of transfers, from the apartment her brother had found for her to the quiet, tree-shaded avenue ending at Hamilton Park, her heart was in her mouth and her knees were weak; but she felt a great sense of elation, convinced that the most difficult hurdles of her life lay behind her. The past having been accomplished, the future could hold no terrors. She had been granted permission by the college to matriculate *in absentia,* and she had passed the Civil Service examination with a high enough rating to win a place in what was considered one of the best-run and most desirable branch libraries of the City. She was innocent about what this might mean, but her niece, who had failed to pass the same examination, assured her that she had been very fortunate indeed.

If she noticed that Bernardine McLaughlin's smile was a little frozen, she must have thought this proper in one occupying the post of head librarian in an important branch. If the other young women, junior and senior assistants, regarded her with open curiosity but acknowledged her name with only a slight nod, then this must be customary on such auspicious occasions. She, Katherine Dunham, by some miracle still confounding her, had in one grand movement left behind the Town, the West Side Cleaners and Dyers, the flat on Bluff Street, the cottage on Elmwood Avenue, the unawareness of her mother, the tyranny of her father, corporal punishment, financial insecurity, the disintegration of the dust wheel, the morbid attraction of the quarry, the loneliness of the room with the single star piercing its window, the uncertainties of her questing childhood and defeated adolescence.

If her new colleagues—of Irish and Scotch and Italian and Polish and just plain American heritage—did not at first recognize her as one of them, that would come later. They were looking at her so strangely because she had come from somewhere else, and it would take time to know one another, as it had in grade school and high school and junior college. If the patrons regarded her strangely, it was because they must sense her amazement at what had happened to her, must even be wishing that they, too, could enter into this magical state of frightened exaltation. As she turned from her locker to her first duty, she felt suddenly alone, but she quickly recovered, reasoning that it was no more than just that her guiding spirit be given a respite. The rows of books were familiar and comforting, and by noon of the first day she had mastered the simple routine of entering and discharging books, even of selecting them by catalogue number.

It did not seem at all strange that the head librarian held a meeting around the polished round oak table in the inner reading room, barring all patrons for the time and excluding her alone of the staff. She sat on a high stool at the front desk with ink pads, date stamps, filing cards, and returned books neatly arranged before her. Her innocence went so far as to leave her all unsuspecting when, immediately after the meeting, a new schedule of lunch hours was posted and a third period was instituted for her name, which had earlier been grouped with several others. Because she knew no one, this meant little to her.

When the time came for her special lunch hour, she relinquished her position at the front desk to a dark-haired, sparkling-eyed girl named Florence Hazzard and received in return a warm smile, her first of the day. The smile was a little pitying, too, but she didn't know that.

The late spring air was warm, and she walked out of the park into shaded avenues that reminded her of Delavan and her morning walks with her Uncle Ed as she had first known him. She wandered along several thoroughfares lined with budding shrubbery, but with no sign of a restaurant or lunch room. She wondered vaguely where the other girls had eaten lunch, whether they all lived in the neighborhood. Before her hour was over, she returned to the park and sat on a stone bench not far from the low building housing the library. She could see Bernardine McLaughlin bent over the typewriter on the desk of her private office, and watched her for some time, wondering what document so absorbed the attention of the head librarian and if she always bit her under lip when she typed.

Suddenly she remembered that she was hungry and resolved to bring her lunch the following day, wondering if it would be the right thing to do and if any of the other girls brought lunches. She wondered, too, what would happen in wintertime, whether then she would sit like this in the park by herself. The invisible figure of her nocturnal excursions drew closer, protecting her from learning too soon about the conspiracies at that moment under way. But even if she had known the startling effect of her innocent descent upon the heretofore sacrosanct confines, she might have accepted it with complete aplomb.

The great wide world opened before her. Her lunch hour was over, and she went inside.

11 December 1958

Habitation Le Clerc—Port-au-Prince, Haiti